VICTIMLY INSANE:

The Frank Jarvis Atwood Interview

George Kayer

Published by Freebird Publishers
Box 541, North Dighton, MA 02764
Toll Free: 888-712-1987 Text/Phone 774-406-8682

Website: FreebirdPublishers.com
Email: diane@freebirdpublishers.com
ISBN 10: 0-991359-8-6
ISBN 13: 978-0-9913591-8-9
ESN:

Attention Prison Libraries:
Request your free copies of this book. Send us an email with your name, title and contact information. Include the number of reading areas in your facility.

Attention Non-Profit Organizations:
Purchase in bulk and save your members money. Review this book in your newsletter and receive an additional 10% discount. Excellent for your next fundraiser.

ACKNOWLEDGEMENTS

Thank you: Frank Atwood. It's been a blessing and honor to do your interview and help tell part of your storied path.

To Nancy Miars, who inspired me in 2001 to begin writing again. We all love and miss you. RIP 2016

To Diane at Freebird Publishers for the courage to publish this work.

To my legal team for preventing the State of Arizona from executing me- so far.

To the staff at Browning Medical Unit for keeping me alive: not easy.

To Jasmine for sharing your wisdom, and coming to visit me the past 10 years.

To Krista at Cyber Hut Designs for enduring my 48 design revisions.

To the Warden and mail room staff here at death row for honoring the Constitution's First Amendment.

DEDICATION

To all childhood rape victims:
May your life story not end on death row.

CONTENTS

WHAT IS VICTIMLY INSANE?

Victimly Insane: 1. A general term describing a victim of intense or long-term criminal abuse, resulting in serious mental disorders. (Lack of proper treatment often results in a lifetime of substance abuse and incarceration).
2. The title of a book by George Kayer, Freebird Publishers 2017.

PREFACE

Please don't hate me, it's so easy.
Kill all the Death Row prisoners - I used to believe – then I became one.
Then I became America's most published prisoner on Death Row.

Please don't hate me, it's so easy.
"The worst of the worst are on Death Row" is fake news, an "alternative fact" as Kellyanne Conway would say.
This is a slogan prosecutors and politicians use during news conferences, knowing before they speak this statement it is a factual lie.
My trial attorney told me flat out, "Your case isn't a death penalty case, but Judge Kieger is running for election and must look tough on crime."
Now that's a fact.

Please don't hate me, I'm not the worst of the worst.
Is Frank Atwood factually innocent? I know, there's damn little factual evidence to support his conviction.
Simply review the Ray Krone case. We now know that prosecutors shopped around for months until they found and paid whores to testify (lie) to the exact script prepared by prosecutors to insure a conviction – AND – Arizona did this twice to the same innocent Ray Krone, until DNA identified the real killer.
Guilty until proven innocent is American justice reality.

Please don't hate me- hate the game.
People and prisoners in here ask me: "Why are you doing this book? Why associate with this monster, why give him a voice? People and prisoners asked the same questions about Ray Krone- that's why.

Let's talk facts: Nearly 70% of citizens sentenced to death in Arizona get off death row. Think about that number for the day. Based on this fact there's a nearly 70% chance Frank Atwood is telling truth: "I'm innocent." Based on the lack of any serious evidence and the new evidence of detectives planting and tampering with evidence—yes. I'd say Frank is innocent.

At its roots, this book, this journey is about one child, his multiple encounters of childhood rape and that victim's path to Death Row. It's a true crime story that needed to be captured and written and shared.
I hope you agree, but if you don't-
Please don't hate me, it's too easy.

George Kayer

CASE UPDATE

At the time, this book went to pre-press, Frank's last opportunity to prove actual innocence was argued before the Ninth Circuit Federal Court of Appeals on June 7, 2017. Despite unequivocable exculpatory evidence, no court has appointed experts or held the required evidentiary hearing (where evidence and witnesses/experts are presented) to support the reality of extreme law enforcement misconduct. What has been uncovered thus far centers precisely on government having hidden that the victim was buried and the police having manufactured paint evidence. Grave wax (adipocere) proves burial and the state, desperate to deny the existence of a grave, contended a body on the desert's surface can develop adipocere. This has never occurred and government could not provide an expert to back this scientific impossibility.

Of note is:

The time necessary to have dug a grave absolutely exonerates Frank and someone had to exhume and place partial remains where they were eventually found while Frank was incarcerated.

Insofar as police fabricating paint evidence:

Within several days after Frank's arrest in Texas, the bumper was removed (according to FBI photos).

While dismantled, the bumper journeyed to Tucson (from where the victim disappeared) and was photographed by Sheriffs on their evidence platform, next to the victim's bicycle. Prior to its Texas return and misaligned reattachment to Frank's vehicle (as seen in FBI photos).

An FBI photograph, supposedly from the night of Frank's arrest and purporting to show paint from the victim's bicycle on the bumper, was a fake. None of the five FBI agents seeking connection between the car and bike observed any paint that night. Also, this fraudulent picture differed from others in the set because it was in focus, taken from an odd angle, and shot with a different camera.

The several inch-deep dents (allegedly from the bicycle pedal) in the gravel pan seen in police photos in 1985 was not present in FBI photos when Frank was arrested in 1984.

In conclusion:

All of this evidence proving law enforcement misconduct was developed by pro bono efforts of several experts helping Frank's attorneys. Hopefully the Ninth Circuit will order the evidentiary hearing so experts can thoroughly investigate and expose all government evidence tampering.

George

ARIZONA'S HISTORY OF SENTENCING INNOCENT CITIZENS TO DEATH: 12 SINCE 1989

Source: AZCentral.com

Debra Milke

Debra Milke, 51, spent 23 years on Arizona death row after the December 1989 murder of her 4-year-old son, Christopher. She was accused of arranging for two male friends to kill the boy so that she could collect an insurance payout. A court decision freed her from prison in March 2015 after a Maricopa County prosecutor's appeal was denied. Milke's conviction and death sentence were previously thrown out in March 2013 by the 9th U.S. Circuit Court of Appeals. The appellate court returned the case to Maricopa County Superior Court because the original prosecutor failed to disclose evidence that might have helped Milke's attorneys challenge testimony from a Phoenix police detective. The detective, Armando Saldate, claimed that Milke confessed to him, but there were no witnesses to the confession, nor was it recorded. And the prosecution did not turn over the detective's personnel record, which showed misconduct in other cases.

Robert Charles Cruz

Robert Charles Cruz, a former Tempe businessman, won instant freedom in 2005 after more than 14 years behind bars. Jurors returned verdicts acquitting him of murder and other charges in the 1980 contract killing of Phoenix print-shop owner Patrick Redmond and his mother-in-law, Helen Phelps. Cruz was tried five times in the murders. Two trials ended in mistrials; convictions from two other trials were overturned. Prosecutors claimed that Cruz hired and paid three killers as part of a plot to take over the business and win lucrative printing contracts from Las Vegas casinos. However, Cruz claimed that he was framed. Jurors said the overriding reason for acquitting Cruz was the lack of credibility of some of the witnesses.

Ray Krone

For 10 years, Ray Krone was thought to be the "Snaggletooth Killer," a postal worker with no criminal record who inexplicably one night raped and fatally stabbed a Phoenix bartender. Krone was convicted twice of Kim Ancona's 1991 murder and spent nearly three years on death row before DNA tests proved his innocence. Krone walked out of an Arizona prison in 2002.

Lemuel Prion

Lemuel Prion was arrested in 19-year-old Diana Vicari's murder five years after her arms were found in a plastic garbage bag in a dumpster just north of downtown Tucson in October 1992. He was convicted in January 1999 of first-degree murder, kidnapping and aggravated assault in the killing, and sentenced to death. Prion's conviction was overturned in August 2002. The Supreme Court's unanimous ruling said the trial judge should have permitted Prion's lawyer to introduce evidence indicating that another man may have committed the murder.

Christopher McCrimmon

Christopher McCrimmon was one of three men convicted in 1994 of killing Frederick Gee, 45; his uncle, Hwang Ze Wan, 77; and clerk Raymond Arriola, 32, on June 24, 1991, at El Grande Market in Tucson. He was also convicted of armed robbery, attempted armed robbery, aggravated robbery, attempted aggravated robbery and first-degree burglary. McCrimmon's conviction was overturned in 1996 when the Arizona Supreme Court found the trial judge pressured a juror into making a decision and should have declared a mistrial. McCrimmon was retried and acquitted in September 1997. He continues to serve up to 36 years in prison for the near-fatal robbery of Mariano's Pizza in August 1992.

David Wayne Grannis

David Wayne Grannis was convicted of first-degree murder in 1991, along with Daniel Ethan Webster, then 22, for the murder of Tucson investment broker Richard Sutcliffe, 47, in 1989. His conviction was overturned in 1995 by the Arizona Supreme Court, saying photos of homosexual activity may have biased the jury. In a unanimous opinion, the high court ruled that the photos should not have been admitted at the trial because their value as evidence was far outweighed by the danger of prejudice. Grannis was freed in 1996 after Pima County Superior Court Judge Bernardo Velasco dismissed murder charges against him in a retrial, Grannis' lawyers said.

Jimmy Lee Mathers

Jimmy Lee Mathers was one of three men convicted in Yuma

County Superior Court and sentenced to death for the June 8, 1987, shotgun slaying of Sterleen Hill and the wounding of her husband, Ralph. His attorney appealed in September 1988 and in 1990 the Arizona Supreme Court voted 5-0 to uphold the other men's convictions and 3-2 to acquit Mathers for lack of evidence.

James Robison

James Robison, who spent two years on death row in the 1976 car-bomb murder of Arizona Republic reporter Don Bolles, was cleared in the case in December 1993. Robison's conviction was overturned by the Arizona Supreme Court in 1990. The jury that acquitted Robison after 2 1/2 days of deliberations, following a nearly two-month trial. Members of the panel later said they didn't believe that the prosecution proved its case against Robison beyond a reasonable doubt. They also said that they found John Harvey Adamson, the confessed killer of Bolles, to lack credibility. Adamson had testified that he planted the bomb and Robison detonated it.

Jonathon Charles Treadaway Jr.

Jonathon Charles Treadaway Jr. initially was convicted -- based primarily on a palm print and a hair that microscopically matched his in color and texture -- and sent to death row for killing Brett Jordan, 6, in August 1974. But the Arizona Supreme Court threw out the conviction and he was freed after a second trial in 1978. DNA tests, conducted more than two decades after the murders of Doris Morris, 3, and Brett Jordan, linked Treadaway to semen found in Doris' underpants and hairs found on Brett's body, police said. Treadaway died before the final DNA tests could be completed.

1

PRELUDE TO INSANITY

In this book-length interview, an innocent Frank Atwood reveals from Death Row the information the public and the jurors had never heard, and the story the lynch mob media doesn't want you to read: How this sweet, rosy-cheeked, silver spoon teen, who went by "Frankie J," arrived at perversity, at the crossroads of victim and victimizer, and the precise manner in which he intrepidly and painfully clawed his way out of a victim's dungeon and a victimizer's lachrymose guilt.

Frankie J was a normal, silver spoon kid, raised during the 1960's in what many have described as like the TV shows Leave it to Beaver and Father Knows Best idyllic lifestyle. One summer day in 1970 at age 14 Frankie J and his 11-year-old friend were kidnapped. In the ensuing hours, the kids witnessed a molester in his twenties forcing young, naïve Frankie J to be fellated, a tragedy compounded by Frankie J having to confront his attacker in court several weeks later.[1]

The pubescent Frankie J had been commonly characterized as emotionally sensitive, a vulnerability having endured significant distortion from his sexual traumas, resulting in his psychologist, Dr. Brandt, recommending attendance at the Melrose School in the autumn of 1970. This is an educational school designed for silver spoon children with emotional difficulties.

During our three months of interviews, today's Frank Atwood depicted in detail the warpage in thinking patterns sustained, the onset of a deviant attitude having plagued the once innocent, but now defiled child. This permanent damage to Frankie J (and to all

[1] In October of 2013 a hearing was held in the United States District Court in Arizona for the presentation of evidence in support of Mr. Atwood's PTSD. References and attachments herein are from transcripts of this hearing.

childhood sexual assault victims) was undoubtedly consequential. Predictably, the demon of escapism took up residency in Frankie J's heart. Diagnosed with Post Traumatic Stress Disorder,[2] Frankie J retreated into extreme substance abuse, resulting in a trip to juvenile detention a few weeks after his 16th birthday. Still gullible, the handsome, rosy-cheeked kid accepted an invitation [by other inmates] to meet in a secluded location, purportedly to discuss ways out of lockup. Of course, the plan was to get Frankie J alone. They beat him, making him perform fellatio on each of them.

Later that day Frankie J was released. As he sat in his father's car, still soaked in the remnants of his disgrace, further psychological damage was done.

Like many rape victims, Frankie J persisted in both increased criminality and seeking escape via rampant drug use. This obsessive interest in chemically induced oblivion led Frankie J to make many irresponsible and dangerous decisions. While on vacation in Aspen with his parents he befriended a local musician. Later the promise of free hashish at the vagabond entertainer's home, Frankie J happily embraced the opportunity. Now, not so friendly, the musician transformed into a nefarious pervert and forcibly raped Frankie J.[3]Our once innocent, rosy-cheeked, silver spooner is now a burgeoning misanthrope and a seasoned petty criminal.

In and out of minimum security psychiatric facilities, Frankie J graduated to California's maximum security psychiatric facility in early 1975. Again – or still – the drive to escape through drugs traveled with him. The promise of an injection of really good cocaine led to another patient on top of Frankie J. With a razor blade at his throat he was brutally sodomized. With four sexual assaults in a five-year period between the ages of 14 and 19, Frankie J became just Frank—and a sexual predator.[4]

---

[2] See four-page diagnosis in chapter four.

[3] See transcript page 33.

[4] Of import to our disclosure on Frank's multiple sexual assaults is his MMPI-2 verification of his being truthful about all four assaults. See transcript pages 162 and 188.

How I met Frank Atwood?
Since September of 1997, the past 20 years, Death Row has been located at ASPC-Browning, a supermax unit where Frank and I reside. Prisoners here are locked down in solitary 24 hours a day, except for six hours per week. As part of the psychological deprivation design there are only ten prisoners per mini-section, known as a pod, a block of five cells on the bottom and five cells above in a two-story building. (See photos in back of book.) So, it's not like I can open my door, walk over to Frank's cell and enjoy a keepsake afternoon of football and hotdogs.

Over the years, Frank has authored six books. I first became aware of him and his writing from an ad I saw for one of his early books around 2008 in the Prison Legal News. I knew then I'd like to meet him someday.
Someday turned out to be eight years later, November 23, 2016. After Arizona prisons lost a few recent lawsuits,[5] judges agreed it was "cruel and inhuman" to keep a person locked in a box for "extended periods" of time. In my case the "extended period" has been 20 years.
Long story short, the short version is Arizona prisons must now provide Death Row prisoners more "out of cell time" and has shuttled some prisoners around. I wound up in Frank's pod, two cells from him on the bottom floor.
I presently know very little about Frank Jarvis Atwood; I just read his earlier book last week, which sparked this project. And, I've never seen his rap sheet information nor viewed any of the TV programs about his case. I rarely view those crime reenactment programs. After all, living on death row is enough crime/drama for me. I prefer comedies.

My daily routine may surprise you. I get up between 4:30 a.m. and 7 a.m. and work six days a week. Not as a prison porter, rather I labor indomitably in my cell (work from home) on publishing projects I feel will elevate the understanding of people on both sides of America's prison gates. Hopefully this project-book will ideally prevent a few kids from following in our footsteps to death row.
Since I arrived next to Frank, we've talked about numerous topics: He favored Trump, I preferred Clinton; he's Greek Orthodox

[5] See civil suit, Federal case #2:15-CV-02176- DGC--JZB

Christian, I'm Buddhist. Not off to a great beginning. I was really impressed to learn about Frank's years-long anfractuous path from life-long criminal to the relatively normal Frank of today. I asked Frank if he'd be interested in a book-length interview to share his methods for change, not expecting him to say yes. Frank said, "If you can find a publisher, I'd like to do it."
I presented the project to Freebird Publishers, who specialize in prisoner publications, not expecting them to say yes. They did. Well, crap! I really didn't want to write another book, but the stars have aligned on this one. Okay, we know something of who Frank was, and has been, who is this man now?

Who is Frank Jarvis Atwood today?
Who is this long-haired, gray-bearded person sitting next to me in a raggedy prison-issued wheelchair wearing a skoufo? None of you reading this know the person next to me, but you will. The only Frank Atwood you may know is from Google.com; YouTube.com, Murderpedia.com, Wikipedia.com, the TV programs FBI Files, Medical Detectives, or from the printed shade of the meat grinder media who spit, "The rich kid from Hollywood gone wild story."
So, who is Frank Jarvis Atwood and why should anyone advocate for him or anyone else on Death Row? As morally repulsive as this sounds, death row lives matter. How could this be possible you ask? Well- shocker LC most children aren't born with larceny in their hearts and the Devil inside. Often the seeds of the Devil are injected into them within the sperm of their abusers.
Later in life, when these victims regurgitate their flagitious childhood all over Society's white picket fence in the form of murder, rape or a mass casualty event, society's first response is, "Kill that godless turd, and by the way God Bless America."
Those people in the criminal justice arena will joke, "We're all fans of the death penalty until we are the ones on death row." From my 20 years of experience on The Row I can assure Arizonans: hypocrisy is not the case. Gang members and tattooed-knuckled criminals are pro death penalty. However, being criminals, they'll do what they can to escape their responsibilities to society.

Many of the people on The Row never had the chance as children to hear someone say, "I love you," "you're unique and beautiful," or "your happiness is important to me." These children of years of abuse don't realize any value in their past or future life, so their death or execution is of little consequence to them. Your life also has little value to the criminally abused.

I've seen many here on The Row require five, ten or fifteen years to deprogram their viruses of distorted thinking. Others become vacuous and lost. Anyone who completes a successful rehab program is absolutely not the same person or personality who was convicted of their crime(s). This is why death lives matter.

Okay, back to who Frank is today.

Born Frank Jarvis Atwood, an only child on a sunny afternoon, January 29, 1956, in Los Angeles and raised in Brentwood, California. Attended Brentwood Elementary School, followed by Paul Revere Jr. High School and Brentwood Military Academy.

Frank's father, John Atwood, was the president of Theta Cable Company in Los Angeles and a retired U.S. Army General. He passed in May 2008.

Frank's mother, Alice Atwood, was born in Austria and with Frank's birth assumed the traditional role of stay-at-home mom, always with a smile and snacks for the neighborhood children: she passed in January of 2010. When Frank speaks about his parents I am aware of a kind, almost reverent tone, yet tinged with sincere sadness and regret in his voice.

I've lived on The Row for twenty years. In this time, I've found three types of people end up here:

Serial criminals- killers.

Semi-normal people who had a bad week.

The mentally ill.

Group A is perfectly at home on The Row and proud of their zip code.

Group B, more often than not, do their introspective soul search and return to a relatively normal, positive life path in a few years, perhaps writing a book or teaching Bible study or prison programming.

Group C, Frank's group, those with both mental issues and a criminal history from their teens, rarely find their way out of their negative, baneful, criminal habits- why would they? If you're surrounded by like-minded bro's, having a (relatively) good time, there's no motivation to attempt some abstract search to improve oneself. Improve what?

For a career criminal with underlying mental issues to change or seek change toward a non-criminal or Christ-centered life is equivalent to a bright red Republican realizing they've been oppressive control freaks, with their governmental and corporate policies handcuffing minorities and women. It would be like dropping LSD and seeing compassion for all humans for the first time in their lives. It's that grandiose- and rare.

With most prisoners, achieving a master's degree from a legitimate university creates such a super moon event, they're usually written up in the local papers. Not Frank, not any citizen convicted of killing a child. These prisoners are persona non-grata in the press, with prison administrators, even other prisoners- and the rest of the world. Even though Frank has maintained his innocence since his arrest, and continues to vigorously appeal his conviction, he is treated as a child killer by prisoners and everyone other than his wife, priest and attorney.

> **Loneliness is a Health Hazard.** "Social isolation is a growing epidemic- one that's increasingly recognized as having dire physical, mental and emotional consequences. Loneliness is especially tricky because accepting and declaring the fact of our loneliness carries with it a most profound stigma. Admitting we're lonely can feel as if we're admitting we've failed in life's most fundamental domains: belonging, love, attachment. It attacks our basic instincts to save face, and makes it hard to ask for help." Dhruv Khullar, M.D., M.P.P., is a resident physician at Massachusetts General and Harvard Medical School. Read complete article: New York Times of December 22, 2016.

While the average citizen might regard solitary confinement in a remote cell as a condition of perpetual boredom, nothing could be further from the truth for Frank Atwood. His life in prison is hell, full of daily angst, anxiety and apprehension. A few weeks after we hit it off, Frank told me, "You're my first friend in eight years." Wow!

It is unlikely that any outsider could begin to understand that level of loneliness and isolation, that depth of being hated by everyone, every prisoner, every staff member. I certainly can't.

The court may sentence a criminal to spend the remainder of his life on Death Row, but the true punishment comes from the prisoners and guards who carry out the malicious, interminable psychological attacks.

Frank said, "I doubt you know the isolation in which I've had to live. Other prisoners would go hungry or without coffee rather than ask me for anything, nor would they offer me anything of theirs. I'm always paranoid about others, of their motives (when they do speak to me), dislikes and jealousies leading to screwing me over."

I knew I would take some heat from other prisoners about my association with Frank, but I didn't expect the wave of condemnation I received one day after Frank left our pod for a visit. One by one, each prisoner piled on, assaulting me for continuing to talk to "that piece of garbage" If we were on an open yard both Frank and I would be in physical danger- daily, hourly. Guilt by association is alive and well in prisons.

> A few days after this writing, all on death row were notified we'd be moving to an open yard at Central Unit, Florence. More anxiety.

Shortly after Frank landed on the row he began his education and transformational soul search. Listed below are most of his accomplishments:

2017	Completing Ph.D. in Theology
2013	Theology Degree St. Stephen's 3-year program
2000	Tarot Master American Tarot Association
1998	Masters in Literature, California State University
1995	Bachelors in Pre-Law & English, Ohio University
1991	Associate of Arts, Ohio University
1990	Associate of Arts, Central Arizona College

View the back pages for "Additional Titles by Frank Atwood" page. Frank converted to Greek Orthodox Christianity, was baptized in 2000, receiving his Christian name- Anthony.

Everyone (and as a non-fiction writer, I rarely get to use this word) is eyebrows-in-the-air skeptical of a prisoner's jailhouse religion, yet damn few prisoners write five books on religion, pray two hours a day, and visit their priests every other Wednesday. Frank lives a monastic life, participating in a (to me) plethora of various fasts and seldom speaking to anyone, only myself, the guard, and a "Fed-X" when necessary. A harsh sentence and way of life that has driven many a weaker man to suicide.

There are a lot of two-faced hypocrites who, during their interview, give all the answers we want to hear or read, and a half hour after their interview they're looking for an eight-ball, or in bed with a hooker, or whatever actions contradict what was said in their interview.

My point is, for Frank to agree to an interview at all is a writer's dream; for Frank to agree to an embedded 24/7 type of personal interview over the course of three months is an extraordinarily brave decision for any human, outside of celebrities seeking to ruin their marriage or career. In addition, I asked Frank hundreds of questions and he answered all of them. How many people could endure that- and still remain friendly and cooperative?

So, we ask again, who is Frank today? He's not skipping rocks on the ocean.[6] Even for this writer, who has little in common with Frank, certainly not in our politics, (He's called me "a lying godless Hilary supporter" and worse.), nor our religion or personal views. Are we friends? My definition of a friend is someone I've known a few years and who can be trusted with sensitive information under pressure. Could Frank become my friend? That's entirely plausible. Currently, I'd say Frank is a respected acquaintance and colleague. I admire the guy for crawling out of the demon-infested genocide of his mind, find God, reconnect with his parents, develop a loving relationship with a woman and celebrate a 25th wedding anniversary with her. Wow!

Is he guilty as charged for crimes in Arizona? Upon reviewing the case, there is little to no evidence to support a conviction, further, the ninth circuit court has agreed to consider new evidence of police tampering with or planting evidence. (June 7th, 2017) We all hope Frank will do a "My side of the story" book and let the public decide. This book and interview cover who Frank was and how he became who he is today.

Our interview takes place on Arizona's Death Row- Browning Unit. There are few places on earth where everyone who crosses the threshold feels a chill of fear, not the mega rollercoaster type of fear, rather the amygdala type of fear, humans never want to encounter or contemplate outside the comfort of a 107-minute horror movie.

---

[6] Taylor Swift

The massive steel door begins its long, slow, six-second crawl to open, slamming loudly to announce its arrival onto the left wall- we flinch. Every first timer does.

In front of you lies a 200-foot hallway, institutionally clean and shiny, and an echo chamber where one's fear bounces off the haunted walls, metastasizing in every bone in your body.

Enter any other men's prison yard, look around at the prisoners, and your imagination runs wild: "Oh, he's cute," or "I wonder what those two did? Perhaps unpaid parking tickets, maybe rob a bank?"

Here on The Row the price of admission is first-degree murder. Death is in the air, ghosts of the executed roam the hallways, and you're more alive and alert than you've ever been in your life....

“Hello, Mr. Atwood....”

THE INTERVIEW BEGINS

GK Hello Mr. Atwood- may I call you Frank?
FJA How's it going George, and yes, you may call me Frank.
GK Thank you for trusting me enough to do this interview.
FJA Hmm. My wife and priest constantly warn me about being overly naïve, it's my Achilles heel. I've learned the hard way about involvement with unchanged felons. In fact, prior to the contemplation of this project, I had ceased speaking to any inmate while in my cell (other than occasional comments to a porter) as the means to protect against continued hostilities, both verbal and physical. You approached me as a decent human being: as someone not wrapped in prison gamesmanship, not in need of material items, and having both compassion and intelligence. When coupling this potential for companionship with the opportunity to have a work published that I strongly believe will help society, I opted to endure the self-sacrifice involved (the public exposure of my past, a possible repeat bad experience, etc.). My involvement is, at its base level, an act of Christian love for people and I gladly embrace the risks.
GK So I misspoke. You don't yet trust me–perfectly understandable. What is the primary message from this interview that you hope sticks with our readers?
FJA There may actually be two primary messages that morph into one another. First, that people not just from low

socioeconomic backgrounds are subject to criminality, that the entirety of the human spectrum has risk. The second message centers on the ability of absolutely anyone to climb out of the darkest abyss. Society has been brainwashed to believe government and the media, so despite my innocence there remains the initial public opinion of me as the lowest of the low, as a child victimizer and killer. Let's go with that illusion, use it to our advantage, to demonstrate to readers how even a scurvy waste of human skin like myself can successfully complete a program for change. Please, I pray dear God, allow every reader to take away this message.

GK The average citizen or victim has no idea of the painful, cumulative psychological deprivation endured by prisoners in these supermax lockdown units. To most victims it's all about "execute that bastard now." If only these folks understood—some of those on the row for 10 or 20 years, welcome the opportunity to end their suffering: some on the row execute themselves. As bad as living conditions are here for the run of the mill murderer, daily conditions are much worse for most of those with crimes against children. Please speak to some of these differences and share some of your personal experiences.

FJA Please permit me to draw a portrait of abuser vs. abused (i.e., differences between prisoners without and with a child murder case) by tracing examples I suffered since the 1984 arrest. Thus, consider:

When in a small county jail in Texas, awaiting a hearing to combat extradition to Arizona, there were bomb threats ("get Atwood out of here or we'll level the building") which led to my being illegally removed by Arizona authorities.

My return to Tucson involved false reports to the press on which airport I would arrive at, me in a bulletproof vest, an escort with multiple cars, police snipers on rooftops enroute to the jail, and other security measures.

Once entering the housing pod, [at the county jail] the doors of nearly every cell were being kicked by inmates screaming death threats.

Having to be kept completely isolated from all inmates (except for brief periods before trial) across the span of more than three decades.

The walk to my initial death row cell was accompanied by prisoners screaming obscenities and threats, lighting fires, and throwing things as I passed other areas (guards simply laughed).

Having continued to suffer verbal abuse, threats, having feces thrown at and on me, stabbings/spearings/dartings, etc.

As is readily evident, the child murder conviction (i.e., me as the abused) results in severe isolation and attack (the abusers, mostly non-child case inmates). Please keep in mind, "We must through many tribulations enter the kingdom of God" (Ac. 14:22).

GK In 2005 you wrote a tutorial on depression titled: Holy Scripture and the Church Fathers on Depression. In that writing you equate "depression(s)" to various demon intrusions upon one's personality. You discuss having a profundity of depression and how to avoid it. So, do you suffer from depression of the clinical psychiatric type? I know on occasion I do.

FJA Given the need for special education to accurately identify clinical pathologies, I find it a bit difficult to self-diagnose depression. However, I believe anxiety dwells as my top tier mental problem, a consequence of overarching post-traumatic stress disorder (P.T.S.D.). Anxiety floating from P.T.S.D. can include temporary feelings of depression. Yes, I've experienced symptoms of depression and been diagnosed with depression as a secondary (to anxiety/P.T.S.D.) disability.

GK When have you felt the most tested during your transformation from godless hedonist and criminal to a Christ-centered life?

FJA I again see two existent primary realms: One involving life in prison, and one pertaining to events beyond these prison walls. In prison, there occur experiences that test my faith, trust, reliance on God. My spiritual father (a monk at a nearby monastery) continually leads me toward seeing abuse from prisoners and guards as beneficial, because therein my prayers for patience, humility, love of others is answered. Just as physical muscles require physical exercise, so does spiritual strength demand spiritual experience (no pain = no gain) and henceforth the assaulters function as my benefactors.

Just the other day I went to recreation outside, where ten 10'x10' cages reside, and two inmates started uttering references to my case; comments like, "I bet he loves watching all the little boys at the Little League World Series," and this tested me. Temptation to view this as something requiring aggressive reaction floated by, then the provocation toward, defensively, stating that my expert (the Director of South Carolina's Department of Corrections, Mental Health, and Juvenile Justice violent sexual predator units) concluded that I am not reoffender

risk. Only then did smiles cross my face, mind, and heart as I thanked God for the opportunity to enter purification and to pray for others. Yet, it was indicative of what tests me. The other area that tests me results from both the decision of courts and attitudes by the general public. There have been developments with evidence that unequivocally prove I had no involvement in this case. These judicial and societal travesties all too often test me. Nota bene: God is loving and good, for: "God our Savior, who desires all men to be saved" (1 Tim. 2:4) and
"We must through many tribulations enter the kingdom of God" (Ac. 14:22).

GK After all those years of running wild, what were your motivations to stop thinking like a twisted criminal? And what year did you begin this process?

FJA Often, for criminals, it requires incarceration to then reflect upon the consequences of their thinking errors and criminal behavior. For me, I neglected several such opportunities—this now, subsequent to change, actually helps to make sense of why I landed on death row when innocent; it simply took this drastic of a fall to gain my attention—and after several months of having been condemned I started to contemplate how much failure my thinking and action created (on self and others).

I began by attendance at a university, believing the discipline of rigorous study would be of benefit; this resulted in continued education pursuits for the next ten years (late 1987 to early 1998). Added to this, within a year after my arrival here, I recommitted my life to Christ (benefit/change from university flowed into seeking more interior alteration through religion; success bred success). I also worked with a well-known psychologist (confidentiality agreements preclude disclosure), which more firmly entrenched me on the road out of criminality in the mid-1990s. It has been a long and arduous path, but so very worthwhile.

GK Generally, neither prisons nor their administrations were ever designed to become the nation's mental health care systems. Mental health care has been forced on prison systems by politicians and the courts. With those factors in mind, are your basic mental health care needs being met? Please describe briefly.

FJA In 2016 I saw a psychologist in June, a lawsuit settlement (between the ACLU and AZ prison healthcare) required therapy sessions at least every 30 days. The next appointment wasn't until November and formal complaints by myself were answered with the "you are being appropriately seen per protocol" standardized response. This exemplifies prison mental health care in AZ; toss pills at inmates, lie about and refuse to provide court ordered care, and treat us with disdain. No, mental health care needs are NOT being met.

GK What, if any, mental health issues are you currently being treated for?

FJA Since having initially been molested at age fourteen I began treatment for post-traumatic stress disorder (PTSD, a little known mental illness in 1970). Misdiagnosed for decades, and very resistant to uncovering the trauma from sexual assault, I wandered in and out of mental hospitals, "treated" by a seemingly endless line of mental health professionals for anxiety, depression, sexual deviancy, family malfunction, et al. As of about 2011 I have been treated here on death row with therapy and medication for the anxiety and hyper vigilance flowing from PTSD.

> Frank is so soft spoken and kind, yet so nano second quick to respond in visceral burst of indignations at maximum volume, becoming the exact opposite of the humble monk persona he holds of himself.

GK As we sit here today are you prescribed any psych meds, if so what do you take?

FJA I just completed a six-month run on Paxil, due to an increase in anxiety. The BuSpar I still take, and have done so since c. 2011-12. Efforts have been made to keep me on numerous other drugs including: Paxil, Zoloft, desipramine, amiltriptyline, nortriptyline, and Tegretol. Recently, I was placed Celexa.

GK My son suffers from autism and displays similar symptoms. Have you ever been tested for autism or Asperger's Syndrome?

FJA No, to my knowledge all testing by experts in 2012-13 never involved either syndrome and any previous examinations throughout my lifetime likewise did not cover either.

GK Ok, we've known each other what now, three weeks?

FJA Since November 23 and it's December 14th, so yes.

GK And you amazingly agreed to this imbedded interview, not placing any restrictions on possible questions, yes?

FJA Yes.

GK You do understand this interview process will require weeks and hundreds of questions, reliving many aspects of your life, are you sure you're ready?

FJA The short answer is, absolutely.

GK These past few weeks I've noticed several unexpected outbursts of acrimony and a proclivity for abusive, denigrating verbal attacks on guards and others. So, my question is, are you still working on responding outside of anger and, if so, what tools are you using?

FJA Yes, and my occasional rage is a failure to accept whatever God allows (guards in my face), this absence of my obedience is unacceptable in God's eyes. As for the tools, to cease being the author of my self-destructive actions I employ asceticism to facilitate my process of acceptance, which results in the reduction of angry responses. Specifically, what is known in Greek Orthodoxy as the "Jesus Prayer," i.e., "Lord Jesus Christ, have mercy on me." Repeated with full concentration upon each word.

GK Ok, with respect to your religious pursuits, jailhouse religion is seen as facetious by guards, prison parole boards and ruled a temporary escape by psychologists. I too dove into the spiritual studies for myself—yes, and to show the world I'm not the monster society makes me out. However, for you and me religious studies were more than superficial busy work, we've both written extensively on this topic. In your case you've written five books in the religious genre.

Two questions: At this point in your life, 30 years on death row, do you still give a crap about what society thinks of you? And, have you found peace within—regardless of the outcome of your appeals?

FJA Society's attitude toward me recently hasn't really been a major concern or influence. Perhaps I've constructed a shield to curb feelings of sadness over being seen by literally millions as a monster. However, what God thinks is, for me, the crucial component in life. I now see as life's purpose the cooperation with God's grace and from this viewpoint, the Commandments of God function as the most essential factor in my existence. Similarly, I do not see my residency on condemned row, nor a future execution, as involved in my sense of peace. Peace is an ongoing process.

> *I do not see my residency on condemned row, nor a future execution, as involved in my sense of peace.*

GK So, 30 years on the row and three years in county—where are your legal appeals at now and what are your options as your appeal(s) move forward? Please

respond in non-legal terms for our readers.
FJA In general, the process subsequent to a guilty verdict and death sentence includes a direct appeal to the Arizona Supreme Court, which has a near 100% denial rate. Next is a return to the same court (trial court) for your P.C.R. (post-conviction relief petition). This is an opportunity to present all new evidence discovered after trial. If denied, and 98% are, one can appeal to the Arizona Supreme Court and get denied there. Then the case enters the Federal court system, where many of the judges are upset at our Arizona courts for backwoods arrogance and refusal to follow the rule of law. I initially entered the federal district court; this ended as a mockery of justice. Now I'm in the federal circuit (appeal) court hoping they will issue a decision to hold a new jury trial on all charges. If denied, I'll go to the U.S. Supreme Court.

Update–February 2017 Breaking News
We just found out oral arguments have been set for June 2017 in Seattle 9th Circuit Court.

GK Do you have any regretful tattoos?
FJA I have 666 in two locations and had Satan on my ankle. I rubbed off the S with salt, it got infected. I had to go to medical every day to have the wound cleaned and fresh bandages: not fun.
GK That sucks. I don't have any tats.
FJA How can that be?
GK Yeah, I don't know. I've been around bikers and was in the Navy—I almost got a "Mom" tat one day, but got sidetracked.
GK It's been nearly 30 years since your conviction; most people hit the federal court seven to twelve years after conviction, so why has it taken your case so long?
FJA Everything in this case always takes inordinately long times. Case in point: after the AZ Supreme Court denied the direct appeal in 1992, the five years being far more lengthy than average at the time, no final notice issued for over a year—a routine clerical duty normally done within a month. Similarly, what had been estimated by the court as under a year in 2007 for pre-evidentiary hearing investigation and interviews, spanned more than three years...all a waste. The court then refused to hold the hearing contemplated.
I cannot definitively conclude why these delays transpire. Officers

of the courts have suggested that the justice system's awareness of my inculpability has inspired lengthened processes to keep me confined. What can be stated is that delays continue; attorneys claim it takes 2-6 months for the Ninth Circuit to schedule oral argument hearings, and I have waited for about two years and counting.

GK What do you enjoy reading?

FJA I take the Casa Grande Dispatch newspaper. Virtually all magazines are Eastern Christian: The Orthodox Observer, The Orthodox Word, and The Orthodox Heritage are ongoing. I hope to receive The Writer's Digest and fairly routinely get catalogs for Orthodox Christian items (books, religious jewelry, etc.).

GK What TV shows do you enjoy after a long day at school and work? Any religious programs in your schedule?

FJA Sports, the major ones, are first on the list. A station with 1960's-1970's game shows is a favorite, as are cop shows ("Law and Order," "CSI," etc.). The West's distortion of first century Christianity (see my book West of Jesus, by Anthony; Regina Orthodox Press 2006; reprint Xlibris 2012) makes televised religious programs difficult to watch.

GK Prior to exploring all the layers of who Frank was; how you survived and transformed yourself, I'd like to give our readers an idea of who Frank is today, right now. What is a typical week of activities for you?

FJA Having been wheelchaired in 2015 certainly muffled my activities, however, I try to at least remain busy. On Mondays, I'll get up at 4:30 am (the guards serve a combo breakfast/lunch sack around this time) to complete the daily two-hour prayer rule, then shower, and from 8 to 10 and 11 to 1 pm I am able to have non-contact visits with my wife.

Once back in my cell I usually take a nap, wake up before 4 pm, eat supper at around 5 pm. The rest of the evening is filled with a mix of reading, writing or watching television.

Tuesdays I'll go to the 11'x22' exercise pen (the 20' high walls preclude seeing any scenery or contact with others). During the summer, I'll stay out usually the allotted 2 ½ hours and during winter I'll generally return to my house after an hour.

The rest of the day (as well as on Wednesdays, Thursdays and Fridays) I will pray, study, watch TV and nap. Every other Wednesday I have a two-hour visit with my priest, I make confession, take Holy Communion, and receive spiritual instructions.

> The Cycle of Violence
>
> Researchers studied childhood events of 43 men on Death Row, they found:
>
> 59% admitted sexual abuse
>
> 83% witnessed domestic violence.
>
> 94% had been physically abused.
>
> Researchers: David Lisak and Sara Beszterczey at University of Massachusetts Boston.
>
> Published by: American Psychological Association

Every couple of months I'll see one of my attorneys, hour long visits are on Tuesdays and Thursdays. Out of cell exercise periods are also available on Friday afternoon and on Saturday mornings.

Most Saturdays a friend will visit me, and on Sunday mornings there's a class I attend. This offers an opportunity to be out of the cell; otherwise the weekend routines are similar to weekday routines.

GK Before we slide into the past let's complete this who is Frank today: do you still have criminal thoughts?

FJA I would say that who Anthony (my baptismal name) is today centers on my relationship with the Greek Orthodox Christian Church. Upon arising each morning, I perform the several hours prayer rule assigned by my spiritual father. Throughout each day I "pray the hours" (set prayers at 9, 12, 3, and sunset), and then do the Small Compline prayers prior to bed every night. When considering involvements with others--watching television, listening to the radio--in everything I seek Christian-minded participation. So, my entire life is immersed in pursuit of God's grace. That is not at all to infer that I never fall; unfortunately, I do so several times a day.

However, I would not describe my lapses as "criminal" (profanity and fits of anger are my most common transgressions). Perhaps life on death row being so terribly controlled incites desire to govern more aspects of daily existence; therefore, becoming upset when unable to control ensues. Some of this manifests as attempts to manipulate events, which reveals my weakness of faith, too frequent disobedience to my priest, and a definite need for far more humility.

GK You mentioned a dual autobiography of you and your wife coming out soon, and the publisher is a monastery in Cyprus; that's amazing, please explain how this came about and how a death row prisoner in Arizona gets published in Greek and English.

FJA Interesting journey. In 1998, I read a book on "mystical Christianity" (Riding the Lion by Kyriacos Markides) and was so blown away I wrote one of the book's protagonists, Metropolitan Athanasios (of Limassol, Cyprus). His response initiated my entry into the Greek (Eastern) Orthodox Church; I was baptized in July of 2000 by my spiritual father, the Abbot of a monastery in Arizona.

Macheras Monastery in Cyprus is under the supervision of Metropolitan Athanasios and the Abbot. Bishop Epiphanios visited me here on death row in May of 2007; his instruction to author the autobiography gave birth to my wife and I beginning to create And the Two Shall Become One, a dual autobiography. The writing process followed by translation into Greek, has been a long arduous process, the book is now being edited. Glory to God!

GK I know it's an autobiography, but can you share a further idea of content?

FJA The central theme revolves around my wife Sarah's straightforward road to Orthodoxy (conservative life, and from Protestantism to the Orthodox Church), contrasted by my circuitous path (Episcopal, crime, occult, Protestantism, Orthodoxy) to evidence how very different lives can come home to the One Holy Apostolic Church and experience the hope of salvation.

3

PSYCHOLOGY AND CRIMINAL CAUSATION

GK While the emphasis of this interview is how you thought and functioned as a criminal, provide a few words on how across the centuries societies have taken different views regarding crime and criminal causation.

FJA Circa the nineteenth century scientific studies of criminals began in the form of the Positivist Movement. Positivists considered law as a changing social institution and determined crime originated from both an individual's disposition and environmental forces. Positivists also questioned whether criminals were responsible for their behavior and established an insanity defense via the "M'naghten Rule" cite as 8 Eng.Rep.718 (1843). Under this rule an accused isn't criminally responsible if: (1) laboring under such defect of reason from disease of the mind as not to know the nature and quality of the act being performed, or (2) not knowing what was being done was wrong." From this standard's onset in 1843 until today criminal law continues to recognize an insanity defense.

GK Have you ever used an insanity defense?

FJA No.

GK I've observed reference to this definition of legal insanity on television, but Arizona has denied and rejected all mental illness defenses since the Jewish American Princess murder case. To what else did the Positivists attribute criminality?

FJA When investigating whether criminals were responsible for their behavior Positivists began understanding one way crime developed involved organic causation. That is, according to the Positivists, crime stemmed from biological as well as sociological sources. This led to the revelation some criminals were born and at the mercy of genetic factors. Other findings included knowledge that nature makes the raw materials, to which society then provides circumstances as a foundation for conditions leading to criminal behavior

As the twentieth century loomed, science began to consider hereditary and genetic causations of crime in greater depth. For instance, it became known human personality was reflected in observable bodily features; in other words, hereditary features determine one's physical and mental capacities. The environment then necessitates the use these abilities adapt. In addition, theories such as the belief that genetic factors predisposed the development of the criminal personality also developed.

GK So Positivists were the first to perceive society as playing significant roles in the emergence of criminal thinking and behavior? Tell me more.

FJA Other theories of organic conditions existing as causal agencies of crime include: organic brain conditions (e.g., lesions, etc.), severe head injuries accompanied by unconsciousness and/or concussion, abnormal EEG'S, mental disorders and diseases, cortical immaturity, and frontal lobe dysfunctions. As for myself, psychiatric professionals have repeatedly and consistently found my having been beaten into unconsciousness by the Los Angeles Police Department in the 1970's along with mental disorders were leading causes of my criminality.

GK Are there further theories on sociological causation, as opposed to organic factors?

FJA Sociological conditions have also been unveiled as determinants for a criminal personality. For instance, when criminality results from inimical social conditions, accompanied by adverse organic states. Thus, causation also occurs from outside the individual; from factors such as poverty, familial dysfunction, broken homes, and a "sick" society.

GK Interesting, but how did those social causatives infect you, especially in terms of criminality?

FJA A common theme for myself, during hundreds of therapy session hours with numerous mental health professionals, centered on my having been severely mistreated by classmates and sexually molested as a young teen. These events played key roles in my subsequent need to achieve control and excitement via criminal means throughout my teen and early adult years.

GK Can you describe this further, in more general terms?

FJA Environmental factors normatively play a crucial role in sociological causation; a fact also revealed when considering the differences in what constitutes crime among variant cultures, or even within a single population, and social circumstances into which a person was born as determinants of whether or not they would be prosecuted. I still recall many times police let me go with merely a warning or a slap on the wrist for even serious crimes as a consequence of my white upper middle-class environment, contrasted by having often witnessed African Americans taken to jail for minor offenses in impoverished neighborhoods.

GK I'm curious. I also grew up in Southern California but didn't have any Blacks for neighbors or as classmates. When and where did you frequently observe Blacks in poverty-stricken areas hauled off to police stations?

FJA In 1972-73, at ages sixteen to seventeen, I dealt a lot of marijuana and cocaine in what was called "The Jungle", an area in South Central Los Angeles, and other predominantly colored places. I sometimes saw police cart people off to jail just for seemingly hanging out on the street.

GK Oh, okay. I believe we were discussing sociologic causation?

FJA Yes. This also evidences existence of environmental pressure to fit in. As an example, criminals being influenced by the company they keep (the contagion theory). My having been abused by junior high school classmates caused overwhelming rejection and shame. Consequently, criminal enterprises provided a semblance of control, an outlet for frustration, and the means to punish society for what I misperceived as allowing abuses to have transpired. Much of my criminality was compelled by environmental conditions such as the above, and having been the victim of several sexual assaults.

In general, other ingredients of sociological causation include: deprivation, competition, neglect, child-rearing practices, media, school, destruction of self-esteem and war. Once again, my inability to fit in at school and abuse—resulting in destruction of self-worth from maladjustment and desperation – led to inappropriate attempts to regain self-value by imposing control via criminal activity.

GK In addition to organic and sociologic influence what other schools of thought address development of a criminal personality?

FJA Psychoanalysis considers continuity of mental life and how early experiences impact and alter development; the adult is related to the child she had been. This underscores why a person acts and thinks. As for myself, psychoanalytic sessions often focused on the impact of my abusive suffering and sexual molestations, on how these events functioned as causative factors of subsequent crime.

Psychoanalysis also perceives oedipal guilt (a child's subconscious sexual desire) causing need for punishment (i.e., analytic persuasion). Therefore, criminals both engage in acts that invariably end in punishment and project self-guilt onto others to then become the punisher. I engaged in felonious enterprises while knowing sooner or later I would be apprehended and disciplined, yet projected my guilt onto others. I believed society must pay for my mistreatment sexually and by schoolmates, resulting in many criminal actions against the community.

> New studies show that trauma biologically alters the brains of young boys in ways that affect their adult behavior.
>
> The Biology of Trauma
> By Alex Hannaford. 6-22-15
> https://www.texasobserver.org/author/alex-hannaford/

Moreover, I often justified property crimes by considering those I burglarized as incredibly greedy and deserving of being robbed. By giving away most proceeds I distorted my criminality into a Robin Hood scenario: my being the hero by robbing the rich to give to the poor. I also misconstrued my own failure, to fit in, with society as having mistreated me, turning this into a reason to commit crime by penalizing society's "misdeed" against me.

Finally, insofar as psychoanalysis, it's believed all criminals have immoral ideas but the strength of id, ego, and superego exist as critical factors in both causation and manifestation of crime. The id impulses in me overwhelmed my weak and underdeveloped ego, not to mention my poorly developed superego's inability to protect my ego from the id's blind, animal reactions. As a result, my mental state(s) were controlled by id and generated criminal thinking ending in unlawful action.

Of course, this brief overview of psychoanalysis does not exist as definitive or comprehensive discussion, many other factors- family dynamic impact, parental fulfillment inadequacy and unwitting parental prompting, deeply felt emotional discomforts – must also be considered.

GK Having heard antisocial personality disorder and post-traumatic stress disorder are frequently confused, what are their distinctive features?

FGA Antisocial personality disorder includes pervasive abuse of other's rights, onset commonly in early teen years, most frequently criminal conduct manifests, and generally prominent poor socioeconomic conditions (i.e., protective necessity prompts, deceit, aggression, fighting and risk taking conduct) .

One prerequisite for antisocial is having been diagnosed with a conduct disorder by age 15; my never having conduct disorder precludes an antisocial diagnosis (please see the appendix).

Post-traumatic stress disorder, in my case, required having experienced sexual violence followed by intrusion symptoms:

A. Affliction from reminders of repeated sexual assault.
B. Anger, particularly toward authority.
C. Guilt, shame and extensive wariness, (with temper tantrums featured).

> "There is nothing to say that a person can't have psychosis and PTSD," said Claude M. Chemtob, a professor of psychology at New York University who has studied the link between PTSD and aggression. But, he said, the two disorders are characterized by different symptoms.
>
> PTSD sufferers can struggle with anxiety, sleeplessness, flashbacks and anger. In rare cases, the disorder results in increased violence and aggressiveness. But paranoid delusions are not typical.
>
> Excerpt from article by Dave Phillips, New York Times 1-19-17

A most devastating impact of my PTSD centered on risk taking behavior, for me, it most commonly manifested in extreme substance abuse and reckless driving.

The Appendix provides further details.

GK In what ways did PTSD intrusion symptoms affect you?

FJA PTSD differs from antisocial personality disorder, which has been a suggested misdiagnosis attributed to me –other personality disorders may be confused with antisocial personality disorder, because they have certain features in common (DSM-5, p. 662) – however, similar affects include: not profiting from experience (especially no behavioral alteration from punishment), inability to form meaningful relationships, poor impulse control, and significant emotional immaturity. I frequently sought immediate gratification, failed to consider others (commonly ascribing blame to society for my shortcomings), and did not view myself as part of the community. The DSM-5 further states, “Individuals with PTSD are 80% more likely than those without PTSD to have symptoms that meet diagnostic criteria for at least one other mental disorder.” (p. 182), which is why my PTSD characteristics must be analyzed conceptually for accuracy in diagnosis and understanding.

CRIMINAL IDEATION, EARLY CRIMINALITY AND FAMILY RELATIONS

GK Did you fantasize often about crime?

FJA There were many phases comprising each criminal act, including: fantasies about illegal actions prior to actually making plans, plotting details of a specific crime, making necessary preparations for carrying out plans (commission), ensuing fear, and actions following my crime. Additionally, other components depended on whether apprehension occurred or detection had been escaped. To dissect and comprehend each of those features of a single crime is imperative, because understanding each element of a felony promotes more "effective deterrence," tactics required for change can then be implemented with greater success.

GK Was criminal fantasy extremely prominent in your thoughts? Please explain.

FJA The pervasiveness of criminality was so intense I would experience hundreds of ideas and fantasies daily regarding illegal enterprises, even though only one of these innumerable notions could be implemented at a time. In other words, felonious thoughts flowed through my mind in a steady stream and criminal thinking permeated all aspects of my life. For instance, whenever I entered a place of business there immediately existed thoughts regarding theft, rather than any consideration of legitimate transactions. While "casing" the joint occurred automatically upon entering a store selling merchandise—like a discount house, where I'd look for video surveillance and notice where employees were positioned, to determine the feasibility of my walking out with a stereo or television set—I also sought opportunities to steal from establishments as seemingly innocuous as insurance companies (to pilfer and forge forms) or doctors' offices (to snatch syringes, drugs, and prescription pads).

GK Were there variations in theme; was there a pattern,

randomness, or a combo?

FJA I generally experienced these pervasive criminal ideas in one of two ways: (1) fantasy, thoughts of illegal deeds without planning details, and (2) scheming, the careful and deliberate designing of a particular crime's logistics. That is, at times I would fantasize about smashing a store window, grabbing merchandise, taking my loot to a drug dealer to trade for narcotics, and then having a party with friends where I'd play big shot. On the other hand, I often began scheming after having learned about desired objects. For example, one evening I overheard some acquaintances discussing the details of a major drug deal, their conversation revealed where and when the drugs would arrive. I then spent the next several days canvassing the location where "my" drugs would arrive to familiarize myself with the perimeter and any security arrangements.

Then again, in addition to imaginings and mental plotting, talking to other felons about crime also provided a charge. As an extreme criminal, all three categories of unlawful conduct (property, sexual, and assault) were constantly discussed and considered. That is to say, as a hardcore lawbreaker I was capable of nearly any type of crime, especially when having suffered a put-down and increase in criminal thinking became overwhelming. It must also be stated that not only did criminal ideation pervade my thinking, I even considered crime as my career.

GK There exists a difference here between random on the spot criminal ideation and careful planning. Which was more prevalent?

FJA Having mentioned pervasiveness and my overwhelming nature of criminal thinking, we arrive at another key concept regarding my past lawlessness- impulse. Inherent in considering whether a crime had been committed from impulse must be determining if the act was sudden. In other words, to be an act of impulse, hardly any time can elapse between thought and action; impulsive acts are not deliberated or premeditated. Additionally, along with impulse, compulsion must also be considered. For an act to be compulsive, one must be unable to avoid acting in a certain manner despite seeking to avoid the behavior. Finally, impulse and compulsion must be contrasted with premeditation- an act that was planned in advance.

GK Please give an example of an impulsive crime.

FJA Of special import when considering impulse and its

applicability to crime, is the appearance of immediacy. Generally, impulse possessed a history of fantasy behind it. An example of an impulsive felony would be: (1) having instantly considered the potential possible fun from the proceeds of a crime, the drugs and the ability to play big shot; (2) having spotted an unattended cash register, and (3) stealing the money inside of it. In this example, the requisite nexus of scheming and premeditation were absent. On the other hand, to have fantasized about having lots of money before carefully planning details of an elaborate burglary would function as a premeditated crime.

Interviewer: Below is a list helpful to parents, students, and criminals needing to identify traits, actions, and thinking of deviant personalities:

1. Continuous and pervasive thoughts about crime.
2. Fantasizing or scheming about crime.
3. Crime compelled (whether by impulse or premeditation).
4. Development of super-optimism and positive opinion of self.
5. Deterrents temporarily defer action.
6. Erosion of deterrents.
7. Deterrents are cut off.
8. Decision to act.
9. Pre-fear crime arises and is cut off.
10. Crime actually committed.
11. Post-crime celebration.
12. Arrest.

> Pedophile Predators & Kidnapping:
>
> The Polly Klass Foundation estimates fewer than 100 children a year are kidnapped by strangers.
>
> Eli Lehrer-President of the R Street Institute wrote in the journal National Affairs: Parents wanting to protect their own children should worry much more about their own friends and relatives than random strangers.

GK Would this list function as a generally accurate pattern of criminal endeavor progression, and do you think it clarifies for readers the basic process of thought to action?

FJA These phases of criminal operations are loosely stated, and it should be remembered they can occur nearly instantaneously or over a period of time. Even though most crime generally has a history of rampant criminal thinking behind it, whether a crime is impulsive or premeditated usually reflects how rapidly the various stages of a crime occur. A single criminal enterprise with a relatively short life span, an impulsive crime, would have been primed by antecedent fantasy, even if having occurred on the spur of the moment. Consider, as an example, how I walked through the park one day, spotted a bicycle, hopped on it, and drove off. There was little concern of being caught and since I merely intended to use "my" bike momentarily I did not really consider this a crime—super-optimism and my view of self as a good person had manifested. Still, there existed some remnant bad feelings about depriving someone of their property (conscience, an internal deterrent), however, they weren't using it (erosion) and I meant no harm (cut off). Just when I decided to take the bicycle I wondered if I would get caught but a quick look around assured me I would not be detected, so I got on the bike and drove off. Of course, later that evening I bragged to several friends about how I stole a bike in broad daylight from a crowded park. The elapsed time from when I first considered taking the bicycle until riding off on it—from conception to execution; a process involving impulse, development of super-optimism and an inflated image of self, experiencing deferment due to deterrents, eroding and cutting off deterrents, deciding to act, cutting off pre-crime fear, and committing the crime—took less than thirty seconds.

GK And for premeditated crime?

FJA A premeditated crime may take considerably longer to traverse a criminal operation's elements. For instance, an expensive Italian sports car. A criminal would scheme, wondering whether to hot-wire it on the spot, push it several blocks away before starting it, follow it to see if the owner parked it someplace where it would be easier to steal, or do a carjacking.

GK We have spoken in detail about criminal thinking and behavior patterns. When involved in this lawless world how did you define "crime" or "criminal?"

FJA I did not apply the designation "criminal" to myself, unless some benefit accrued. I employed the term only against those committing action I disdained. To me "crime" meant behavior such as informing on illegal activity or infringing upon criminal enterprises in other ways. A fairly common occurrence was tracking down and dealing with those who had informed on me for having committed what I believed to have been a grave injustice. Of course, when confronted by the police later, I also perceived them as acting unfairly for having questioned and interfered with my right to punish an informant, or a drug customer for non-payment.

GK So, you were a criminal and a hypocrite?
FJA And how! I only considered right and wrong when someone else raised the question, and issues of what constituted proper and improper conduct were always subjective to me. Basically, I believed what I'd done was right, except for getting caught, and while I knew society had ordained some acts as illegal I still deemed them proper for me and remained satisfied with my "ethics." If challenged, I enumerated my virtues and sought to demonstrate where others were wrong and I was right. I also believed others had no authority to make laws controlling my behavior, that is, I saw myself as possessing the ultimate authority to govern my conduct.
GK What other distorted concepts did you believe?
FJA My concept of right and wrong also included not having perceived the many crimes I had committed almost daily as criminal behavior. I considered these actions as my job. Drug manufacturing, transportation, and dealing were my career and crimes committed to obtain sufficient funding was a legitimate part of my chosen profession—these distortions to reality enabled me, and every criminal, to be able to stomach the physical, mental, and financial harm caused. In general terms, my ideal of permissible and impermissible action involved what I wanted to do at any given time, impropriety did not exist in the act itself but rather in getting caught. In fact, when held accountable I believed I had been wronged. In other words, I failed to connect the relationship of having been apprehended to any idea that I had committed an offense.
For me, nothing regarding criminality, from the viewpoint of responsible adults, applied to myself; it was these skewed opinions—concepts having originated from (and which were maintained by) severe mental illness—enabling me to build up the perception and delusion of myself as a good person. (Please review ensuing [4] pages with PTSD diagnosis).

Dr. Donna Schwartz-Maddox
Sept. 2013 Report

On 5/6/01, he noted in a grievance that The Arizona Department of Corrections web page had him listed as molesting his present victim. The site was amended.

During the interim between his first and second evaluation, Mr. Atwood reports he was attacked "again" in July. He states that the guys write "stuff" on the walls in Pod 1, like: "Atbitch, you rot." He states another inmate ran up the steps three or four feet from his space and spit on him.

Mental Status Examination

10/11/12

Mr. Atwood was well kempt and looked his stated age. He was alert and oriented. On cognitive examination, he was able to abstract similarities between objects. He performed average on a test of verbal fluency. He was able to register three items and recall them correctly after five minutes. He had difficulty with a visual design task. He was obsessive about providing details about his history.

8/24/13

Mr. Atwood remained pleasant and cooperative. He read the report previously prepared by this examiner and was humorous about some statements and expressed increased insight into his impaired judgment. His cognitive examination was without change. He expressed frustration that he has not been receiving some of his prescribed medications. He was able to provide many more details about being sexually pressured while confined.

Neurological Screen

He did have some nystagmus. He was able to perform rapid motor movements without difficultly. His gait was normal. Since the visit was noncontact, no further examination was completed.

Diagnoses:

Axis I) Post Traumatic Stress Disorder
  Hallucinogen Abuse
  Methamphetamine Abuse
  Cannabis Abuse
Axis II) Avoidant Personality Disorder
Axis III) Headaches by history, Gastroesophageal reflux, Hepatitis C, spina bifida occulta

Discussion of Diagnoses:

Mr. Atwood suffers from an anxiety disorder known as Post Traumatic Stress Disorder (PTSD). The criterion for PTSD, according to the DSM-V, is as follows:

A. The person has been exposed to actual or threatened death, serious injury or sexual violence in one (or more) of the following ways

1. Directly experiencing the traumatic event(s).
2. Witnessing in person, the event(s) as it occurred to others.
3. Learning that the traumatic event(s) occurred to a close family member or close friend.
4. Experiencing repeated or extreme exposure to aversive details of the traumatic event(s).

Mr. Atwood had been exposed to serious traumas before his charges, which threatened his physical integrity. The different occasions of sexual abuse during his development have been described above. His first sexual trauma at the age of 14 is well documented and resulted in the conviction of the assailant. He has also been exposed to threats on his physical integrity since his incarceration through assaults by other inmates. He has since recalled numerous other instances where sexual violence was threatened.

B. Presence of one (or more) of the following intrusion symptoms associated with the traumatic event(s), beginning after the traumatic event(s) occurred

1. Recurrent, involuntary and distressing memories of the traumatic event(s).
2. Recurrent distressing dreams in which the content and/or effect of the dream are related to the traumatic event.
3. Dissociative reactions (flashbacks) in which the individual feels or acts as if the traumatic event(s) were recurring.
4. Intense or prolonged psychological distress at exposure to internal or external cues that symbolize or resemble an aspect of the traumatic event.
5. Marked physiologic reactions to internal or external cues that symbolize or resemble an aspect of the traumatic event.

Mr. Atwood re-experiences his traumatic stress in two ways. He experiences psychological distress when exposed to external cues that symbolize or resemble an aspect of the traumatic event and he has physiological activity when exposed to cues that remind him of the traumatic events. For example, ADOC records reflect that Mr. Atwood was recently placed on suicide watch because he indicated that he would harm himself due to the threats he was receiving from other inmates. Even after he was taken off of suicide watch, he expressed his desire to be moved because of his fear of other inmates. He reports feeling scared whenever he is in proximity to larger _____ in population.

C. Persistent avoidance of stimuli associated with the trauma event(s), beginning after the traumatic event(s) occurred, as evidenced by one or both of the following:

1. Avoidance or efforts to avoid distressing memories, thoughts or feelings about or closely associated with the traumatic event(s).
2. Avoidance of or efforts to avoid external reminders (people, places, conversations, activities, objects, situations) that arouse distressing memories, thoughts or feelings about or closely associated with the traumatic event(s).

Mr. Atwood avoids dealing with inmates. He was raped by juveniles and an inmate and assaulted by inmates while confined at ADOC. He does not speak to inmates and avoids interactions with them. He therefore avoids conversations, places, and significant activities. As referenced in Dr. Nelson's report, Mr. Atwood has acted as a legal aide to various inmates in the past. He was paid for that job and also reports he performed that job for others so that he could gain favor with them to avoid being assaulted. During previous confinements before his present conviction, Mr. Atwood would request "being in the hole" or be in a form of protective custody to avoid inmates he felt were dangerous. He has been assaulted again since his first evaluation. He has avoided being in general population and previous institutional assignments where he would be housed with large numbers of inmates.

D. Negative alterations in cognitions and mood associated with the traumatic event(s) beginning or worsening after the traumatic event(s) occurred, as evidence by two or more of the following:

1. Inability to remember an important aspect of the traumatic event(s) (typically due to dissociative amnesia and not to other factors such as head injury, alcohol or drugs).
2. Persistent and exaggerated negative beliefs about oneself, or others, or the world.
3. Persistent, distorted cognitions about the cause or consequences of the traumatic event(s) that lead the individual to blame himself/herself or others.
4. Persistent negative emotional state.
5. Markedly diminished interest or participation in significant activities.
6. Feelings of detachment or estrangement from others.
7. Persistent inability to experience positive emotions.

Mr. Atwood has blamed himself for his assault when he was 14 years old and has done so until recently. He reported that since he did not say no, he believed he was at fault. He has downplayed his guilt over the years by telling people he liked it and didn't mind. He has blamed himself for his assault at Atascadero because he was seeking drugs and placed himself in the situation. Mr. Atwood has also had a persistent negative emotional state. He has been angry and has history of treatment for anxiety over the years.

E. Marked alterations in arousal and reactivity associated with the traumatic event(s) beginning or worsening after the traumatic event(s) occurred, as evidenced by two of the following:

1. Irritable behavior and angry outbursts typically expressed as verbal or physical aggression toward people or objects
2. Reckless or self-destructive behavior
3. Hypervigilance
4. Exaggerated startle response
5. Problems with concentration
6. Sleep disturbance

Mr. Atwood has evidence of numerous outbursts of verbal aggression towards corrections officers. He also had an episode where he destroyed property and brandished a knife at his mother. He has a twenty-year history of reckless and self-destructive behavior, soon reoffending after his release, and abusing drugs. He is hypervigilant in situations.

F. Duration of disturbance is more than one month.

Mr. Atwood has a history of psychiatric treatment predating his offense, amounting to well over 1 month. He also has documented anxiety and treatment for anxiety in his corrections file.

G. The disturbance causes clinically significant distress or impairment in social, occupational or other important areas of functioning.

Mr. Atwood has a long history of treatment for anxiety, which has impaired his functioning.

H. The disturbance is not attributable to the physiologic effects of a substance or another medical condition.

The highest rates of PTSD are found among survivors of rape, and military, political combat and captivity. Environmental factors also reveal the greater magnitude of the trauma, the greater likelihood of PTSD. Individuals with PTSD are 80% more likely to meet diagnostic criteria for at least one other mental disorder such as depression, anxiety or substance abuse disorders.

GK Please provide an opening statement about your early criminality.

FJA I committed hundreds of crimes, before ever being caught and considered a "first offender" at age sixteen. These violations prior to my initially being apprehended were overt (arrestable) crimes. In addition to considering the hundreds of crimes I got away with before my fist arrest we must also consider my well-ingrained criminal thought patterns, fantasies, and schemes that occurred continually, even before having committed my first arrestable crime. Moreover, my criminal history (e.g., police reports, pre-sentence reports) was laden with misinformation, I had corrupted the process by providing interviewers with unreliable and self-serving stories.

GK In what ways did these patterns of thinking and behavior impact your view of self?

FJA Another particularly revealing pattern you'll find was how my attitude toward myself, others, and society exposed my arrogance and self-centeredness along with my willingness to invoke radical extremes to obtain the control I so desperately needed and the excitement I so desperately craved.

GK Give us a few specific examples of positive actions of thoughtfulness that you did as a teen, without expectation of getting something in return: Mother's birthday, Christmas, Valentine's Day, etc.

FJA Your question evokes a few responses. I possessed a great deal of love for my parents, so I always bought, with allowance money, cards for every special occasion and gifts on Easter, Christmas, and birthdays. Some classes at school (shop, art, etc.) provided opportunity for making ashtrays, sculptures, artwork to give as a surprise to mom or dad. At church I volunteered often, so helped teach hymns and Sunday school lessons. Also, I would offer to do chores like walk the dog, wash dishes, clean the pool, or yard work. Some of these examples were more frequent in my early teens but consistency did visit my thoughtful actions done sans any expectation of self-benefit.

GK From birth to around ten years old, how do you remember your parents? Were they kind, positive and supportive or something else? I ask because my mother was kind, positive and supportive yet I still ended up on death row.

FJA My mom supported me all of the time. Took me to practice for sports, was our Cub Scout den mother, helped with school lessons, etc. We spent every day during summers on the beach together, truly a loving mother.

GK And your father? Mine passed when I was five; he died at 39 of a heart attack.

FJA He taught me hockey, baseball, and football, even was the coach on most of my teams. As a family we enjoyed close relations, what glorious times; family vacations, classical concerts, time together. I was cared for and loved. To have become a criminal, having spent most of my life in prison, so brought such anguish on my loving parents, is a major regret. May God forgive me.

GK I too share your regret.

GK What music and movies influenced your criminal tendencies in the late 60's, early 70's?

FJA What leaps out initially is hard rock music. Once I began to gravitate toward the counterculture, music became a huge part of my life; among my favorites were Grand Funk Railroad, Black Sabbath, Canned Heat, and Mountain. The lyrics tended to reinforce new sets of values (pro-drugs, anti-establishment, irreverence, etc.) and acquaintance with major rock stars found me enamored with the celebrity lifestyle.

Movies did not possess as much influence, although I recall an attraction to the cruising across country while stoned depicted in *Easy Rider*. There were some movies—like *Woodstock*, *The French Connection*, and *Super Fly*—that further cemented my changing values, but hard rock music catapulted me into netherworlds never previously contemplated.

GK Let's pick up with attitudes and conduct pertaining to family. What can you tell us about this?

FJA In this instance, family refers to my parents, and as a youth I was seen as "different" by them, as well as by teachers and others with whom I came in contact.

GK How were you different?

FA I tended to engage in extreme behavior after the age fourteen sexual assault and subsequent onset of PTSD. Being an angel one moment and a hellion the next I would claim my excessive behavior resulted from having been a victim of unreasonable and punitive parents. However, no recounting of what I had done to deserve punishment was ever offered.

My parents had legitimately invoked a plethora of available punishments; I was grounded, spanked, lost my allowance and other privileges, was made to do extra chores, et al. Moreover, I was sent to therapy, drug counseling, special schools, and was taken on business trips with my dad—occasions intended to rebuild the close relations from childhood and during which I actually felt normal again. My refusal to alter my downward spiral was so very difficult for my precious parents; for instance, under the guise of a regularly music lesson my father took me to the probation office. I was sixteen or seventeen and to seek, out of desperation, help for me, my dad had pre-arranged for me to temporarily be taken into custody. Upon realization of this, I screamed for my daddy, who was walking toward his car. Years later we talked about this incident, to learn of the heartbreak (both the decision to have me locked up and to not come running to help his screaming son) had me in tears…I still feel so horribly ashamed at what I put both of my loving parents through when I was a teen and young adult. Thus, it was never my family who rejected me, instead I rejected them by having chosen a criminal lifestyle; the fact remained, I came from a loving family and affluent neighborhood.

GK You left him no other option but tough love.

FJA This was after having been assaulted at fourteen, and my attitude, in regard to both myself and my parents, was revealed by selfishness and disregard for others. Take as an example the many times I stole my mom's or my dad's car and stayed out all night partying. Beyond the theft were concerns such as driving while intoxicated, uninsured, without a license (I was fifteen to seventeen), safety and chance of arrest…not to mention the incredible worries I caused my parents. Still, I resented anyone who limited my freedom, and when deciding who was "good" or "bad," the determining factor resided in how much opposition to my ideas the person in question posed. This meant believing I had a "bad" mother when she did not perform as I desired.

GK How else did your relationships at home deteriorate?

FJA Well, there was my failure to see myself as obligated to fulfill mundane requirements at home, believing instead others should fall in line with what I wanted. As such, I didn't appreciate favors, taking them for granted and expecting more next time, being completely insensitive to the desires and needs of my parents. Recounting this is way difficult! Wow.

Even as early as when I was fifteen my mind focused more fully on exciting things, like power, control, and victory, rather than on school or responsibilities at home. I made contests out of everything to achieve these aims and viewed winning any dispute as being far more important than the disputed issue. In addition to winning, what mattered was getting away with things so, not surprisingly, I employed many tactics to get my way.

GK This negative, rude personality, this was after you were sexually assaulted?

FJA Yes. It began to emerge several months after I was molested at 14 ½, then was relatively full-blown at age fifteen. Doctors opined my PTSD led to distrust of others and as a defense mechanism I became angry and tended to rudeness, even tantrums. See subsequent PTSD appendix.

GK Were you basically a spoiled rich kid who experienced sexual trauma followed by a temporary psychotic break?

FJA Temporary psychosis episodes erupted as a consequence of drug intoxication, which was due to self-medicating as a way to minimize PTSD's devastation. While there were psychotic experiences, the underlying mental illness was post-traumatic stress disorder.

GK I'm still trying to get a more complete picture of who Frank was before your assaults vs. after. I've not found the key component yet.

FJA Okay. Prior to my initial rape I was well-adjusted, involved in organized sports, excitedly attending church and participating in related activities, fully engaged in family interaction, a great student, and my house was where all the neighborhood kids gathered (my mom was our cub scout den mother and often included my friends in family activities). Subsequent to the original sexual assault everything changed…for the WORSE. Gone, in short order, were sports, church, family, school attendance, and friends. I became a loner, extreme drug abuser, sexual deviant, criminal, and radical anti-authority/counterculture activist. Sadly, a near 180° turn transpired, one that had me in and out of prison by age seventeen; rather than having attended the United States Military Academy at West Point. For a commentary record on drastic changes please see the Appendix.

> The type of trauma has differential impacts on psychopathology in adulthood.
>
> Our findings based on an incarcerated sample, (confirm previous primarily on community-based research samples) showing childhood trauma has strong negative associations with adult psychological wellness.
>
> And, different types of childhood trauma are independently associated with impacts on adult psychopathology.
>
> Research by: Nancy Wolff and Jing Shi. May 2012
>
> https://www.ncbi.nlm.nih.gov/pmc/articles/PMC3386595

GK How were temper blowouts a factor in your familial interactions?

FJA As an example, in order to "justify" violations I would start an uproar by initiating an argument over the slightest perceived offense, blowing things completely out of proportion, and then use the other person's reaction as an excuse to commit the desired criminal action—like after having picked a fight and then stealing my dad's car or having taken money from my mom under the guise of needing to get away from such an unfair and explosive environment (...of my own making!) I would also dredge up prior interactions and apply them in a different context, however, when something was desired I could "suddenly" communicate effectively or behave well, since it suited my purposes. Occasionally, I would simply make life miserable for my parents by throwing things and threatening violation if not accommodated.

GK The treatment of your parents is still hard to fathom. Did you tell your mother and/or father about your sexual trauma(s)?

FJA Mostly. The first molestation at fourteen became a court case, so my parents learned all details. The next rape was found out by my father and he informed my mother. The third assault was during a family vacation in Aspen, I did not immediately tell anyone, however, circumstances exposed to my parents that something, presumably of a sexual attack nature, had transpired. Finally, the last rape, I did fully discuss with my mom and my dad.

GK Did you tell therapists?

FJA Yes, I did. And for whatever reason this never became a topic covered in depth. My thought is therapists instead focused on the consequences; PTSD was not identified by the psychiatric community when I was attacked (between 1970-75) so attention fell upon the results: anger, sexually provocative behavior, recklessness, anti-authority thinking, heavy drug use; to mention a few symptoms of PTSD I suffered.

GK Why the anger at your parents?

FJA I've wondered about this and all I can come up with is the rage I felt toward myself for having placed myself in positions where sexual victimization could, and did, happen. I've been told that victims of sexual assault often blame themselves, I've certainly done this and felt so much anger toward myself. Consequently, to desperately seek deflection of self-anger I misdirected it onto my beloved parents. May God forgive me.

GK What were some of the results of this on you and your parents?

FJA By age fifteen I had chosen to live a life of crime and felt I had to reject my parents to live a life of secrecy. Many times, teachers, psychiatrists, or counselors faulted my parents for misunderstanding me, or not being involved enough with me, however, I was the one who imposed secrecy and set myself apart. In order to escape detection of my criminality I had to constantly be deceptive and lie. Consider, for example, my telling my mom I was going to visit a specific person to play sports and then I'd proceed to a different place to do drugs.

GK So your parents didn't care where you went or never verified your plans?

FJA They always insisted I relate my plans to them whenever I left home, so asked where I was going. And verification was difficult; as in the example just given, where I knew one friend was going to a park to play football so a call by my mom would result in her being told my friend was playing sports; presumably, I too. If caught lying, my goal was to have made a clean getaway (to depart sans hassle) and if interference would later arise I'd deal with it then.

GK Didn't you still have a close relationship with your parents?

FJA I shied away from familial relations, starting at around age fifteen, choosing to neither receive or give love [I feel so sad right now from recalling having snubbed the unconditional love proffered by my mom and dad]. Even when my parents and I attended functions it was done begrudgingly on my part and occasionally I'd wander off (as happened in Aspen, leading to having been sexually assaulted). Overall, I wanted the comforts of home, I wanted to do as I pleased, expecting family to meet every need; all without contributing to family life or considering the rights of my parents.

GK In what way(s) did your parents try to regain the loving son they once enjoyed?

FJA Out of desperation my mom and dad often sought counseling for themselves and me. The initial problem with counseling involved therapists directing the focus toward my parents, not what I had done. This provided me with a license to act up, worsening our situation, and I'd also lay the blame on my parents. Therefore, while I attended counseling sessions "under protest" I exploited the circumstances; for instance, I used therapists to convince my mom and dad to implement "fairer" procedures (fewer restrictions) at home. Finally, I attempted to manipulate counseling by having asserted a specious claim about requiring confidentiality so that one doctor would treat me while another doctor treated my parents. This enabled more chaos to be injected into home life and resulted in my getting my way.

GK Did you then and/or do you now experience any remorse for your having so badly abused your parents?

FJA Both the frantic drive to see myself as “good,” not as a criminal causing harm to others, and an immature personality (with attendant self-centeredness, etc.) precluded much remorse for horrendous treatment of my parents when in my teen and early adult years. One of the greatest crimes I committed consisted of the untold damage inflicted on my own parents. My mother and father ultimately had their hearts broken, inevitably had their lives disrupted, and were forced to live under extreme stress and uncertainty. Actual crimes against them included stealing cars and money, taking and selling property, abusing credit cards and checks, and concealing contraband (drugs, stolen merchandise, weapons, etc.) in their home. My parents were forced to engender a new attitude and behavior as a result of my exploitation. Then, despite their innocence and all my above atrocities, somehow my parents were blamed for my conduct and attitude—blamed by me, after I had been apprehended for violation, then faulted by therapists, law enforcement, teachers, parole/probation officers, and society. I just do not see how God can forgive me.

GK I sympathize with your familial regrets. I have plenty of my own, have you any concluding comments about the life, the despair you foisted upon your parents?

FJA Understandably, my family became desperate, they loved their son dearly but abhorred my attitude and behavior; the result was constant emotional agony. Additionally, my parents were caught between admitting the truth about their son, attempting to ignore the severity of my conduct, and protecting me. My mom and dad did acknowledge I was different but refused to classify this as delinquency, since to admit my criminality would have somehow caused them to feel they had failed. Instead, they desperately continued to hope I would change. This led to my family enrolling me in one private school after another and clinging

> In Alex Hannaford’s article Letters from Death Row: The Biology of Childhood Truama, Maurie Levin, a capital defense attorney told Mr. Hannaford 100% of her capital case defendants “survived miserable” childhoods rampant with sexual, physical and emotional abuse.
>
> https://www.texasobserver.org/letters-from-death-row-childhood-trauma/

to the false hope that a different environment would resolve problems, even having on one occasion, when I was sixteen, uprooted the entire household to change residences. Eventually, my parents were caught between misleading the authorities and their personal integrity, as they struggled with loyalty to their own flesh and blood, versus honesty with law enforcement. The unimaginable pain I put my parents through has broken my heart.

GK How did you perceive and interact with friends and neighbors?

FJA I perpetuated the belief I was corrupted by the company I kept, and my family, not wanting to believe I was bad, readily accepted this premise. I actually gravitated toward others who were also in pursuit of excitement, and sought out older, more experienced individuals. So rather than my having been, as an inexperienced youngster, sought and corrupted, it was I who chose the derelict company I kept. In fact, once I had become heavily involved in crime as a mid-teenager, I endeavored to guide neighborhood kids down the same evil path; I had become the corrupter. So, while knowing responsible children, I rejected their way of life and found I had less and less in common with them. I began to scorn ordinary means of living and this led to dropping out of traditional groups (church, school clubs, etc.) by my mid-teens because these functions failed to provide desired excitement—crime = excitement at the expense of others.

GK Sticking with involvement between yourself and other kids, please discuss a bit more detail.

FJA Another troubling characteristic I developed as a youngster (i.e., age fourteen) involved going way beyond responsible limits when playing sports to thusly create excitement, and I usually engaged in action that other kids frowned upon. For instance, I refused to ride my bicycle merely for transportation or leisure, instead racing around to be recklessly daring. An example of this dwells in my having terrorized pedestrians by chasing them down sidewalks and then frightening motorists when entering the street by shooting into traffic from between parked cars. Other examples include having ignored rules at swimming pools by jumping off diving boards as closely as possible to swimmers or having leaped out of rides or aiming for head on collisions with bumper cars when at amusement parks. A common antic at Disneyland was jumping out of a car (during "Mr. Toad's Wild Ride," "Haunted Mansion," "Pirates of the Caribbean") to attack walls or figures. When at Magic Mountain I beat up a park employee, who I'd argued with while he was in a troll suit; being escorted off the grounds necessitated a scuffle with security. Also, when playing team sports, I demanded to be the captain and ordered others around, having had no sense of a team working together to achieve a goal, and I rarely sustained hobbies because I was only momentarily attracted due to my need for kicks. For me, I found "fun" in violation—throwing rocks or eggs, putting sugar in gas tanks, damaging property, and other acts of vandalism; anger at self-further being misdirected by projecting it onto society to then be mad at "them."

I just had no consideration for friends and neighbors and often possessed a need to build myself up by tearing others down. To me, people were like money in the bank, they merely existed for me to draw on.

GK Please describe a bit more on your criminal experience.

FJA As mentioned previously, there are three crime groups: assault, property, and sexual. My criminal activity began in the property category when I stole from my parents. Subsequent to that I moved to stealing bicycles, shoplifting, vandalism, and finally burglary. As I got away with crime after crime, I became bolder, and my contempt for responsible people increased. Of course, my awful behavior caused great disdain toward me by society, which, in a desperate move to somehow justify my conduct, I twisted into a reason to engage in additional criminal conduct to punish an "unfair" world. Felonious behavior quickly became ingrained in my life.

GK Of course, the end result was involvements in all three blocks of criminality?

FJA Yes, eventually early patterns in the property crime arena expanded and increased and, especially when criticized, I began to commit assaultive crime. At the same time, I began to involve myself in sex crimes, having even molested a kid. Finally, as I became more subsumed in all categories of crime and grew bolder, the fear of arrest diminished and no longer functioned as a deterrent. In fact, when apprehended I even found excitement in the challenge of escaping or mitigating punishment.

GK Would you please share a few details from your first arrest as an adult?

FJA I was arrested in 1974 for lewd acts; having ridden up to a ten-year-old girl on my motorcycle. I kissed her and grabbed between her legs before driving off. Having back then seen the incident as insignificcant, I felt arrest was wholly unreasonable.

Thus, I thought of myself as the victim and minimized my misconduct. Once my attorney failed to have charges dropped, or to otherwise procure my release, I authorized psychiatric evaluations for contemplation of hospitalization. The anger felt over what I perceived as such an unfair fate gave birth to my career as a very successful and well-known jailhouse lawyer.

5

EXAMINING MY THINKING ERRORS

During our two months of interviews, today's Frank Atwood depicted in detail the warpage in thinking patterns sustained and the onset of a deviant attitude having plagued the once innocent, but now defiled child.

GK Hopefully, by exposing the criminal characteristics you possessed, others will be better equipped to comprehend their criminal personality and apply correctives. Please provide a brief synopsis of your personality during your days as a criminal.

FJA As a criminal, I did not label or think of my personality traits as deviant, nor did I believe my characteristics were erroneous; no criminal does. This facilitated my having functioned in ways very different from responsible persons, manners that were harmful to myself and others. The root cause resided in thinking patterns; how I viewed myself and others, along with how I interacted with people and events, comprised the foundation of my criminality. My criminal characteristics existed as a dark manifestation of my thought process. Once I began to understand my thinking patterns, I realized what I had become: a fearful person who was filled with anger because of being a nobody. Of course, these personality traits were not unique to myself; each and every criminal possesses many of these distinct features for various reasons.

GK I've heard about "concrete thinking" and "fragmentation." Please explain these and detail how they influenced your thinking and behavior.

FJA One of my more prominent and debilitating aspects of criminal personality involved thinking in terms of isolated events, failing to recognize similarity between situations. For example, I perceived drug use as a teen as something distinct from school or family functions. I simply failed to grasp how one set of actions, such as drug use or crime, impacted my involvement in responsible activities.

GK I'm pretty sure I did that as well; please continue.

FJA Concepts society took for granted were completely alien to me. Some of these included family, looking after family members, and adapting to stresses and strains each family unit experiences. As for the notion of parenthood, I believed a parent existed to provide me what I desired and, having interest in only what I wanted, the cohesion required in family units was desperately absent. There dwelled no concept of reciprocal relationships; my idea of "relationship" was basically all take and no give, involving merely what I could get from family, friends, and lovers.

GK I see how isolationist ideation severely retarded your personal relations, did this malfunction in perception similarly infect your interaction with the community?

FJA I harbored little conceptualization of social institutions. For instance, there existed a failure to appreciate education as preparation for adulthood, a particularly revealing personality trait exposing my inability to connect present actions with future consequences. Or, as another example, I accepted police officers as responsible for stopping crime…so long as it was not my crime. This demonstrates how I assessed social institutions and others in terms of whether or not they interfered with me.

GK This seems to speak of an altered sense of morality, is that the case?

FJA Concrete thinking also led to my belief that I had to be the sole arbiter of right and wrong. Actually, I did not think in terms of right and wrong but instead considered whether I could get away with an action. Of course, if an operation could be successfully completed (sans detection or interference), it was "right" for me; this included any action, even when the rights and safety of others were at stake.

GK How else did fragmented and concrete thinking affect your relationships?

FJA As a consequence of failing to consider others, I did not maintain a balanced view of people. I could consider an acquaintance who owned a store as a companion when we went to a club or as someone to rob when at their place of business. One day I was driving around Hollywood with a buddy, smoking a joint, trying to pick up women. Despite his having several thousand dollars in his possession there was no thought of robbing him; I would have harmed anyone trying to take his

7 to 11 Rapes Before 1st Arrest

David Lisak Ph.D. Psychologist wrote: Rapists who are prosecuted are convicted on a single count of rape yet typically have raped multiple people, on average between seven and eleven.

82% of child molesters have also sexually attacked adults.

50 to 66% of incest offenders have also sexually attacked children outside their families.

Source: Wikipedia–David Lisak.

money because, during that distinct experience, he was my pal. However, this "partnership" was not enduring, since the next day I showed up at his car dealership, demanded the use of an automobile, then beat him and borrowed a car once he refused to provide a vehicle.

GK Did he call the cops, were you arrested, was the car returned?

FJA The police weren't summoned, nor was I arrested. I suppose our use of drugs discouraged his involving law enforcement and perhaps he considered the car's cost as "severance pay" (worth its miniscule value to be rid of me). I did return the automobile after a several days joy ride.

Overnight my "friend" became an enemy as a consequence of failing to accede with my plans. As can be seen, my focus was on only one situation at a time, to the exclusion of all other events, causing me to be burdened with an extremely limited perception throughout much of my life.

GK This sounds a bit Jekyll and Hyde? I tried to stay away from people like that.

FJA My readily apparent inconsistency in behavior and attitude permeated every aspect of my life. The contradictory nature was a standard component of my personality. Fragmentation involved fluctuation in mental states and action occurring over relatively short periods of time. For example, I would revere a person one moment, such as a love interest, yet cause the same person untold anguish soon thereafter if my desires didn't pan out. A common manifestation of this characteristic involved displaying a helpful attitude and a hateful disposition within minutes, with the degree to which I changed revealing my depth of fragmentation.

GK Is that to say your fragmentation and concrete thinking carried equal detriment?

FJA Fragmentation is connected to concrete thinking. This can be seen by recognizing that I viewed responsible living as a set of concrete, isolated acts—such as going to work, attending church, and so on. I had no comprehension of responsibility as based on concepts such as ethical or moral standards.

Moreover, a most common consequence of fragmentation manifested in an eminent pattern of beginning something, then quickly changing my mind. I recall deciding I'd put together a complex system of stereo components, and even began to build a cabinet for them. Then I wanted to add accessories to my motorcycle and dragged out necessary tools. Finally, I decided to watch a football game on television, before halftime I was on the way to a friend's house. This all happened within several hours and not a single action had been pursued to completion. Severe fragmentation compelled me to move from one event to another in a frantic search for excitement. This pursuit of excitement, a key precursor for criminal thinking, served to greatly expand unlawful involvement. Of course, violations that were once exciting quickly failed to produce requisite excitement, after which criminal patterns broadened at an alarming rate.

GK Please illustrate further how fragmentation hampered your thinking.

FJA Fragmentation also led to viewing others by considering what I desired and whether someone else agreed. In the preceding example, where I had been on friendly terms with a car dealer when he posed no threat to my plans (while we got stoned) and treated him as an enemy the very next day, as he refused to acquiesce to my ridiculous and unreasonable demands. Fragmentation even caused me to lack a consistent view of myself, a defect also altering how I perceived others. During these events, I also saw others as responsible adults, but as potential marks. However, when involved in a scam I then viewed myself as unpredictable, and this engendered my belief others behaved as deceitfully and erratic as myself. In general, my severely fragmented personality caused me to be at the mercy of whatever I wished for at any given moment.

GK Now, for concrete and fragmented thinking errors, how did you correct these?

FJA Recalling past errors and responsibly viewing long-term consequences of behavior deflect fragmentation and concrete thinking. However, new patterns had to be developed in myself. I had to, with force, compel myself to dwell intensely on former patterns, in order to learn from past error. I then had to develop and sustain the feeling of self-disgust. That is, I began to correct tubular vision by maintaining constant awareness of past thinking and behavior errors. Furthermore, in order for a realistic evaluation of progress to occur, I had to be able to contrast present ideation and conduct with previous characteristics.

As for the long-term consequences of my behavior, I generally viewed only my present when contemplating a crime. Obviously, I had to broaden my sense of time perspective. I began the process by learning to plan for my future. For instance, I attended a degree program at Ohio University with the intent of developing skills I could employ several years later, and budgeted monthly finances in a way that provided savings for potential emergencies. This enabled me to begin considering possible positive consequences of my new thinking.

> As of 2016 there were more than 805,000 registered sex offenders in the United States. About 33% are considered at low risk to reoffend and roughly 15% fall in the sexually violent predator category.
>
> In 2006 there were 541,000 registered sex offenders. About 26,000 new sex offenders are added each year. Or 73 per day.

This shows I also had to learn what a responsible goal was and needed to work toward the disappearance of excessive pretensions by developing the filters of logic and reason. In other words, to grasp how patience possesses many rewards, my sense of urgency had to be abated, I needed to recognize precipitous actions always resulted in disaster.

GK Especially since your concepts of family, work, and future were being modified.

FJA Yes, I lacked so many basic social concepts—such as family, education, time, work, money, and religion—it became necessary to learn how to conceptualize the nature of personal relations and social institutions in order to facilitate responsibility, this existed as an imposing impediment, because early in the change process focus was limited to a series of concrete events. What I mean is, I perceived something as commonplace as going to work to be simply a solitary act to complete—get in the car or on the bus, go to the job, perform whatever tasks were required, and return home. In no way did I ever contemplate how this work fit in with or served society. Part of the reason for this was so I could shield myself from the harm I did through criminal enterprises, like when having sold myself for sexual favors to older men and perceiving each occasion as a single innocuous event rather than part of a broader pattern concerning problems with health and other risks.

My failure to have conceptualized individual acts constituted a major obstacle to my learning from experience, to correct this I took each single episode in my daily journals and related it to other events. I did this by authoring a list of experiences, then looked for ways to apply them to other situations that were far removed in nature (sort of like a personality puzzle or game). This enabled me to learn each act could be generalized and conceptualized to apply to a variety of people, events, institutions, and even the nature of my existence. The failure to have acquired this skill earlier in my program for change had severely retarded the process, however, once developed I found it far easier to pursue responsible living.

GK What were some of your challenges in developing a new constant personality?

FJA It is important to note my fragmentation didn't exist as a discontinuity in thought, rather (at least early on in the change process) it manifested as an impossibility to know what reaction I would provide on any given day or at any particular moment. The main impetus for this involved having relied on people and circumstances for satisfaction, which, especially in a supermax prison, is a certain prescription for disaster. There were times when having been promised the delivery of some coveted property item I would take on an exuberant mood; when the property failed to arrive, I'd become despondent and snap at others.

The corrective existed in learning to conceptualize beyond momentary thoughts and feelings, so regardless of what ups and downs life brought I could remain on an even keel. Part of this was achieved by realizing others did not exist to cater to my rapidly changing desires. In other words, I had to develop a realistic and responsible concept of what a lover, parent, or acquaintance involved. Another corrective was to restore rational perspective by constantly reminding myself of my three basic options: crime, suicide, or change.

With practice, an objective outlook existed as a strong antidote to my fragmentation and was essential to my modification program. Only then was I able to accurately review previous phenomenological reports, contemplate future actions, and generate responsible perspective—all of which reduced fragmentation by enabling me to apprehend and appreciate these "objective outlook" successes.

GK I found it rather interesting for you to connect your concrete thinking, fragmentation, and work. Please discuss how your thinking errors and PTSD impacted your perception of work.

FJA Work?!?!

Seriously, one of the diagnostic features of PTSD centers on impaired functioning. For myself, I experienced detriment in multiple areas; including social skills, educational endeavors, and work. Consequently, I commonly believed the workplace had to adapt to my demands instead of my adhering to the requirements for the job. This also involved deciding how I thought the job should be performed, as opposed to how the boss had instructed me to do the work, and having imposed my own work schedule by showing up when it suited me. Other ways my pursuit of power impacted how I interacted, aside from the work arena, included embellishing speech to make an impression, or sporting radical styles of clothing—at times having worn Kelly green and bright orange two-toned pants and/or a fur coat—and grooming to set myself apart from others.

The bottom line, insofar as my maintaining control, involved believing I was invariably right and others were wrong. This meant others, no matter who, had to shape their normal thinking to fit my twisted mind. For instance, workers were not perceived by me as knowing as much as I did, at least among areas in which I had serious interest; therefore, it was up to me to educate them.

I also had to believe I was exceptional, or would at some point during my life perform some extraordinary feat, but only lip service was given to what was required to accomplish such lofty aspirations. Still, in this manner I was able to maintain the internal concept of myself as a powerful person.

GK What else can you tell us about your approach to employment?

FJA I possessed three characteristics toward work that existed on a continuum: (1) work was scorned so I refused to get a job, (2) having put forth a half-hearted effort to hold a job in order to provide a facade of working, and (3) having worked only to use the job for criminal enterprises. Obviously, I had no concept of a career and no long-range goals. Nevertheless, I believed I should have been an immediate success without being required to start at the bottom and work my way up.

GK Thus, you saw no value in earning a living, of establishing yourself in a job of your choosing?

FJA My general attitude toward work was it would never get me anywhere, there were far better and easier ways to get what I'd desired. I also saw following a routine set by others as offensive and demanding, so refused to take orders or be a subordinate. In other words, I resented doing work I considered beneath me, and because I thought I knew more than the boss I perceived him/her as an "inferior." Besides, I knew I didn't have to take orders in what I considered to be a debasing job, because I could have more money pass through my hands in a month of crime than in a year of work. As a result, I rarely worked at all or drifted in and out of part-time jobs.

GK Unfortunately, there was a time in my life when I acted the same way.

FJA Ah, so we're in good company! Occasionally I worked to appear responsible, as a front, or because my family and probation/parole officer required me to work. The few times worked I did ended in embarrassment, since it became obvious I knew little about work processes. Moreover, because I could care less, I failed to learn about job hours, pay schedules, tax deductions, or benefits, and this also exposed my ignorance. Yet I still believed the job had to conform to me rather than my adapting to its requirements. With these attitudes about work I failed at every job before ever having shown up for the first day.

GK On the days you did show up, what kind of relationships with co-workers did you have?

FJA If I decided to show up at work I would usually steal from my employer or cheat customers. One job that I held for about a month was at a car rental business, and the sole reason I stayed longer than the usual couple of days was for the

Sexual Predator Numbers:

Only 7% are strangers.

The victim usually knows the attacker – 93%.

80% are the victim's parents.

6% were other relatives.

9% are female and 3% are unknown.

34% are under age 12.

Typical effects of child sexual abuse:
Drug Use
PTSD
Depression

opportunity to cheat customers who paid by credit card. Then again, this on-the-job theft occurred not from a need for money, but rather for the thrill of getting away with it. This led to learning about co-workers, where they lived and their habits. I'd then burglarize them when they were away from home. Even if not involved in job theft, I was still heavily involved in other crimes. Additionally, other on the job violations included drug use.

GK And as for education, how did PTSD impair your studies?

FJA I began having serious problems in school during age 14. This was at Melrose School, when problems worsened. I'd been sent to this school for children with behavior and emotional actions upon the recommendation of a psychologist treating my family soon after I was raped, competing interests arose; truancy, theft, destructive acts increased in number.

However, I was well aware of school personnel who were sympathetic to me and would manipulate them mercilessly. I saw a great teacher as one assigning little work and who was lax in discipline.

Eventually misbehaviors at school lost their thrill, I basically quit attending high school to seek greater sources of excitement and entertainment.

As for the response by schools, rather than deal with a troublemaker they just recommended a transfer to get rid of me, citing my need for professional help. (See school report below)

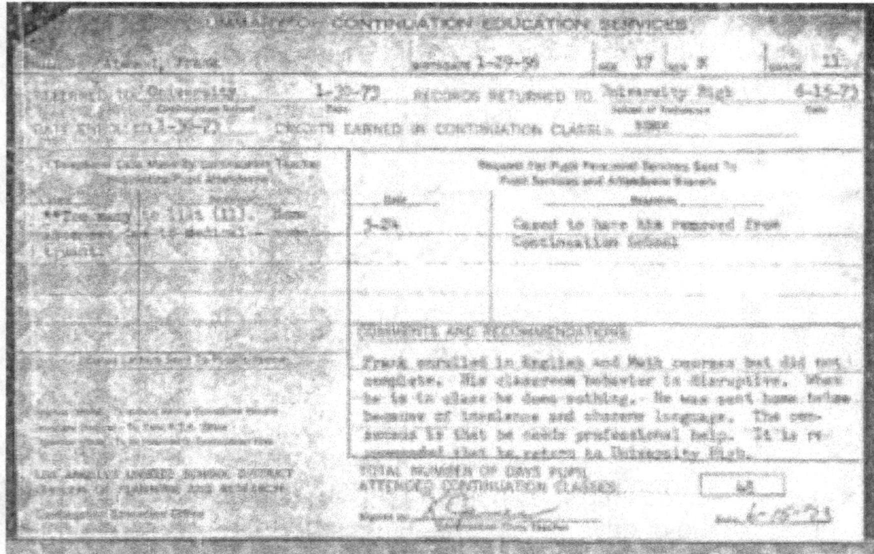

CONTINUATION EDUCATION SERVICES

RECORDS RETURNED TO

CREDITS EARNED IN CONTINUATION CLASSES

Caused to have him removed from Continuation School

COMMENTS AND RECOMMENDATIONS

Frank enrolled in English and Math courses but did not complete. His classroom behavior is disruptive. When he is in class he does nothing. He was sent home twice because of insolence and obscene language. The consensus is that he needs professional help. It is recommended that he return to University High.

TOTAL NUMBER OF DAYS PUPIL ATTENDED CONTINUATION CLASSES

GK Why did you stay in school as long as you did?
FJA I treated school as an arena to inflict disturbance, and harbored little concept of education. I stayed in school not to prepare for a career, but because of parole and family pressure. School served as the lesser of two evils, as something to endure because if I dropped out I would've been forced to get a job--something I certainly sought to avoid at all costs.
GK So, you actually didn't see any benefit from learning when in class?
FJA To me, academic and vocational education were irrelevant to what I wanted in life. I often joked about wanting to enroll in lock picking classes, or any courses to make me a more successful criminal; public school was a waste of time. Moreover, I believed I was superior to the common herd, felt I could become whatever I wished, and all it would take was my decision. Thus, I always reserved for myself the right to determine what was important, and thought I already knew a great deal, and could always learn what I desired at a later time.
GK By the way, did perspectives toward work impact your financial aptitude?
FJA My attitude toward money did influence my thoughts about work. I didn't value money, failed to see money as providing financial security, advantages to my family, and material comfort. Nor did I anticipate future requirements. Concepts such as budgeting were alien to my way of thinking. Consequently, I viewed money only as an index of my success as a criminal. In fact, I experienced a significant thrill in giving away money. To labor at a job I disdained for money I didn't value was incomprehensible to me, and despite all the money I stole, I never had anything to show for it.

These work patterns were the same whether I was on the streets or in confinement. However, I worked more often when in prison because there was less to do, and it provided the possibility of an earlier release date.
GK What about learning how to use money and budget responsibly?
FJA For me the ultimate goal had to involve cognizance of legitimate financial obligations, so I could fulfill them automatically in a responsible manner.
GK What other maladies in cognition affected you?
FJA I experienced widespread, persistent, and intense terror after having been initially sexually violated at age fourteen. This

all-encompassing fear spawned states of hopelessness as my self-esteem hit rock bottom; I believe I had failed in every way. This perception of worthlessness, coupled with a sense of guilt and shame, possessed three main components: (1) the basic view of myself as nothing, (2) the belief everyone shared the view that I was worthless, and (3) the belief my condition would last forever.

GK How did this fear manifest, in what ways did it affect you?

FJA My three greatest fears were of injury or death and of put-downs. In general terms, a put-down consisted of any situation in which I had no control. As a result, I harbored an intense dread of losing control and was saddled with the inability to handle criticism. I feared being a nothing without redeeming qualities. Of course, being afraid also existed as a put-down, as a consequence of having viewed myself as fearful, and a vicious cycle ensued.

Anxiety over injury infected nearly every aspect of my life. For instance, I avoided dentists and doctors like the plague; fear of immediate pain being far more extensive than concerns about future potential harm.

GK At first blush, it would appear you experienced a life of fearlessness, yet you have also referenced examples of being fearful. Please speak about this.

FJA I possessed many more fears than most other teens. For instance, I experienced an inordinate intolerance for pain that resulted in an unreasonable fear of physical injury. Unfortunately, this failed to deter me from having initiated many heated arguments in order to dominate another person, as well as to achieve victory from having temporarily conquered the dread of physical injury. Interestingly, this shows I could readily override fears to more effectively be able to pursue desires, sometimes even to extremes.

GK In what other ways did fear impact you?

FJA I possessed a childish reaction to disease and pain, which served as an impetus to insecurity, because I believed to suffer constituted a personal affront. I was either overly concerned about an illness or entirely neglected my condition. Additionally, psychosomatic ailments were prevalent, especially if I was bored, and I used infirmities (whether imaginary, feigned, or real) to gain sympathy and to exploit the situation.

Having mentioned insecurity, my inordinate fears also led to my having constantly downgraded my appearance. This meant I saw myself as ugly and unattractive in numerous ways, so was insecure about all of my physical features: my face, build, genital size, etc.

GK How did you deal with this?

FJA Despite far-reaching, constant, and intense fright I did everything within my power to conceal this, to appear fearless. As an example, if confronted about having missed a dental appointment I, would allude to some made up deficiency in the dentist to then express an empty intent to see another dentist. I also frequently exhibited machismo by engaging in physical confrontations or would drive cars and motorcycles in absolutely foolhardy and reckless manners (often exceeding speed limits by 30-40 mph). My capricious behavior also involved acts of bravado to cover underlying fear, like pulling up next to a car in traffic and breaking the windshield or denting the hood with a chain. But keep in mind, when it came to my own personal safety I was an excellent judge of character and would select victims who I knew would not retaliate or pose any threat.

GK You actually exited your car and slammed a chain into the vehicle behind you? That's crazy! What if they wrote down your license plate?

FJA I had in mind an incident where, while under a freeway bridge, I stopped at a light and upon its having turned green I failed to immediately move; the automobile behind me honked. I took the hidden motorcycle chain from under my seat and ran to the other car, smashed the hood, and after returning to my vehicle drove off. A second occasion unfolded when a driver cut me off and honked as if I were wrong. Having then swerved in front of her to prohibit her movement, I grabbed the chain, went to her car, broke the window and sped off. I suffered no repercussion from the first incident and was arrested on the second one…for "attempted murder!" Thus, occasionally my evils ended in arrest while other times only the tragic damage I inflicted was the result.

GK While some of your behaviors—such as these involving property damage—involved an element of criminality, in what other ways did your fear contribute to your criminal thinking and action?

FJA Being so afraid of condemnation operated as a cornerstone to many other criminal characteristics. Misgivings over criticism also created unreasonable thought patterns. For example, hypersensitivity in interpreting the attitudes of others toward myself, abhorring being told what to do, or detesting having to ride the bus rather than driving a fancy car. I was also

> Why Older Stats Don't Identify the Damage of Sexual Abuse in Male Children
>
> 20 years ago, the Bureau of Justice Statistics (BJS) found:
>
> A. 16.3% of murderers were abused before admission to state prison.
>
> B. 18.8% of males convicted of sexual assault were abused before admission to prison.
>
> Researchers now understand better the importance of the circumstances and who's asking sensitive, sexual abuse questions. When and where questions are asked makes a difference. Asking a person, were you abused as a child is nearly useless, we need to know the type and frequency as well.
>
> My research shows when properly trained mitigation specialists are able to gain the confidence of their clients, then ask specific questions about sexual abuse, we see results in the 60 to 80% range.
>
> These results are in sharp contrast to the 16 and 18% 20 years ago.
>
> For more discussion on this see Appendix: Personal comments about sexual assault research.

unable to accept intimacy from someone who did not act as I expected. I couldn't handle anyone disagreeing with me. In fact, occasionally I even refused to acknowledge that other viewpoints existed. Included in this was having perceived whatever I expected as an actuality, as a sure thing. Thus, whenever I decided my parents would chauffeur me somewhere, an obligation had been conferred upon them to do so and all that remained was informing them when I wished to depart. All of these were frequent results of my fearing put-downs.

GK It seems that, especially in today's world, people unfortunately and routinely endure offensive situations—perhaps on a crowded subway or elevator by being pushed, did perceived insults really impose such deleterious effects on you?

FJA Another way of expressing how pervasive my terror became is that I felt doomed when the world did not meet my needs, or when I failed to get my way. Actually, during such times I often reacted with unfounded suspicions of others, even threats of violence issued, because of not accepting what I mistakenly perceived as undeserved criticism, insult or rejection.

GK My son has similar symptoms and suffers from autism, have you ever been tested for autism or Asperger's?

FJA No, I haven't.

GK Okay. Tell me a little more about fears, maybe include an example.

FJA Misperceptions of emptiness occurred frequently with me because I assessed situations in extremes, I had no gradation between being number one or feeling worthless. Moreover, states of utter hopelessness often caused consuming anger, although not always expressed, leading to a dangerous situation. I recall having experienced an apparent rejection from a lover who had innocently gone to dinner with someone in our apartment building.

GK Was this a male or female?

FJA Perhaps "lover" was an unartful term here. It was a male I lived with, however, we were emotionally not sexually intimate.

GK And what happened?

FJA I became enraged, left, and returned to my parents' estate at speeds in excess of 100 mph, extreme danger to myself and others being disregarded. A two-day crime spree ensued, all of this in a desperate attempt to overcome a prevailing sense of worthlessness resulting from a rejection that never actually occurred. Interestingly, despite my view of self as a failure while in a state of meaninglessness, I still maintained the view of myself as a good person by placing blame for my helpless condition either on circumstances or others.

GK Whatever became of your fear? Did you transcend or transform it?

FJA I developed a healthy fear, allowing frightful premonitions to guide me. The main method of utilizing fear as a guide to accountable living involved the use of deterrents. For example, I had to initially develop consideration and dread of instant and future punishment. However, in conjunction with this I also had to create an attitude of having achieved gain. In other words, for the fear of punishment to be effective, I had to have something to lose. Once fear of discipline and loss, along with the sense of having enjoyed success, had been developed, I was able to begin constructing a responsible life. Friendships, reliable functioning, self-respect, and so on became permanent personality features. Moreover, terror of punishment was no longer limited to mere confinement. I began to fear all I'd gained being lost: honesty, open communication, respect, and a host of other virtues. I also developed the capacity to experience guilt as an enduring deterrent. That is, guilt had become functional (as opposed to merely transient), and this working sense of blameworthiness led to my having so utterly installed considering others as a quality that I began avoiding injuring them automatically.

GK How else did you use fear in positive and responsible ways?

FJA I discovered fear was an ally, not an enemy, in the lives of responsible people. This required having to eliminate my worries of being put down and using phenomenological reports to focus on and correct thinking errors connected with insecurities. This correction compelled my learning to evaluate the merits of criticism, and led to attaining a perspective that provided balanced assessments of myself.

As I progressed in the process of change, my prior thoughts of violation became habitually deterred by fear. Consider how on one occasion a prison guard walked up to my cell, called me several derogatory names, threw my mail on the floor, and left. Previously, this sort of put-down would have at least resulted in a verbal confrontation, but fear had become such an ingrained feature by the time of this experience that, as revealed after I studied the day's reports, I failed to even experience any thoughts of anger. The fear of punishment and losing all I'd gained was now a functional and automatic deterrent.

> Childhood Trauma Research in UK
>
> Over 20 years of researching why young people become violent–Gwyneth Boswell, a professor at the University of East Anglia, identified two trauma experiences in childhood that are prevalent in violent children:
>
> 1. Pervasive Abuse
> 2. Traumatic Loss (death or loss of contact of a parent)
>
> 91% of the 200 young, violent offenders had experienced abuse and/or loss.

GK While understanding your PTSD contributed to outbursts of anger, it still seems you suffered excessive instances of rage, what can you share about this? Especially in terms of your intense desire and need for control?

FJA In order to neutralize pervasive dread and worthlessness, I employed two favorite strategies: anger and control. However, before elaborating on these tactics a word about energy is in order. I was an extremely energetic individual when it came to pursuing actions involving criminal enterprises. To exert several hours of hard labor to break through the roof of a pharmacy was no problem, whereas chores as simple as making a bed or washing dishes seemed the same as running a marathon.

As can be deduced, I possessed an intense quality in actions pertaining to my pursuit of excitement and engaged in thought patterns that did not include random ideation. They were rapid, continuous, and highly concentrated—a purposeful flow of ideas regarding what was interesting and exciting occurred on a consistent basis. Again, this intense mental and physical vitality was not used for activities involving responsible living. To maintain the desired homeostasis, my mental and physical energies had to be directed exclusively toward excitement, in general, criminal behaviors. This explains why I was only indolent or bored when not pursuing a criminal conquest. That is, once ideas of triumphs re-emerged my intense energy was restored.

Consider how, as I sat in my room one day, a sense of exhaustion overwhelmed me once my mother asked me to help move boxes, subsequent to my father having repeatedly told me to mow the lawn. Neither chore could produce the requisite excitement. Then the telephone rang, and a criminal associate queried me about transporting some drugs up the coast. My energy suddenly returned and, as I hopped around my room to gather necessary materials, I once again felt on top of the world.

As for control, emerging on top was my primary concern, and I recognized no limits on my own power. As such, I was unable to deal with restrictions in a constructive manner. Also, seeking control was most prominent when engaged in crime, where conquest existed as my ultimate goal. The experience of causing someone to do what they did not want to do, such as handing over their precious possessions, functioned as the supreme victory. Consequently, I'd pursue control by seeking dominion over the destiny of others, which included building myself up as more powerful, especially if the person I sought to control was influential. This meant that coercion, exploitation, the threat and/or use of violence or sexual desire, and manipulation (power over others by deceit) were common devices.

Additionally, pleasure and excitement were derived from controlling others through fear and suffering, as when employing an implied or actual use of force. At the extreme of these spectra existed death, the power to destroy. For me, this ultimate fantasy of control never became a reality. However, as I lost control over external events I began to contemplate consummate control of the internal via suicidal thinking.

> A child who is the victim of prolonged sexual abuse usually develops low self-esteem, a feeling of worthlessness and an abnormal or distorted view of sex. The child may become withdrawn, mistrustful of adults and possibly suicidal.
>
> Source: US Dept. of Health & Human Services, Children's Bureau (2012)

GK With control such a predominant factor in your thought patterns, how does anger fit into this personality feature?

FJA It was obviously impossible to maintain control, the primary catalyst for why I was chronically angry. This anger would usually begin with a petty or imagined isolated episode, spread to other events and people, then shortly all perspective would be lost. This one isolated episode could then result in illogical thought and opened the door to criminal ideation—contemplating, or at last fantasizing about, crimes that would give me control over others. Furthermore, my chronic anger was so frequent and so intense, serious repercussions often occurred to myself and others. As an example, after having been out committing crimes for several days I returned home with plans to take my girlfriend to Disneyland but needed direction to get there. When my father refused, because I was way too intoxicated to drive, I ended up breaking a window and becoming involved in a physical confrontation with him. I never made it to Disneyland, but residual anger led to a couple of physical confrontations that evening in a nightclub's parking lot.

GK In what other ways did your temper manifest? Was there a specific triggering mechanism?

FJA The most common contributors for my anger were fear of put-downs and any interference with my objective. A frequent pattern included suffering criticism; my ensuing anger and interjection of irrelevant or illogical issues deflected attention from misperceived chastisement to regain the upper hand. Keep in mind an essential element during these cycles involved overlooking my own misperceptions- my mistakes of blaming others and then taking out my frustrations on them. Thus, the antidote for put-downs I employed was angering to re-establish control over others and get my way.

GK And another cause of anger?

FJA Boredom (boredom = restriction from pursuing excitement and triumph), anger definitely stirred up energy and excitement. Moreover, it was rare for me to disagree without using anger, especially with another criminal, since both of us desired control; the issue was almost never a legitimate difference of opinion. If things didn't go my way I'd react as if my entire existence had been threatened. An example of this was when a classmate (with whom I got stoned nearly every day) and I were in my room talking about sex. We began to lie about our sexual exploits, this led to a heated argument about who had been involved with the most partners. This challenge to my carefully contrived image presented such a threat to my sense of control it actually resulted in a physical scuffle.

Finally, others often misconstrued my anger as rebellion against anyone or anything representing authority. While I did engage in many antiestablishment actions of the criminal nature, this existed as distinct from the use of anger to re-establish control.

GK With anger and hostile outburst as one of your most debilitating PTSD symptoms, how does this affect relationships?

FJA It destroys budding friendships fast. I still really struggle with these outbursts. I've received numerous write-ups. After being molested I've been chronically angry. Instead, I had to deal with anger rationally and consider it as a thought process.

Because anger still exists as a part of my life, I have to work at initially deterring its expression as I implement new methods of prevention. One way in which I tackle this daunting task is by closely examining the outrage expressed in my daily phenomenological report; my attendant thought processes, costs of anger, and my contributions to its development are all considered. Also, I cannot allow myself to express the view of anger as irreversible or natural. To do so, enables me to excuse my excessive anger and build insurmountable obstacles to lessen rage. This avoids overcoming blow-ups. In eliminating anger, I need to realize all loitering resentment, (be it from having never committed murder yet residing on death row for over three decades, the continued attacks I endure, or any other stimulating factors).

As I began my program for change, I viewed prison staff as my captors and oppressors, other prisoners as constant sources of danger and aggravation, society as out to get me, the justice system as wholly corrupt, and law enforcement as the epitome of evil. I was filled, consumed, and obsessed by an all-pervasive bitterness. Along with this I still must keep in mind how the mere expression of anger produces adverse outcomes every time- to myself, my wife, the Church, etc. Built up rage explodes, anger is misdirected, and confrontation ensues. This means I must still aim at avoidance of venting anger, and to focus instead on eliminating the thought process causing anger. This concept is similar to not merely attempting to banish criminal action, but rather to eradicate my incipient criminal thinking. Any failure to abolish internal sources of anger will enable an underlying state to remain in which violation looms. I need to apply correctives at the first indication of anger (not an easy task), and must work toward handling irresponsible people, prisoners and guards, in a responsible manner; which was irritating as hell at first and still remains problematic. This means accepting that human beings make errors; are rude, manipulative, and can be annoying on a variety of levels. Only then can I expend energy by directing it toward remedying situations, rather than to waste it on expressing anger.

Eventually, as my correctives for thinking errors are more consistently applied, and I learn to monitor my emotions (including anger), and to implement deterrents, I am able to preempt more of my rage by approaching life in a rational and mentally prepared state. This includes allowing fear to guide me and leads to the capability of eliminating anger by choice—I pray God aids me in this endeavor.

GK I've noticed your lapses; for instance, the time you let a file folder caught in front of your cell piss you off, until you finally fished the object of your anger back into your cell and ripped it to shreds. I also hear your display of anger at people on TV when you curse at them. Are you aware of these thinking errors?

FJA Unfortunately, yes, I am painfully aware of these transgressions. It remains quite a fierce war to conquer my remnant anger. Besides, with Hillary Clinton, et al, there's much to be upset over!

THE WITNESS: "He says he has been having a problem with shortness of breath. He's been checked out medically and says he was told it was -- it was something due to anxiety."

MS. HARMS: Okay.

THE WITNESS: "He wants to start Zoloft. Says his wife recommended it."

BY MS. HARMS:

Q. Okay. I think I'd like to turn now to the fifth criteria for PTSD.

Could you explain what that is.

A. Yes. That's just the -- that's the old -- Your, Honor, I have to go back -- and I apologize. The DSM-5 just came out and said this is a little bit different. Normally I could tell you these things, spew them off.

It's been changed and now what this is, is a marked alteration in arousal and reactivity associated with a traumatic event. And what this is -- that's a physiologic manifestation that may be able to be observed by others. And the symptoms that he has, irritable behavior and angry outbursts with little or no provocation. Typically expresses verbal or physical aggression towards people or objects.

And again, as I mentioned, his records were replete -- there were many times where he's approached by a corrections officer for something and in some cases they're

GK As for control, this permeated much of your life, what were some correctives you implemented?

FJA My criminal power and control patterns were so habitual and deeply ingrained, I failed to consider their exploitive and injurious effects. However, my daily phenomenological reports revealed these patterns and exposed how they saturated my relationships with everyone. This demonstrated why one of my tasks needed my being aware of the pervasive nature of my desperate search for power and control; on how I endlessly pursued conquests, the purpose it served, and the effects on myself and others.

For instance, my having been assaulted in recreation cages: had this ended in my having hit someone with a rock, there not only would have been injury to him but my wife, myself, and the Orthodox Church would also have suffered. There would have been disciplinary proceedings and ensuing punishments, such as loss of television and store, against myself. My wife and I would have endured visitation and phone call loss. There also would have been the disappointment and shame visited upon myself, my wife and the Church. Finally, additional criminal charges could have been leveled against me. Indeed, devastation would've been significant and widespread.

It was reviews such as this, regarding the costs to others and myself, that constituted the onset of reduction in my unrealistic pretensions. Only then was I able to more comprehensibly consider other criminal characteristics and apply correctives. These additional patterns in criminality included defaulting on obligations, lacking interdependent relationships, and failing to consider others. So, it was essential for me to have remained alert, and my daily journals had to be monitored closely to uncover any thinking reflecting former power and control patterns. A part of this required I learn to differentiate between power derived legitimately and power obtained through irresponsible behavior at the expense of others.

GK Out of curiosity, were there any strategies you used to ease your conscience?

FJA One common to each and every criminal involves a sense of sentimentality (known as mawkishness) which materialized in my having been overly kind one moment and then suddenly extremely vicious the next instant. For example, I would revere my mother, even to the point of having been willing to die for her; the next moment I would verbally abuse her if having failed to get my way. Another manifestation of mawkishness existed in the propensity for doing good deeds enroute to a crime, a sporadic sense of kindness and honor used to reinforce the concept of myself as basically a good person. In my convoluted mind, I was somehow able to offset, for example, the financial and emotional damage I had inflicted during a burglary through such insignificant acts as giving someone a ride or directions, opening the door for a stranger, or letting a driver cut in front of me in traffic. Of course, my "sentimentality" never eliminated my criminal thinking and action patterns.

GK I'm wondering if sentimentality, or mawkishness, was transformed into a healthy emotion, how did you treat sentimentality?

FJA As I embarked upon the process of change, my fragmented sentimentality often reared its ugly head as I overemphasized my good deeds and noble ideals. It was essential to realize my boasting about any sense of nobility and worth applied not to enduring personal features, and any kindness to others was still merely transitory. This forced me to face the fact that I was not compassionate to others, especially when having considered those who had been an obstacle to my objectives. This awareness resulted in my painful realization that despite my claims of altruistic ideals I had always readily sacrificed others in pursuit of my own gain.

Additionally, in the past I had freely given things away, whether out of transient sentimentality, as a con, or to play the big shot. There was a need for me to have recognized the absence of permanence in my passing mawkish states, and to halt the pattern of indiscriminate gifting by learning that any presents had to be compatible with long-range responsible interests. Coupled with this was the need to recognize any miniscule goodness from my charity was completely outweighed by the injury I caused to my family and society; consequently, my kindness could in no way be construed as a redeeming quality. With this frame of reference firmly in tow, I was able to utilize daily phenomenological reports to reveal how sentimentality had actually encouraged crime by making it easier to have lived with myself.

Another area of concern was how frequently an episode of sentimentality had manifested in pseudo-religious involvement. One example of this, prior to my Arizona incarceration, was my need to boost self-confidence by imposing a momentary sense of order in my life. I attempted to accomplish this by implementing a rigorous religious routine of meditation, yoga, and studying various sacred texts (e.g., *The Vedas*, *The Tao Te Ching*, Lao Tzu's works). Of course, I quickly grew bored and, despite fervent reentry into drug realms, pronounced myself "cured." Or, as another example, when I felt lonely and missed home I tried to reconnect with what I perceived as the happier times of childhood through a passing involvement with Episcopalian precepts. Actually, what I longed for was action, and under circumstances such as this, any superficial interest in Protestantism was never sustained.

GK Please tell me about your initial participation in religion.

FJA I was raised from birth in the Episcopal Church; I really enjoyed services, classes, gatherings, and a host of other related activities. I was confirmed at age twelve.

> Over 11,000 cases of rape or sexual assault are reported every day. (12 years old and up)
>
> U.S. Dept. of Health & Human Services, Children's Bureau–2012.

GK Did anything in your beliefs about God change after having been the victim of a sexual assault?

FJA I began to stray from the Episcopal Church soon after the age 14 ½ assault, not so much from a change in belief but due to competing interests; thus, outward acts of religious devotion expired, absent interior adherence. I justified my movement away from Christianity in various ways, such as with claims of it being pointless to follow an "unjust" God (when I was the unjust ingredient), contending God didn't exist, and criticizing the human foibles of a congregation or ministry as a way to disparage God—all of these being nonsense, being cover-ups for rising competing interests.

GK In the next few years, did you seek solace in God again? If so, what did that look like?

FJA There were momentary returns to God out of expediency. That is, I sought miracles from God, in the form of drastic changes in myself, to avoid having to undergo or be responsible for the task of my progress. Of course, once miracles failed to happen and no change occurred I was then able to blame God rather than myself. Eventually I moved from traditional faith (Christianity of the West) to more mystical belief systems whose tenets were more compatible with my emerging philosophy and were easier to implement (more flexible, lenient).

GK What religions and belief systems did you pursue?
FJA I had interest in tarot, astrology, and ancient Egyptian religion (including planetary magic). I also ardently studied Eastern beliefs—Buddhism, Taoism, Hinduism—and became adept at Shaolin martial arts.
GK Did these studies continue during your incarcerations in California and your current imprisonment?
FJA In California, yes. I temporarily turned to religion in confinement because of a guilty conscience or as an attempt to portray a phony rehabilitation, as "evidence" of change. While I was diligent in my training, the problem resided in rarely having implemented what had been learned, and these conversions were not sustained.

While in the county jail this time (1984-87) I played at pursuing some of these various religious belief systems, and until entering the Greek Orthodox Christian Church in 1998, I did study a few disciplines. Martial arts have been a mainstay (albeit, I've been wheel chaired since 2015).
GK In what ways, if any, do you find that your crimes affected your involvement in religion?
FJA Having been raised in the Episcopal Church, ever since childhood I had seen God as an all-powerful, all-knowing Being who knew and saw everything all of the time. There existed the prevalent belief that in order to be in God's favor one had to be a consummate and perennial saint. Thus, as a criminal I justified my criminality by asserting since it was impossible to be good at all times there was no point in even making any attempt at all. In other words, it was God's fault (for knowing and seeing everything) that I was bad and a criminal. Additionally, my fragmentation and concrete thought caused an inability to see Christianity as a way of life, as the pursuit of a life in accord with Christ (i.e., the example He gave while on earth). Concrete thinking caused me to think in extremes; for instance, people were either good or evil, no gradation existed.
GK Is that to say, after a crime spree you engaged in no religious activities?
FJA I often used religion as a last resort, mostly when imprisoned or in a jam. As an example, when in juvenile hall I called upon God to get me out and in exchange promised to no longer act criminally. Thus, the burden was placed on God as I disowned all responsibility. Of course, my deep sincerity was transient at best and I would reject Christianity as a way of life—

pursuing instead my own warped ideals upon release from imprisonment.

GK How have you made corrections in this area?

FJA Understanding that Christianity, the Christ-centered life, requires obedience to God, a concept that is foreign or undesirable to criminals and much of America. This explains why most jailhouse conversions are either transient, phony, or both. There exists an absence or obedience that relegates a criminal's often impressive knowledge of the Bible to mere intellectual fodder, which cannot be and is not applied to daily life. This reveals how and why my Greek Orthodox Christianity is both sincere and effective. My Christ-centered life is thoroughly grounded in obedience, and thus I live and am guided by Christian precepts.

GK In furthering our discussion on religion, have you anything else to add?

FJA Yes. Having cited my own instances of phony conversions I find it essential to outline the relatively hopeless turning to Protestantism or Catholicism (i.e., Western "Christianity") by prisoners and to contrast this with the Eastern Orthodox Christian Church, our soul saving spiritual hospital. The West relies on "scholasticism," a process whereby the rational faculty is said to be able to learn about God; that is, the futility of each created (and fallen) mind engendering its own conception of God—so someone retains "control," even over God! In the East (Greek Orthodoxy) knowledge of God develops via asceticism (e.g., fasting prayer, prostrations, obedience to one's spiritual father, etc.) and through the apostolic line of succession—rather than current personal opinion, we rely on what has been believed by all of Eastern Christianity, everywhere and always, since the first century.

Many jailhouse conversions are sincere (some are phony, made for ulterior motives), however, reliance on merely intellectual ideas condemns these experiences generally to worthlessness, this is why my 1988 death row conversion to Protestant persuasions left me interiorly empty and in search of something more. I discovered total inner fulfillment once I came home, to the Eastern Christian Church. The time since my baptism in July of 2000 has been spent in obedience to my spiritual father, and the centuries of Church Father tradition, in order to steadily pursue the process of purification. Subservience is essential in Christianity, and has quickened movement from criminal patterns of thinking.

GK So, you've adhered to Greek Orthodoxy for going on two

decades, how else has this enabled transformation?

FJA Greek Orthodox (Eastern) Christianity centers on interior transmutation through adherence to Church Tradition. From this subservience, I was able to enjoy correctives—or to reinforce the ones I had by this time (late 1990's) fostered—by subordinating my criminal pride to the authority of Church fathers. Not to stray too far into the woods, but in Greek Orthodoxy the aim is to return attention to single-minded focus on Christ, which in itself extinguishes many thought patterns of a negative persuasion. The return of my mind to only God, and spiritual progress, placed me squarely on the path to the Kingdom of God within…how could I not persist?

GK Right on! I'm interested in any other Trump-ego infections having afflicted you, or having contributed to criminal thinking patterns.

FJA Vainglory, defined here as abnormal and irresponsible pride, existed as a successful way to recover from put-downs and to conquer fears. Normal, responsible pride may include satisfaction from having achieved something worthwhile by honorable means. This could involve being proud as a result of fulfilling an obligation or task when obstructions have been overcome. However, the type of pride I engaged in included conceit, arrogance, egotism, and vanity. This often took forms of ensuring other criminals knew about, so could admire, my exploits and was the result of my need for an extremely inflated evaluation of self in all of life's aspects. Further, I considered myself being above others; beyond mundane chores or work—having regarded employment as for only laborers or suckers. The existence of vainglory also resulted in having taken what I wanted, in having outwitted or overpowered others to always come out on top; great antidotes to put-downs because if I ever submitted to another person or system, or even modified a belief as a consequence of an argument or persuasion, my very sense of manhood would have been at stake. For instance, there was a time when the pastor of the church my family attended visited me in juvenile hall and one topic of discussion was my criminal involvement. While our priest proffered excellent reasons why, from both spiritual and humanistic perspectives, I should abstain from any further criminal pursuit I simply could not implement any of his advice; to do so would have subordinated me to another person. As a consequence of vainglory, even continued self-destruction and jail seemed preferable.

GK Quick query, you just said "church my family attended" rather than our church, should we presume you didn't attend church? At what age did you stop attending church?
FJA At age sixteen in 1972, I'd ceased attendance. However, this did not mean I'd ceased considering St. Alban's Episcopal Church as "our" church; it was where I grew up and had learned foundational life lessons. The cessation of attendance (having begun at age fourteen) occurred due to competing interests and the results of PTSD having distanced me from family and societal life.

Interestingly, my resumption of a life after Christ in 1988 led to having arranged for an Episcopal priest (Father John) visiting me monthly from the autumn of 1988 until his move to Guatemala in 2015; I had maintained my ties to the Episcopal Church.
GK Neat. Please provide another example of vainglory.
FJA I even took pride in my criminal modus operandi and condemned how other criminals operated. This meant when involved in robbery I'd consider burglars as sneaks; as cowards for not "standing up like a man," taking with force what they wanted. Of course, when engaged in burglary I would accuse robbers of being idiots for risking identification by witnesses and for lacking the skill required to pull off high stakes burglaries. Then again, subsequent to having committed a particularly odious offense I could always assert "at least I'd never killed anybody." These utterly ridiculous stances often meant adhering to "principle," insisting whatever I believed in had to be right—even if doing so appeared silly and seemed to court punishment or resulted in my engaging in self-destructive behavior. The example cited above, regarding my preference to remain involved in a life of crime (whatever the consequences), exposed my abject folly of criminal, vainglorious pride. As now seen, I always had to insist I knew it all, had to maintain my misguided sense of vainglory, and this closed my mind to any contrary view. Therefore, I always imposed my opinion on others and rejected what anyone offered.
GK The vainglory, or criminal pride, ownership, sense of machismo, and similarly related thinking errors certainly took their toll on you. What steps did you take to eliminate these?
FJA My misguided notions of manhood existed as a foundation of my distorted sense of pride. While warped ideas had to be removed from every aspect of my life it was especially important to focus on specific realms of physical and sexual toughness—arenas in my life in which the sense of machismo had to be

radically redefined. I had perceived sexuality as the pursuit of conquest and an ownership operation, and so overcame fear by physical domination and damaging property—enduring postures that ceaselessly infected all aspects of my existence. Thus, I had to pursue manhood as involving the ability to face life's problems responsibly, requiring doing one's best to resolve daily complications.

GK Your sense of superiority and always having to be number one, which I've experienced, how did it lead to misguided cognition?

FJA Insofar as uniqueness, there was a constant emphasis on what I perceived as my total difference from others. I harbored a pervasive sense of being one of a kind, which constituted the foundation of my self-image. There existed beliefs such as being so distinct that no one could have the thoughts I experienced; that no one could truly understand me. This sense of me as unparalleled, I expressed everywhere: I considered classmates as a herd of cattle, society as mindless sheep, all other criminals as part of a common pack, and responsible citizens as fools.

Beliefs like thinking only others needed training, so I could step right in and do better than anyone else, were also prevalent. To accept training, or even advice, meant my loss of superiority and sense of unique identity. Thus, I saw myself as knowing it all, as knowing what should be right and wrong or legal and illegal, but these determinations changed to suit my purposes at any given time. There was no acceptance of being bound by society's restrictions, rules applied to others but not myself. This belief in being better than everyone not only helped overcome put-downs but also comprised an all-important component of my sense of self. However, being unique never sufficed, I had to be unique and number one.

GK This sounds like an incredibly lonely existence, possessing this unparalleled sense of self, how did it affect your relations with others?

FJA Since I considered myself to be one of a kind, set myself apart from others, I isolated myself and functioned as one against all of the world. This led to secrecy, to tell others about my plans would have resulted in objections and/or interference. Obviously, to inform my parents I intended to sell a few sheets of LSD, or was on the way to do a burglary, would have posed significant obstruction. Additionally, many of my criminal

Social Isolation

Social isolation is a growing epidemic–one that's increasingly recognized as having dire physical, mental and emotional consequences.
The evidence on social isolation is clear. What to do about it is less so.
Loneliness is especially tricky because accepting and declaring our loneliness carries profound stigma. Admitting we're lonely can feel as if we're admitting we've failed in life's most fundamental domains: belonging, love, attachment. It attacks our basic instincts to save face, and makes it hard to ask for help.

Dhruv Khullar, M.D., M.P.P, is a resident physician at Massachusetts General Hospital and Harvard Medical School.

Excerpt from an article in New York Times 12-22-16

enterprises were too radical for less extreme criminals, so I experienced quite a bit of dissent from even the so-called outlaw element, which functioned as a put-down.

GK I'm guessing these criminals held no interest in bombing utility companies?

FJA They didn't. But even when secrecy was unnecessary I maintained it to set myself apart, to avoid or counteract put-downs while enhancing my sense of unique superiority. Then again, leading such a secretive life caused me to be ill-equipped to become involved with others in responsible or constructive ways. My idea of a relationship was one-sided: how could I benefit? In fact, I could not even apprehend what a conversation was, since I was uninterested in exchanging ideas, preferring instead to engage in a monologue to either promote myself or to display my knowledge. Nor could I have ever viewed myself as equal in a transaction—to be equal or ordinary would have been a put-down and intolerable. For example, those with whom I chose to get stoned were not my equals as I was the one with the best drugs. Or, since I nearly always made all plans for a criminal enterprise, anyone with me was at my beck and call as a flunky.

PRELUDE TO CHAPTER SIX

Frank and the Only Child Myths
I feel it worthwhile to touch on this topic as so much of Frank's interview speaks about his psychology. Frank being an only child certainly factors into his personality, upbringing, strengths and weaknesses.
My sister is 13 years older than I, and off to Hollywood at age 18. So basically, I was raised as an only child. I wonder, what percentage of "only child's" are on Death Row vs. middle and end children?
In my opinion, the worse label attached to us is the untitled label. Yes! We have high self-esteem and a higher index of confidence yet, people around us with even the slightest insecurity complex call us arrogant and entitled–to our face– especially other prisoners and even guards. To us, people who display "entitlement" are Donald Trump and the British Royals, not some lowly human on death row.
Gabrielle Moss wrote an article (April 2015) entitled: *What Being an Only Child Says About You, According to Science*. I list some highlights below:

Twenty percent of American families only have one child.
We have higher IQs.
We're more confident.
We're not actually more spoiled.
We have just as many friends.
We're happier than kids with siblings.
We're more likely to divorce. Well, five out of six ain't bad.
https://www.bustle.com/articles/77486-what-being-an-only-child-says-about-you-according-to-science

The author, Car Pickhardt, wrote an article published in *Psychology Today* about the only child experience in middle or high school that may apply to Frank.
When the "break" from childhood comes and the need for more independence begins, unwelcome conflict typically occurs between indulgent parents and a child who has been bred to be strong-willed. This abrasiveness troubles both only child and parents for whom the past was so harmonious, for whom the

companionship is so important, and for whom displeasing each other can be so hard to bear.

I believe this is why the adolescence of a lot of only children is delayed, often not beginning until middle school or even early high school. When the beginning of adolescence does not occur until early high school, what I call a "collapsed adolescence" can begin. Over a very short period of time, maybe two years, the first three stages of adolescence unfold on top of each other. The negativity and resistance of early adolescence is jammed up against the increased push for freedom and propensity for conflict of mid adolescence that is jammed up against the need to try more grown activities of late adolescence. This is a lot of fast change and high tension for only child teenager and parents to weather.

https://www.psychologoytoday.com/blog/surviving-your-childs-adolescence/200907/the-adolescent-only-child

JUDGEMENT AND AFFECTIONS TOWARDS OTHERS

GK I notice you currently have difficulty expressing gratitude and other real affections toward others.
FJA In all fairness, there's few people here deserving of my affections or gratitude. Probably because of years of mistreatment, I'm leery of everyone.
When people show a kindness–experience has taught me to raise defenses–not say thank you.
GK And was this true in your teens during your criminal path?
FJA It was rare for me to display warmth or tenderness, to express real affection or concern, other than for my own self-serving ends, to have done so would have caused vulnerability. Again, I viewed others as friends only when they did what I wanted, my affinity toward someone could change to anger within minutes. As a result, I could be enthusiastic and disenchanted with the same person—concrete thinking precluded most concepts of loyalty even though I erroneously believed a single tangible act of kindness made me "loyal."

In conclusion, it must be noted these views of myself imposed a lonely existence for me. This self-induced isolation in prison must not be equated with being a loner. I was a loner only when it suited my purposes and if desiring to be with others I was adept at finding someone to gratify my immediate needs. Consequently, my life as a criminal involved living a life without truly knowing another person. I was a wanderer, a nomad always seeking conquest, who was rarely satisfied.
GK I hate to drop this on you, but yes, you were a textbook loner, as an only child it comes naturally. Anyway, what other personality features and thinking errors beleaguered your functioning as a criminal?
FJA It would indeed be useful to consider several other prominent characteristics I possessed to more fully complete the

portrait of a criminal's personality traits. However, let's first finalize uniqueness and perfectionism. This feature of exactitude applied only to things of my choosing and was not an enduring characteristic. Consequently, my sense of exactitude was quite sporadic and did not appear consistently, rarely lasting long during any one activity. In fact, I even displayed extremism in my application of perfectionism. Take as an example how my room would be immaculate one day and filthy the next, or the times when I feared failing to be perfect and didn't try at all—believing it was better not to try than to try and fail. Also, once having begun an enterprise, then encountering obstacles, I would rarely renew efforts once these stresses or diversions arose—unless an exciting criminal enterprise was at stake.

Extremism and perfectionism also existed in my view of others since I believed both others and myself were either saints or crooks. This enabled me to uncover merely one minimal negative feature in someone in order to obliterate all of their assets, then I'd perceive them as a wholly immoral individual.

GK I think a lot of folks share this finding of one negative feature to then condemn a person. E.g.., being a Republican or Democrat.

FJA True. But for me this justified my own criminality and allowed maintaining the view of myself as basically a good person. My exactitude, no matter how fragmented, bolstered my belief: I was a unique number one.

GK Regarding your sense of uniqueness, was it related to control and how did you overcome this Donald Trump ego?

FJA I treated this error both separately and in combination with others. Having lived around other criminals enabled me to deal with my sense of uniqueness effectively, I became aware of their daily behavior and quickly recognized my own negative patterns in them. As a result, I learned thinking errors are common to all criminals and rapidly began to understand I was not at all unique. In other words, where I had previously believed nobody could have possessed or understood the thoughts I once experienced, there now existed no doubt that literally tens of millions of people functioned in my same capricious ways.

GK Aha, that surely would eradicate the aura of uniqueness. Learning to be ordinary after our star of delusion has fallen, right there with you bro. But look at us now, two of the most published guys on America's death row. Some might say we're pretty unique?

FJA Despite having overcome this sense of singularity I still had to abolish the misperception I was not an ordinary person and my belief I could accomplish whatever I desired. I achieved this by living a consistently responsible day by day life as an average person; I soon realized I had few skills, little job experience, and a rich history of irresponsibility—that is, far from admirable. I owned a background of abject chronic failure, certainly quite a sobering perspective. One of my main correctives centered around interacting with and watching ordinary people handle situations in life, so I could expose my own deficiencies. This resulted in developing a strong sense of humility and assisted in leading a normal life.

GK I'd say it's a good thing you didn't give up your belief that you could accomplish whatever you desire. It requires a mountain full of desire to be perfect to go for your Ph.D. from death row. You know, perfectionism and her sister uniqueness, when internalized are excellent motivators; when externalized they manifest as boastful ego and excessive pride.

FJA Precisely, it became necessary to learn in which areas to strive toward less perfectionism; as a consequence of my tendency toward extremism a middle way or point had to be my new habit. This meant learning to work hard and do my best without excessive obsession over things beyond my control. My work at Ohio University and Cal. State University provides good examples; I initially sought to expend an overabundance of time on studies, to the exclusion of other needs; it rapidly became necessary to impose moderation. Moreover, attempting to study and concentrate amidst the chaos of a prison environment can be most difficult, so there arose temptation to micromanage my surroundings by attempting to control the noise made by others; it required diligent struggle to simply accept prevailing conditions.

Eventually, I was able to curtail perfectionism and maintain a standard of performance, which enabled me to avoid unnecessary actions that previously reduced overall productivity and obstructed responsible living. Prior expectations, such as everything having to go my way, were replaced with my new attitude of taking what did not go my way in stride. Once this sense of balance and proportion had been attained I could then believe there was worth in one's daily work, which led to no longer having felt a need to continually attempt to prove I was better than others.

GK I have to throw you under the bus on this perfectionism issue. Let's remember when I sent you my pages of handwritten

questions with undotted i's.
When these pages came back all my i's were dotted. I'm thinking you may need a little more work on balancing your perfectionism.
FJA Well I'm thinking if you'd dot your i's I wouldn't have to clean up your lack of perfectionism.
GK Classical Frank, deflect and assign blame anywhere but Frank. ☺
Let's talk about your bipolar suggestibility.
FJA I possessed no susceptibility to suggestion, especially when it came to responsible or socially acceptable behavior. Whenever doctors, parents, or friends tried to change me into a responsible person I routinely displayed patterns of rigidity and persisted in former actions, even if possible confinement was the obvious result. And, I was impervious to pleas from my parents. At the same time, if action or excitement were possible then I became extremely suggestible to nearly any type of behavior. When in pursuit of excitement I eagerly participated, rarely bothering to check facts or details; what mattered was simply whether excitement would result and what I desired at the moment.
GK Learning to trust people is always tricky at best–which suggestions and invitations are sincere ?
FJA My program for direction and suggestibility change had a two-fold objective: (1) to achieve contra-suggestibility to crime and (2) to gain suggestibility for responsible living; these goals existed as a corrective to criminal thinking and as an education in responsible ideation and action.

The first step was for me to avoid situations that automatically prompted criminal thinking; like exposure to old law-breaking cohorts, movies or TV programs and magazines or books containing accounts of crime or sex. Having been incarcerated made it very difficult to maintain distance from other felons and not to engage in criminal talk—after all, the penitentiary is a sort of convention for criminals—and it took repeated effort to have firmly assumed an anti-crime position without having been a zealous missionary about it. Eventually I was able to remain indifferent to my neighbors (other prisoners), yet not involved with them, this burned the primary bridge to the only life I had ever known, severed all old ties, and opened me to advice from responsible adults.

Moreover, while this pattern of avoidance of inmates enabled me to have circumvented exposure to negative situations in which

I might have been suggestible to irresponsibility, it only reduced some external stimuli and did not eliminate the inner state of mind that had made me so open to temptation. As change progressed, and I began to experience complete disdain toward my unconscionable traits and other criminals, both avoidance and deterrence no longer existed as my sole toolbox; I was able to engage in more profound deliberations toward suggestibility and responsible living. Most of my contemplations were free of prejudgment and stressed the augmentation of fact-finding. This let me review daily phenomenological reports to seek out mental situations in which suggestibility to crime had previously precluded sound judgment, I also learned to evaluate current patterns from the viewpoint of considering what might happen (worse case scenarios) if I ever reverted back to being susceptible to criminal pursuits. Consequently, suggestibility toward irresponsibility gave way to balanced, rational thinking, with change having resulted in the form of no longer trusting my old thinking. This required seeking advice and opinions from others about responsible living and allowed me to begin to function with an open mind; a very different mind.

GK What role do you find honesty and dishonesty played in your life as a criminal, how did it govern your thinking?

FJA As for lying, this was an integral part of my life. Every criminal incorporates lying into his/her basic make-up, meaning one fabrication leads to more and more deceit until one's entire life

Is Free Porn Societies Most Effective Deterrent

I came across a study, article entitled 'Have Sexual Abuse and Physical Abuse Declined Since 1990's?' It states a 62 percent decline in sexual abuse from 1992 to 2010.

I don't believe it would be a long-shot bet to surmise the decrease was due to free Internet porn. A converse example is here at Arizona prisons. They banned porn-men's magazines in 2009 and you guessed it, violence against staff and prisoners by Inmates has increased every year.

All because women want to work in men's prisons: but they're "offended by our T&A on the wall." I wonder if these same women are equally offended by the increase in violence they've caused?

becomes a web of lies. Of course, my criminal action necessitated prevarication for self-preservation, but there also existed the fact to have obtained something in a routine way, by not having run a game or a con, would have failed to provide the sought-after thrill and could not have been gratifying. Lying was simply a major ingredient of the excitement I so desperately craved and had been a standard in my life since I was a teenager. I would lie about my age, where I was from, or other inconsequential facts just to fool others and obtain a charge from "putting one over" on suckers.

GK I too used to lie constantly to make me feel better about myself, or because the questions people were asking were none of their business.

FJA And probably like your lying, my lying took many forms. For instance, I lied not only to escape being held accountable for crimes or to mitigate punishment but also in order to avoid being considered a failure. While I'd attempt to avoid being thought of as deficient by responsible people—such as lying about having held jobs—my falsehoods more often involved fabrications regarding criminal action. I lied by claiming I had committed crimes that never occurred, or I'd only heard about, as well as by having exaggerated my involvement in crimes I had been a part of to impress other criminals by enhancing my status as a radical outlaw. This ended up playing a major role in my having landed on death row for a crime I did not commit; I lied to my transient traveling companions about a knife fight, a stabbing, that never occurred in order to perpetuate the view of myself as a tough guy who was not to be fooled with; this lie truly came back to bite me.

GK Lying is so much more dangerous than people understand. Were there other manifestations of lying?

FJA Despite these overt, blatant lies the most significant form of fabrication involved lies of omission. That is, lying was never limited to just misstating facts. I would insist I'd been truthful when having not engaged in outright prevarication, even if having told a small part of a truth. A common form of these lies of omission transpired when someone in authority, such as my parents, harbored suspicion about my criminal involvements and attempted to discern my whereabouts. Thus, when I actually went to a fellow criminal's house to pick him up on the way to a crime, I would conveniently omit parts about doing crime and only relate the misguided implication I went to a buddy's house for benign purposes. As can now be seen, these lies of omission comprised

one of the greatest methods of deception in my criminal toolbox.
GK That's an excellent point, many times lies of omission fail to be taken into account yet are brutal, causing as much devastation as well-placed lies.
FJA I was also a master of calculated ambiguity and employed the "con of assent"—outward agreement in opposition to inner disagreement or indifference—to cut short any undesirable situation or to cause someone in authority to believe they had an impact on me. This frequently occurred when caught doing something wrong, then feeding my accuser whatever they wanted to hear in order to escape or ease punishment. A classic example of this is after I burglarized the prison hospital pharmacy and was ratted out by fellow prisoners. Unable to avoid blame, I gave my counselor the appearance of carefully listening to and being influenced by his commentary. Actually, I was discerning what he was attempting to teach me, then rephrased it so I could appear to have gained new profound insight because of the wisdom he had imparted to me in such a clear manner. Having puffed up my counselor's ego, the resultant punishment for this significantly severe violation was minimal: ten days in the hole.

Overall, I simply had no concept of truthfulness as an integral aspect of responsibility and actually even failed to see myself as a liar.
GK That's the slippery slope, isn't it? Once we delude ourselves into believing we don't lie, we're done!
FJA Totally, and this came from my belief whatever I deemed was right for me at any given time was truth. Furthermore, when cornered or caught in an outright fabrication I usually claimed it was a test or I was just fooling around. At other times, when caught in a lie, I would point to the smallest lie by others, turn it into a major point of contention, deflecting attention from myself. The methods of deception I once employed were endless and characterized the way in which I functioned; especially in regard to major aspects of life that are generally incongruent with criminality.
GK Did you study the C.I.A. manual on disinformation?
FJA No. But I thought I possessed an impressive arsenal of tactics with which to obstruct effective communication. For instance, when I was under interrogation the investigator had to be defrauded, cogent discussion would have compromised my freedom. Consequently, I became extremely adept at hindering effective discourse—even if somewhat truthful discourse would

have been benign, deceiving an interviewer was still exciting.

GK You mentioned the example of obstructing communication with those who functioned as threats to you, please shed a little more light on this; especially, isn't this another form of lying/deceit?

FJA I approached interrogators, or any authority, like a criminal enterprise. My initial "job" was to case the investigator. Then I would take cues from him/her, talk about matters that were irrelevant to the investigation, otherwise divert efforts to learn about the issue in question, and receive aid in the achievement of my objectives. I viewed any attempts to establish rapport as weakness and I was usually in control of the interrogation. Only now I know that's what guilty criminals do.

I perceived interrogations as a struggle for survival—survival in this context being defined as anything serving to fulfill desired objectives. Additionally, my overall strategy was to reverse roles.

GK Unfortunately, for the police at the time, few were ever formally trained in interrogation techniques and their primary methods used back then have been found to be unreliable.

FJA I had only contempt for investigators and viewed them as ignorant while having perceived myself as the expert. To reinforce my misbelief, I took the offensive by criticizing the examiner. One common way I accomplished this was having selected, then ridiculing, something about the examiner; such as an article of clothing, their hairstyle, or a facial feature. Not only would this reinforce my concept of superiority but I also seized control of the interrogation.

For me the goal was to gain the advantage over the inquisitor, a person I viewed as an adversary to overcome. Of course, a key feature of these tactics involved my push for dominion to provide desired excitement (here, control over an authority figure).

GK How much of these exchanges were the dance of feeding the interrogator what he wanted to hear?

FJA I constantly fed investigators what they wanted to hear, while doing so I presented the appearance of responding thoughtfully and sincerely to allow examiners to think they had an impact on me. This was more common in counseling situations rather than during an interrogation. For instance, whenever I was called to the guidance counselor's office at school and confronted with some deficiency (poor grades, inattentiveness, being disruptive) I played at admitting the transgression and gave lip service to making improvement. These acts usually satisfied my counselor and demonstrates how the vast majority of the time I merely gave the facade of cooperation. Moreover, by deceiving interrogators I not only achieved expedient objectives and personal advantage but also once again gained power and control over an important person.

GK And, of course, you'd insert topics for purposes of distraction?

FJA I believed I had sole responsibility/prerogative to decide what was important. To me, what was important was anything putting me in a favorable light. In considering the example of having been confronted by school counselors, I knew their objectives included desires to further student involvement in the education system. So, I'd express empty interest for doing better by becoming more involved and inquired about school clubs, tutoring programs, and athletic endeavors to plant the appearance of my renewed enthusiasm for school.

GK How else did you corrupt communication with misdirection?

FJA It was standard procedure for me to maintain a lack of responsibility, to offer excuses. In furtherance of this I proffered many falsehoods, with lies of omission being far more common than lies of commission. Also, when preceding a comment with "to tell the truth" or "to be honest with you" it generally signaled that deception would follow; a ploy today's investigators are now aware of.

Consequently, vagueness as another commonly used tactic of misdirection, I employed a variety of methods to qualify what I said as a way to interject obscurity. One such ploy involved the use of words with idiosyncratic meanings, thus leaving it to others to figure out what I had said. Other examples of my having implemented vagueness include avoidance of giving direct answers to specific questions or having used a genuine opening up in devious manners. Again, considering the example of confrontations with school counselors, I would use language such as "I might look into that as an option" or "yes, perhaps that would be of help" rather than adopting more definite stances, such as "I will...". This would give me an excuse later, once I neglected to follow through, by claiming I had only agreed to take these possibilities under consideration.

GK Please provide another example.

FJA I would offer inconsistent versions of a given event, speaking so rapidly that it was hard to follow, or speaking slowly and listlessly. The intent here was to wear down or exasperate the inquisitor, so these strategies were used for far less severe sessions, when an examiner was not as insistent on having to achieve success. If that failed I'd deviate from initial topics or even occasionally acknowledge a lie to receive credit for having been "honest."

GK And now you know any inconsistency in one's story is a huge red flag to investigators.

FJA I would generally avoid bold lies and instead opt to minimize my involvement in the action under scrutiny. One day I stole some alcohol from my parents' liquor cabinet and when my mother confronted me—I had been the only one home, so obviously took the booze—I concocted a story about having taken the alcohol but not drinking it, as if that minimization of events would somehow excuse my theft. Additionally, there were times when I would conceal the harm I had inflicted by offering deliberate understatements. For instance, "borrow" was a common euphemism for theft.

GK I see, this functioned as merely another form of befuddlement. How else did you inject distraction into examinations?

FJA I inevitably introduced irrelevant material during interrogations and was quick to notice if questioners became interested in trivial matters for me to exaggerate by spending disproportionate amounts of time on their minutia. If held accountable on issues I did not care to discuss I put into motion various strategies to deflect attention away from myself, including: recounting my qualities and good deeds, invoking racial issues, talking about the faults of others (making a lack of integrity in them the issue rather than my violations), and resorting to ideological arguments and tirades on social injustices. In addition to having deflected attention away from my misdeeds another goal when using these tactics was to teach, to reduce the examiner to the rank of student, while attempting to present a favorable impression of myself and to obtain a power thrust. At other times, I resorted to feigning ignorance in order to induce the inquisitor into a demonstration of his/her knowledge as a ploy to divert the course of the session to an innocuous realm.

GK And when you got caught red handed?

FJA I would employ "assent" and appear to agree with the interrogator, only momentarily acquiescing. My intent was to cut short an uncomfortable discussion without alienating the investigator. This was an especially common scheme when what was at issue had little or no relevance to me. For instance, if confronted about having missed school, something I actually felt justified in doing, I had no difficulty in admitting my purported wrong…so receiving brownie points for receptivity to the examiner.

GK Did you ever use silence as a technic?

FJA Silence existed as a potent method through which I assumed control of interrogations, when I invoked the tactic of silence no inquisition could proceed and I enjoyed the thrill of having confounded the investigation.

GK What part did your selective attention and myopic self-perception play in this?

FJA I implemented selective hearing and perception by ignoring everything unrelated to my immediate objectives. I heard only what agreed with my thinking and even construed incongruent statements as being in accord with my ideas when actually the opposite had been asserted. For example, if a counselor enumerated several areas in which I needed change I would misconstrue this as my counselor having acknowledged changes I had already made. As a result, when discussing a conversation with those who had been present they would often wonder when and where the discourse I was now relating had taken place.

GK Were there times you'd ignore people completely during conversation?

FJA As an alternative to or in combination with selective listening I would often ignore everything that had been said, especially if the conversation involved telling me what to do. The tendency was to turn my attention to more exciting ideas and when confronted with having not met requirements I would allege some supposed deficiency in the way these directives had been presented.

GK But I bet you played the diva card by showing up late to appointments.

FJA A condition of my parole was to participate in group therapy (please see next page) and while somewhat enthusiastic at first, I had still not seen a therapist for several weeks after having been released from prison. The newness and excitement of having possibly engaged in the change process wore off and I decided I had better things to do. Not a single session had been attended; that is, I readily ignored appointments once something more exciting presented itself.

Similarly, if being on time conflicted with potential excitement: I would be tardy. There were countless times when I arrived hours late, if at all, for meetings with my parole officer, medical or dental appointments, to pick up someone, or for some sort of job interview.

Department of Corrections   State of California

NOTICE AND CONDITIONS OF PAROLE

You will be released on parole effective 5 16 84, 19 ___ for a period of 3 yrs. This parole is subject to the following notice and conditions. Should you violate conditions of this parole, you are subject to arrest, suspension and/or revocation of your parole.

You waive extradition to the State of California from any state or territory of the United States or from the District of Columbia. You will not contest any effort to return you to the State of California.

When the Board of Prison Terms determines, based upon psychiatric reasons, that you pose a danger to yourself or others, the Board may, if necessary for psychiatric treatment, order your placement in a community treatment facility or state prison or may revoke your parole and order your return to prison.

You and your residence and any property under your control may be searched without a warrant by any agent of the Department of Corrections or any law enforcement officer.

If another jurisdiction has lodged a detainer against you, you may be released to the custody of that jurisdiction. Should you be released from their custody prior to the expiration of your California parole, or should the detainer not be exercised, you are to immediately contact the nearest Department of Corrections' Parole and Community Services Division Office for instructions concerning reporting to a parole agent.

You have been informed and have received in writing the procedure for obtaining a Certificate of Rehabilitation (4852.21 PC), and furnished with CDC Form 807 "Notice of Unemployment and Disability Payments".

You have read or have had read to you this notification and the following Conditions of Parole.

CONDITIONS OF PAROLE

1. SPECIAL CONDITIONS: You are subject to the following special conditions:
   1) To Attend Parole outpatient clinic.
   2) To not associate, nor be in the company of, minor children

   Reasons for the imposition of special conditions of parole:

   History of Psychiatric Problems.

   ______________________ Signature of Parole Administrator   Date

2. RELEASE, REPORTING, RESIDENCE AND TRAVEL: Unless other arrangements are approved in writing, you will report to your parole agent immediately upon release. You will not leave the State of California without prior written approval of your parole agent. You will not change your place of residence without prior approval of your parole agent. You will inform your parole agent within 72 hours of any change in employment.
3. PAROLE AGENT INSTRUCTIONS: You will comply with all instructions issued by a parole agent. Instructions will be given to you in writing as soon as possible.
4. CRIMINAL CONDUCT: You will not engage in conduct prohibited by law (state, federal, county or municipal). Conduct prohibited by law may result in parole revocation even though no criminal conviction occurs.
5. WEAPONS: You will not own, use, have access to, or have under your control: (a) any type of firearm; (b) any weapon as defined in state or federal statutes or listed in California Penal Code Section 12020; or (c) any knife with a blade longer than two inches, except kitchen knives which must be kept in your residence and knives related to your employment which may be used and carried only in connection with your employment.

Frank Atwood 6-4-84 — Signature of Parolee/Number, Date
R. McLean 6-4-84 — Signature of Institutional Staff, Date

Atwood, Frank C26006

CDC 1515 (Rev 11/80)

GK Did you participate in programming during your incarceration?
FJA I quickly learned what was expected of me and generally provided every effort to seem to be in accordance with requirements. For instance, if having had to complete a specific program to improve my chances of release from prison or jail I would present myself as anxious to participate in order to elicit details about the program. This enabled me to be able to pretend to be engaged in personal change while covertly pursuing criminal enterprises.
GK How do we know you're not doing exactly that right now?
FJA I would hardly agree to do an interview project like this. Plus, the body of work I've completed over the years should speak to my sincerity.
GK And I can confirm to our readers that Frank isn't one of the 'cool kids' bangin with the youngsters.
GK How did you use socializing and leadership positions?
FJA I often attempted to assume leadership roles as a tactic to demonstrate positive personal changes and newly found responsibility. Even when momentarily not involved in crime I used leadership as a criminal substitute. I enjoyed the build-up, excitement, and power from leading others. Therefore, I don't see how leadership can be a valid index of change for prisoners or ex-offenders. Likewise, socializing did not demonstrate change in myself but rather provided a source of excitement from criminal talk (bragging about and embellishing violations) and a build-up of self. Socializing also existed as a criminal substitute and, like with leadership, should not exist as a sound indicator of change.
GK Returning to interaction with authority figures, in what way(s) did you approach specific involvement?
FJA I was extremely adept at fashioning my approach to any particular audience; including all authorities, interrogators, friends, and so on. I tailored my approach to dovetail with the personality and views of whomever I was currently in contact with. A parallel method for accomplishing this was to find out what sports or music someone liked in order to develop common ground and facilitate more familiar dialogue. Obviously, I lacked any responsible social interaction skills (please see next page).

medications like Paxil and Celexa and Zoloft. He's also received anti-anxiety agent known as Atarax or it's often called Vistaril, which is for anxiety. And he's more recently been prescribed an anti-anxiety agent known as Buspar.

MS. HARMS: I want to bring up Exhibit 163, which is the psychological report that was done in 1973 which is three years after the molestation.

Could you highlight the sentence that says -- I'm sorry, start a little earlier than I have -- "he is a person". Next to the last paragraph.

Could you highlight a little more, down a little.

THE WITNESS: It's not very clear and it's not the fault, but excuse me if I have an error when I read it.

"He is a person who makes inadequate and/or ineffectual responses to emotional, social, intellectual, and vocational demands placed upon him. While he is certainly not mentally deficient, he does show considerable inadaptability, ineptness, and poor judgment, particularly in situations he finds stressful, which may appear to be minimal to others."

BY MS. HARMS:

Q. Does that statement have any meaning to you in terms of the diagnosis of PTSD?

A. Yes. That one especially. That's what we call

ON LYING AND BEING A JERK

GK We all have a "crazy" story from when we were in the psych ward, what's yours?

FJA I altered meanings so as to render them useless. For instance, if I became angry and expressed that anger in offensive terms, or even violently, I claimed I had been told to be completely open. I recall a time in a psychiatric hospital when I threw a chair across the room, nearly hitting other patients, demolishing the chair, and cracking a window. My "defense" was to assert I simply had expressed myself, per doctor's orders.

GK I could see that. Give us another example of indefinite postponements.

FJA Another common tactic consisted of deferring responsibility. Since I had little intention of doing what was required of me I deliberately postponed things indefinitely. Having never showed up for outpatient therapy, as my parole required, serves as an example of this since I then repeatedly made new appointments in order to have indefinitely extended the time in which to fulfill the obligation and was also able to have produced excitement from once again having assumed control over those I saw as fools.

GK Did you ever use the "thank you doctor, I'm healed" move? Or, "Hallelujah, I can see the light, can I go home now?"

FJA I used them all. Once boredom at attempts to change arose, and the need for excitement became overwhelming, rather than admit my failure to change I would claim that enough change had occurred and then cease further effort. Of course, I knew I hadn't changed, all I really wanted was to overcome restraints and get back into the action.

GK What about putting others on the defensive as deflection?

Bored, Broke and Armed:
The Seeds of South Side Gang Violence
By John Eligon New York Times 12.22.16

During my research for this book I saw this headline and understood these "seeds"; bored, broke and armed extend to many young teens, even well outside gang culture.

While in the Yavapia County Jail a few of the older guys with money would tell a poor kid: "Go pick a fight with that guy over there and I'll give you five candy bars and three cigarettes." Why? You ask, because we had nothing to do 24 hours a day. It was pure boredom, and perversion of social ethics that made the act that much more interesting.

FJA I always struggled to maintain a good opinion of myself and desperately fought efforts to expose me as worthless. As a result of the continuous need to maintain this position I found it was far more important to demonstrate my own knowledge to others rather than to learn. For example, when attending therapy sessions or drug counseling I tried to assume the role of teacher and convert others to my views, even those running the sessions. This concealed my shortcomings while allowing self-promotion. It also allowed me to continue the attempts to show that I was something rather than to be unmasked as the nothing I actually was. Being somewhat educated, well-versed, and intellectually inclined, I viewed myself as operating on a higher plane and this made it most difficult to deal with me. I would also occasionally become extremely offensive or accusatory when attempting to assume control and by putting others on the defensive I was able to take the spotlight of criticism off myself. This tactic would sometimes use anger as a weapon and frequently included an attempt to launch a direct attack on someone by degrading them, both of which were intended to put others on the defensive via deflection.

GK One last question on lying and miscommunication, can you please relate something about language?

FJA Many disagreements arose (something I encouraged and was to my advantage) because I ensured the other party did not understand the terms or content of what I was saying. This involved attaching very different meaning to words, since other people generally possessed drastically dissimilar frames of reference than I did as an extreme criminal. In fact, my vernacular was often so alien one may have wondered whether I was speaking the same language as everyone else. In this way, communication was often confounded, which was desirable when interference with my objectives seemed likely. Moreover, the use of semantics also allowed me to seize control and provided a power surge and excitement.

As an example of attaching very different meanings to words, consider my use of "let's go pick up some…" which to me would infer a criminal deed (theft, drugs), whereas to a non-criminal this would be construed as making a legitimate purchase.

GK Was there any distinction between your perspective toward others and materiality?

FJA Another manifestation of erroneous thought patterns originating from my extreme need for control centered on my concept of ownership. This meant if an object was desired it immediately became mine. Moreover, there existed no sense of permanence, no lasting gratification from acquiring, using, and appreciating an object. Similarly, if I desired a person they became mine, and were expected to do as I wished.

GK So then, this "ownership" applies to both persons and things?

FJA As mentioned, once I desired an object or person it immediately became "mine" and then the mental process of how to take possession (scheming) ensued; I believed I had "earned" ownership of items upon execution of the crime. Consider how one afternoon while driving down the street I noticed a pharmacy and at once regarded its drugs as mine. I went home and planned how to break in and later that night carried out my attack and took "my" drugs—my planning and ensuing burglary, my ingenuity and risk of jail, gave me the "right" of ownership.

Another feature of ownership was it became most pronounced during threats to my power and control. A frequent manifestation of this occurred when confined and I disregarded the fact prison guards had ultimate control over me, believing I "owned" them. That is officers did not exist as those having any authority over me but were peons who fulfilled my desires, such as bringing in drugs. So, yes, both people and objects were subject to ownership.

None of this is intended to convey I did not understand property was owned legitimately by others. My thought patterns simply perceived "want" as synonymous with having, a consequence of my defective thinking. As a result, my idea of ownership extended everywhere, even to people. Just as I drove down the street and eventually took ownership of drugs in a pharmacy, I would spot a girl, then fantasize about picking her up for a date. Prevailing thoughts consisted of hoping" my" girl would stay where spotted and remain safe until I came for her.

GK What else can you share about this concept of owning others?

FJA My concept of owning people, I'd reflect a relatively sustained attitude of dominance. For instance, when imagining a lover, I'd think in terms of possessing them, body and soul. Or, consider how as a teenager I functioned as though my parents were my property. Also, I felt I had a great claim on someone when I did them a favor. This would include, by way of example, borrowing money then, if deciding to pay it back, not thinking the lender had done a favor for me but rather my believing I'd done the favor by having repaid my loan.

GK Thus, consequently, the ownership (or dominance) really just served as yet another method for control; would that be an accurate way to define your thought process?

FJA Understanding these thought patterns I possessed reveals the pervasive sense of ownership extending into virtually all areas of my life. This was evidenced when realizing I perceived my rights as transcending those of others; when noticing how I made my own rules—however, I only followed these rules if they didn't interfere with my objectives. Also, when told by others what was expected of me I reserved all rights whether to comply, all the while demanding others must acquiesce to my every whim. This was evident in my belief I was entitled to know everything about everyone else, despite having led a secretive life; that is, I demanded my own privacy yet invaded the privacy of others at will...since I owned them. Quite simply, ownership existed as part of my view, my rights were unlimited and, yes, control was certainly a primary objective.

GK What did you do to eliminate your "ownership of others" attitudes?

FJA In thinking back from the onset of my phenomenological reporting, there existed numerous instances of "me, me, me" possessive thinking errors; despite the apparent innocuous nature of relatively minor ownership (i.e., others existing to serve my interests) flaws, each one had to be immediately corrected. In order to eradicate possessive thinking errors, I had to replace prejudgment and assumptions with investigating facts and my developing consideration of others. One key corrective for establishing this was to remind myself not everyone would like me or readily do as I desired. Thus, there arose the need to accept people as individuals, to realize each had their own preferences. An additional corrective was learning about social boundaries and how people were accountable to one another for what they said and did. Overall, I had to progress from the view of owning people to realizing I had no claim on others (many actually had claims on me).

GK It seems you possessed sufficient willpower to pursue whatever you desired, when confronted with the distasteful how did you react?

FJA I had several pet thinking patterns at my disposal whenever things failed to unfold as desired. One of these, the "I can't" stance, was a particular favorite, even though I actually believed there was nothing I could not accomplish. Hence, when thinking "I can't" there existed intent to refuse acting responsibly. This defect in ideation manifested, for instance, when responding to a teacher who had asked me to complete an assignment, or a supervisor requesting I perform an undesirable task, by stating "I can't." On the other hand, if my crime partner suggested a burglary I'd respond enthusiastically, no matter what obstacles we had to overcome. So "can't" meant I would not, or did not want to, and "I can't" existed as a dismissal of requirements outside of my desires and interests.

GK Many of your tactics were typical teenager responses, the problem was you didn't adhere to any models of discipline. What other weapons were in your arsenal?

FJA Another favorite was considering myself as a victim when held accountable for misbehavior. That is, contemplation of myself as a victim existed only when confronted, it wasn't part of my daily thinking. Thus, only when facing accusation did I blame others and argue the world had not provided me with what I believed I was entitled to; I was a "victim."

Moreover, when playing the victim, I always pointed to something that was wrong with others, never with myself, and often used excuses such as, "If only it had not been for…". In fact, there were even times I viewed society as unfit for me, rather than my having been unfit for society. Of course, by using these mistaken beliefs of myself as a victim, by deflecting fault away from myself, I was able to hang on to concepts of myself as a good person. That is why I so desperately refused to admit the existence of a disagreeable situation of my own making, to admit to an adverse condition for which I possessed a modicum of responsibility would have constituted an extreme put-down.

GK Can you provide an example?

FJA Consider how a videotaped group therapy session exposed me as extremely hostile; when confronted with this I launched into a litany of reasons why I should have been seen as the victim. When the video exposed these pathetic attempts, I insisted I'd been entrapped, still clinging to the role of victim (which resulted in several days of depression); the point here being the desperate holding onto the victim stance.

> *In fact, there were even times I viewed society as unfit for me, rather than my having been unfit for society.*

GK How would you frame the impact of victimization upon your thinking, can you offer a brief overview?

FJA How differently I approached decision making has now become apparent; unlike a responsible person, I would rarely weigh pros and cons, failing to evaluate various courses of action. By impulsively deciding to engage in irresponsible conduct I increased the opportunity to use the "I can't" and victim postures while absolving myself of any responsibility for resultant destructive consequences. That was why I refused to employ sound reasoning; I almost never engaged in fact-finding, would not evaluate financial concerns, and failed to consider options. Instead, I did whatever was compatible with my current state of mind, employing the doctrine of "cogito, ergo est" ("I think, therefore it is").

My decision-making ability became so flawed I couldn't even make wise purchases at stores, such as at the market or a clothing outlet. I lacked the necessary process and feared asking questions would have revealed my ignorance. However, if facts were needed to conduct a criminal enterprise I never hesitated to investigate and make inquiries.

Truly, when considering my past decision-making ability, the narrow and defective thinking patterns—i.e., failures to have considered and established alternatives, along with the tendency to prejudge—certainly imposed significant restrictions.

GK Picking up on blaming others and placing yourself in the role of victim, describe some "victim, stance" lessons.

FJA The use of daily journaling allowed me to undertake a careful study of the many patterns I utilized to blame others and present myself as a victim. For instance, I frequently asserted I was "born to lose" and could never succeed at anything, or claimed having been so disadvantaged by an extensive arrest and prison record precluded any hope. My victim stance existed as a prepared justification tactic and enabled me to revert to innumerable excuses in rapid succession. This reveals why it was critical for me to negate any focus on cause and effect by concentrating instead on my choices by considering my contributions to adverse situations and recognizing how I compounded difficulties. Moreover, any attempt to blame feelings also had to be thwarted because feelings were often within my control. This meant having to consciously avoid employing a plethora of victim excuses early in the change process.

GK I see, and exactly how did you kill the roots of this ingrained pattern?

FJA Whatever victim stance I utilized there were four ways to combat these postures:

1. By tracing the patterns of my choices in order to expose the role I had played in arriving at my position under consideration.
2. Through realization that others made different choices when faced with similar or worse circumstances and had not turned out as I had.
3. By becoming aware I was a victimizer far more than a victim.
4. Through awareness of having assumed the victim stance and becoming aware of its concomitant opposition to responsibility.

GK Speak about how you overcame your "I can't" attitude.

FJA My specious claims of "I can't" also had to be addressed early on in the change process. Whenever having uttered, "I can't" I had to recognize I actually meant, "I won't," or "I don't want to." I also needed to realize the use of "I can't" indicated criminal thinking had gained the upper hand; requiring immediate correction. In other words, I needed to recognize the "I can't" excuse as it occurred then replace it with "I must." The corrective existed in using my new attitude. I needed to perform what was difficult now, then tackle the impossible soon thereafter. Thus, the corrective involved more than the elimination of excuses, it required doing.

GK Changing streams, I wonder about your sense of commitment, not in a business or contractual format, but insofar as duty and gratitude toward others (whether society or criminal), what can you say on this?

FJA The concept of obligation was foreign to my way of thinking. To me, obligation was indebtedness, it caused the loss of my perceived status as a powerful person because others had assumed control over me. I simply viewed obligation as interference with what I wanted.

Moreover, any sense of duty was alien to my thought process, meaning I possessed no moral imperative toward duty; I only fulfilled obligations, or did as I said, if a criminal objective could be furthered and nothing else more exciting loomed. Thus, I may have satisfied a debt as a self-serving operation; possessing zero genuine inner sense of duty meant it was impossible for obligation to have existed as a functional concept in my life. At the same time, I was tyrannical in requiring others to fulfill what I considered to be their obligations to me. Also, I was adept at avoiding situations in which new duties may have been incurred. I was an expert at having others indebted to me as an ulterior motive.

Finally, as far as obligation, I generally responded in one of the four following ways:

1. With blatant disregard.
2. Avoidance of new indebtedness to others.
3. Fulfilling duties out of transient sentimentality.
4. Satisfying obligations to advance exploitive schemes.

GK Sounds like you were a real jerk. Expound upon avoiding obligation(s).

FJA In addition to the failure to assume obligation I also refused to accept responsible initiatives—they simply did not provide the desired thrill. I failed to assume responsible initiatives because they didn't guarantee there was anything in it for me; I nearly always required absolute assurance of personal gain. Another obstacle to responsible initiatives involved my inability to comprehend the concept of responsibility; thus, by having refused to take responsible action I was able to avoid initiating events, enabling me to escape having appeared ignorant as a consequence of my failure to apprehend responsibility.

GK Please provide another example, for clarity's sake.

FJA A classic example of my failure to have assumed obligation or taken responsible initiatives—unless in pursuit of a crime, when I'd demonstrate enthusiastic and energetic actions—occurred one day when my father had been after me to clean the pool, something I'd promised/obligated myself to do but continued to postpone. My dad finally mumbled something about a lazy bum as he left for a meeting, at which time my mom began questioning me about when I was going to stop sitting around and to start looking for a job. I merely gave lip service to calling employers to arrange interview appointments. Suddenly, my crime partner telephoned to let me know some primo hash had hit town; I at once made around a dozen phone calls, traveled to a handful of houses and clubs across the Los Angeles and San Fernando Valley area—anything but a lazy, haphazard course of action had been embarked upon when something desired and illegal (exciting) arose.

GK In other words, the emphasis fell squarely upon what was at stake at that moment rather than a consistent thinking pattern?

FJA My general refusal to have fulfilled obligation and taken responsibility meant I failed to perform as society required. For instance, responsible functions like work or school held little or nothing of value to offer me, and competing interests precluded me from acquiring the requisite skills and knowledge to progress in the mainstream world. Excitement was my guiding light, I was simply governed by action…rejecting what others had to offer while still desiring benefits of what I had rejected.

GK I'm wondering, did you feel you owed other people and/or had accrued a debt against yourself once some change transpired?

FJA I did experience onset of a real sense of obligation, and in learning about this ingredient of a responsible way of life I had to differentiate between two forms of obligation: one included requirements of daily life (e.g., work necessities, prayer rules, writing my wife, etc.), in which there could be little to no choice. These obligations mostly concerned what others expected of me. The other type involved an inner or moral sense of responsibility. I'd never thought in these terms, having instead always considered people and possessions as existing for my use.

Obligation—defined here as duty to others, so my need to act in a specific way, even if undesired at the time—is the antithesis of control. Because I had always perceived the world as having to cater to me, it was a new concept. I learned the need for me to become aware of old patterns as I did something for another person while undergoing the process of change. For instance, I had to consciously avoid helping others as a way to obligate them to me. I also had to cease helping criminals; to aid felons generally established anticipated exploitation.

Also, I had to concentrate on obligatory concerns, as opposed to leisure activities based on preference; personal desire had to become balanced. This necessitated cultivating an attitude where I would immerse myself in something, stick with it, and allow non-criminal interest to develop. Enjoyment could follow once knowledge and skill had been achieved (meaning my new knowing and expertise generated appreciation), which enhanced my self-confidence and resulted in change.

GK Rather than others being able to trust you, what about your ability to rely on and trust others?

FJA The existence of my "self-important" perception meant that to trust another person was a rarity. I generally used the term "trust" to indicate someone had done as I desired. In other words, even though criminal endeavors required some level of trust among participants—such as relying on a getaway driver or depending on an arrested associate to keep his mouth shut—I never saw this as a matter of trust. Instead, I thought my influence over others commanded a kind of obedience. A good example of this was the time when I relied on my crime partner to be at a hotel for a crucial meeting involving a major drug deal. Suffice it to say he risked both incarceration and death to be on time, yet rather than having viewed him as trustworthy or reliable I simply took it for granted that he had merely done as I had ordered. Clearly, my perception of "trust" was the equivalent of not interfering with my intentions and basically agreeing with me, a posture revealing that as a criminal my notion of trust was tied to the element of control. Unless, of course, the issue involved others trusting me, something I demanded from others without equivocation.

> Children Report False Accounts?
>
> Historically, professionals promoted the idea that children frequently report false accounts of abuse. Current research, however, lacks systematic evidence that false allegations are common.
>
> Allnock, D., Children & Young People Disclosing Sexual Abuse.

Obviously, trust is needed for social cohesion—even when involving confidence in those one doesn't know; i.e., with store clerks, factory workers, doctors, attorneys, and so on…trust must exist. Unfortunately, I failed to comprehend this concept and considered putting faith in others as a weakness. For me, trusting others resulted in dependence, the antithesis of control, so I refused to believe some interdependence was a necessary part of existence. I thought of dependence as an infirmity, as causing vulnerability. At the same time, I feigned wanting dependence if I didn't want to do something. For example, I often played the role of helplessness as a ruse, encouraging others to do things for me.

GK Considering the change process in the context of ridding yourself of criminal characteristics, doesn't this require trust?

FJA Absolutely, others could not provide me with a rationale for implementing my program for change, nor could I be persuaded into uncritically believing a program would induce lasting alteration of my thought and action patterns. Change necessitated my seeking and discovering on my own the requisite faith and desire to activate new thinking and behavior structures. This functioned as the sole method through which I could determine whether my trust was warranted; that is, I could not be led into being a believer in recovery, instead I had to become the initiator.

The trust by those involved with helping me to change could never be violated (privileged communications had to be steadfastly maintained) and mutual openness was a perennial requirement. Additionally, my confidence had to extend beyond those helping me as I engaged in this process by correcting errors brought out in my daily phenomenological reports. For example, after having recorded all thoughts and feelings experienced as a result of interactions with others throughout my day I would then carefully examine these printouts of thinking objectively to determine their veracity, or lack thereof. As a result of this evaluation of situations, followed by reaching responsible decisions, I began to trust even those who were not close to me. Along with this, I also learned a person's qualities emerge over time; deciding when to trust was a slow process. In addition, when learning whom to trust, I needed to begin showing others I was worthy of their trust.

GK How about your need for parental dependence?

FJA Herein dwells another example of my defective concepts on dependence when observing how I refused to seek or accept affection from my family. I pushed my parents away and sought independence from family requirements and expectations. In fact, not only did I push my parents away but I also exploited them by demanding the comforts of home while contributing little to family life. My abhorrence of dependency even led me to think of my parents' bailing me out of trouble as an entitlement rather than as a form of dependence; my teen years witnessed my abandonment of familial dependency.

GK Having lived an isolated, negative path, with reliance only on yourself, how did you develop an ability to accept assistance from others?

FJA I had to recognize my fresh yet fragile interdependence didn't project weakness but instead enabled a responsible independence. I also had to grasp the fact that interconnected living produced greater and more fulfilling latitude than was possible while engaged in an irresponsible life. It became essential to learn my dependence constituted a part of normal existence and was not a put-down.

By examining my daily journals, I was able to assimilate the nature of interrelatedness as a result of having expanded tubular vision beyond my power and control concepts so my perception included an understanding of how responsible people rely on each other. For instance, even in prison I must rely on guards to feed and clothe me, and to bring mail. Thus, I had to subject my thinking to their criticism, and my correction, so old patterns (such as blind hatred of prison staff) could be differentiated from emergent responsible motifs (i.e., dependence on and respect for others).

GK What was it like to come down from your big shot pedestal?

FJA Because I had always viewed myself as a bigwig, and as the unique number one, a most difficult task involved my having to start from the bottom and progress slowly by responsibly earning positions and items I desired; by developing a realistic perspective of my place in life. Both qualitative and quantitative aspects, in terms of altering pretentiousness, had to be attended to; meaning I had to develop constant awareness of what I expected and of how much I hoped for from others—being careful not to demand but rather to ask.

I also had to study and to then grasp what realistically constituted a success or a setback, a process I daily pursued by evaluating problems in order to learn achievement. Eventually, people's benign comments no longer existed as humiliation and by meeting ordinary everyday problems I learned experiences of abasement possessed more significance than any one specific final result.

Again, my daily phenomenological reports functioned as an essential component in helping me to develop an entirely new perspective, one in which I accepted setbacks were an unavoidable aspect of life. Only then was I able to discover failure as a guide and inspiration, something that led to instituting my improvements. At first, I had to encourage these correctives from definitive specific events or thoughts contained in my daily journals before the concept could be applied to my entire life. This was an excruciating mental and physical process, but I was ultimately able to view myself in more realistic terms and with a humble pie modesty as I strove to do my best to function responsibly in pursuit of progress. This actually exemplifies my program for change: movement away from intense cravings for continual excitement while a criminal and toward functioning as a responsible adult by diligently fulfilling my new life's ordinary everyday tasks.

GK When imagining crimes, obviously you've put many ideas into action without getting caught, did getting away with so much lawlessness play a role in your plans?

FJA Insuperable confidence existed as an extreme form of optimism and manifested as a rising certainty of not being caught. This assuredness of evading arrest increased until having reached a state of unsurpassable certitude. Then again, personal experience supported my confidence of not being apprehended. Take as an example how I sold many different kinds of drugs literally thousands of times before ever being arrested; the possibility of my capture was extremely low. Then again, insuperable confidence was not a consistent state of mind, despite all of the crime I got away with I occasionally acknowledged the likelihood of eventually being caught, but I never believed it would be "this time."

GK Insofar as your acknowledgement of potential arrest, in what ways did this impact your decisions to act illegally?

FJA Another facet of insuperable confidence arose as a consequence of experience having led me to believe even if arrested there existed many proceedings before conviction or sentencing, many opportunities to work the system. I routinely observed motions to suppress evidence, variant technicalities, and plea bargains to serve as effective strategies. Thus, I expected to either beat the rap or receive a light sentence (such as probation). I remember having departed a resident drug program and being arrested for several felonies; the following morning I was released on bail. After several months of maneuvering, my attorney got everything reduced to a couple of misdemeanors...I plead guilty and received probation. Even a string of serious charges resulted in merely a few hours behind bars.

Also of interest is how since around age fifteen I considered possibilities and assumptions as accomplished facts. Meaning, ideas or potentialities existed as reality—an actuality briefly pointed to when providing examples of how once I saw something I desired it existed as "mine." So, for instance, having espied a pretty girl the possibility of a date became an accomplished fact, all that remained for me was to decide when to pick her up. Having considered potentialities as reality fit in with the state of insuperable confidence because in both instances there existed attitudes everything would function as I saw fit in every situation. That is, I viewed everything as stacked in my favor at all times; when in a super-optimistic state, I perceived the completion and success of a criminal act as a fait accompli. This can be seen when realizing I'd already spent the proceeds in my mind prior to having actually committed the crime.

GK What I hear you saying is if the police would have done their job, i.e., arresting you, repeatedly jailing you, your extreme confidence wouldn't have emerged and developed your insuperability.

FJA No, police and courts merely perform their duties; it's my responsibility, to the extent PTSD's intrusion symptoms weren't at work! I'm only trying to explain my unsurpassable certitude, once having emerged, gave credence to self-aggrandizement, the false belief I was a good person, which existed as a powerful factor in wearing down deterrents. Consequently, as crime was either fantasized about or actually planned I still maintained the notion I was a decent human being. Therefore, my contemplated action appeared to me as acceptable, I saw others as foolish not to engage in similar behavior.

GK It seems inconceivable that you maintained this sense of benevolence, please explain a bit further.

FJA Self-aggrandizement also encompassed the sentimental stage of criminal enterprises, a passing phase of kind and generous acts to assuage any lingering guilt from prior unlawful exploits and restore the positive view of myself as a good person. In fact, even enroute to a crime I often engaged in acts of compassion to reinforce this warped perception of self. Consider how one day my crime partner and I were on the way to rob a business when we encountered a lady with car trouble, we pulled up, fixed her flat tire, then congratulated ourselves on what nice guys we were. This enabled us to distort the fact we were about to commit an extremely serious crime into our being friends of the down-trodden; after all, we were simply liberating funds from the fat cats.

GK Does this mean you possessed no intent to change, to cease your felonious conduct?

FJA Insuperable confidence and self-aggrandizement had significant influence on deferment. For example, I continually delayed self-reform and deferred responsibilities incompatible with committing crime because I already saw myself as a good person (self-aggrandizement) and was overly optimistic (insuperable confidence); that is, I believed I could establish myself in the world as a citizen of good standing whenever I chose to do so, however, implementation was always put off. Moreover, responsibility was also deferred because it simply did not exist within my realm of interests. Responsibility took away from more exciting pursuits and did not provide the desired power and control. In fact, I'd even defer what was in my best interests if more exciting pursuits became available.

GK Let's talk about overcoming your Donald Trump super-optimism.

FJA At the onset of my change process my male macho bravado assured me there would be nothing to it; nearly immediately thereafter, as error after error was exposed in my daily journaling, I rapidly discovered my smugness was wholly unfounded. Moreover, despite the belief of my having held a somewhat firm grasp on the principles of my modification program I could never adequately apprehend any new concept of belief until having applied it to daily experience.

GK Was that the death of your super-optimism?

FJA Not yet. Once initial overconfidence had been shattered I diligently pursued the arduous process of change, however, as each error was corrected I again mistakenly believed complete success had been achieved: super-optimism persisted. To unmask and expose my super-optimism as unwarranted and destructive I searched my daily phenomenological reports for any semblance of pride; the corrective was humility, and this via trust in God to provide what was in my best interests (not trust in myself). It was crucial to slay my tendency toward overconfidence and complacency about change, it being a real danger to my program. For example, whenever I believed I'd done it all my performance slacked off, daily journals became incomplete, and violation was far more likely. Therefore, above correctives had to be implemented immediately, usually on an hour by hour basis, in order to violently combat this super-optimism obstacle.

There were several other useful correctives for super-optimism, examples include: (1) anticipating the worst may occur (i.e., Murphy's Law), then plan for it, (2) operating with an open mind (seeking the opinion of others), and (3) remedies employed once I'd learned responsible decision making.

> Our brokenness tells us something about who we are. Our suffering and pains are the foundations to our uniqueness and intimate selves. I feel, privileged when someone shares their brokenness with me. I get to see the real 'them'. Their soul is bare, their heart exposed, the greatness of their daily struggle to overcome is revealed. That is why it is an incredible sign of trust when I disclose something to you of what I struggle with, I'm trusting you with my most vulnerable self.
>
> The Author
> nwtauthor@icloud.com

GK I too had to endure much of the same process. It seems the first threads of recovery we must develop are rediscovery of one's abilities to make sound decisions, would you agree?

FJA Yes, I had to acquire the rudiments of sound decision making to plan for my future by implementing all correctives so I could elicit responsible determinations. However, even if all other thinking errors had been corrected, decision making for my future still stood alone and had to be treated separately.

While it was necessary to ask questions and to discover how to research information, I also had to develop the habit of considering the options generated by my research. That is, I could not look at these concepts as mutually exclusive but rather had to learn to implement them as a congruent parcel; I needed to consider future options as a way to determine where to gather facts, to establish both options and priorities.

GK Plus you had to restrain your reptilian thinking long enough to consider logical, well researched options?

FJA Another important consideration I needed to assimilate was to deter decision making until I possessed the facts, developed alternatives, and established priorities; this included delaying decisions until I was composed and calm enough to realistically evaluate these ingredients of sound decision making: easier said than done. I also had to maintain cognizance of the fact my anger precluded logical thinking and only poor decision making would result while in a state of anger. I also needed to remember that when under stress conclusions could not be made for me; while I could receive assistance in evaluating the process by which decisions were made I had to reach my own conclusions in order to become a responsible adult.

GK What cognitive deficiency were you dealing with at the time?

FJA This example of my defective thinking included lacking time perspective; that is, my time frame existed mostly in the present so instance pervaded my thinking. I refused to defer gratification, demanding immediate triumph. I also disregarded the future as a result of my inability to understand concepts such as the length of a lifetime.

GK I think half of America's youth fits this description.

FJA Probably so. While in my mid-teens I never thought I would live past the age of thirty, so never considered the impact of my current actions on later life. Thus, appeals for me to remain in school to obtain training needed for adulthood appeared superfluous, since I planned to be dead. Similarly, cautions that tobacco and drugs could be injurious to health failed to influence me, as a result of thinking I'd never be alive long enough to experience possible health complications. Also, during the few times I had been employed I expected to be on an immediate par with those who had worked a lifetime, demanding the achievement without having performed the work.

The absence of time perspective also caused me to be unable to really benefit from prior experience or to plan for the long term. While I dwelled on or recalled the past, this did not serve as a guide to the future. That is, the only time I learned from prior experience was if it happened to be in line with my objectives, criminal enterprises; I never considered the long-term impact of a current action.

GK Was this consequent to your PTSD and immature, underdeveloped personality?

FJA Yes, unless criminal undertakings were at stake I made no effort and refused to endure adversity. Effort and adversity involved doing things contrary to what I preferred; only if something I desired (such as crime) was involved would I endure hardships and attempt to overcome obstacles—my failure to endure hardship or exert myself only existed when responsible living was involved. Keep in mind I perceived difficulty as either my failure to maintain control or as things not going my way.

GK It is surprising to learn how the criminal harbors such diverse energy sources, or lack thereof, how did this fit in with your need for control?

FJA To make any change in my approach to life, even if change was desired, required exertion and was rarely pursued. Furthermore, if things did not go smoothly or as planned, and effort was needed, I usually quit. For instance, having landed in the state mental hospital I decided since I was there I may as well gain the benefit of a few positive changes. Well, first of all, I insisted changes must be in areas I desired, along lines acceptable to me rather than in accord with what doctors knew was needed and what society required. One such pursuit of "change" involved seeking to be free of paranoia accompanying the commission of a crime or driving past a cop. Once told my only way to avoid paranoia was by abstention from crime I at once decided this change business was for squares and losers; I quit then and there. Too much effort.

CHANGE AND HEALING SEXUAL DISTORTIONS

Do sexually abused children go on to become abusers? The easy answer is yes. Due to Franks circumstances and the subject matter of this book I did extensive research to answer this question for our readers and myself. Unfortunately, I found no consistency in studies on this question.

I used to volunteer at our local YMCA day care center when my son was a toddler. A group of 5 or 6 kids had a sheet over a table, playing campout. One seven-year-old male (the oldest in that group) had his penis out, encouraging the other kids to touch it. It was pure luck that I looked in to check on them at that critical moment. I kindly said, we don't play that way here, and asked him to come with me.

Was that event sexual assault–or kids being kids?

GK Change couldn't have been easy, talk about the effort required and put forth by yourself.

FJA Effort, defined as the physical and/or mental power to do or refrain from doing what one wants, had never been used in my teen and early adult years toward responsible objectives. This indicated my need to utilize my phenomenological reporting as a method for learning correctives for my lack of responsible effort; a process involving focusing my attention on transcending boredom, absence of interest, and fatigue. For instance, the recognition that fatigue resulted from mental states such as anger and self-pity allowed me to opt into responsible thinking and thus generated the requisite energy flow.

I had to discover responsible effort meant pushing myself toward obtainable goals, only then could I learn to accept my limitations. Pushing myself was necessary to achieve change in thought processes and in action, meaning the ultimate goal became making it a habit to press myself in order to establish new thought and behavior structures. For me to continue to assume initiatives, accept problems, and resolve adversities responsibly there had to exist a self-generated exertion and enthusiasm motivated by my developing abhorrence of the old Frank Atwood.

GK We've spoken of single correctives, but tell me, should correctives also be considered cumulatively?

FJA Yes, because had I adopted a responsible time perspective, the need to totally eliminate fragmentation (hence, all of its many infections) remains. Consequently, complex correctives for criminal traits must be taken together...great point George.

GK Once on the road to change, how did you manage your time, and was it difficult to stay on track?

FJA During my process of change I functioned better when over-scheduled than when under-scheduled or idle. For instance, by taking numerous courses through Ohio University I had to study at least six hours daily and by having adopted such a heavy day to day program I possessed much less time and energy for criminal thinking.

GK "Idol hands are the devil's playground" was golden for me.

FJA Exactly! At the same time, my tubular vision had to be broadened so I wouldn't become too focused on one part of life and default in other areas. As such, it was necessary to handle many new responsibilities at once; if excessive energy was expended in any one aspect I had to recognize it: time budgeting was my applied corrective. Note well, no one stood over my shoulder correcting me whenever my train for change ran off the rails...I failed a lot.

GK Can you provide an example of time budgeting?

FJA Sure, consider my heavy caseload. While the simultaneous variant courses helped me to broaden perspective I still needed to fulfill other responsibilities; such as answering mail, doing legal work, completing daily exercise, prayer, writing phenomenological reports, and so on. Learning to manage my time certainly became a necessity. On the other hand, occasionally I would try to do everything at once, when this occurred the applied corrective involved my establishing priorities with respect to energy expenditure. Moreover, I had previously chosen to utilize the tremendous amount of energy I possessed for irresponsible objectives but now afforded myself the opportunity to employ this energy for change pursuits by harnessing and directing it toward purposeful, constructive activity.

GK There appears to be opposition between weak ego and

self-esteem, would you please explain why puffing up one's view of self transpires from a feeble ego?

FJA The manner in which I thought of myself, with extreme pretentiousness and a highly exaggerated sense of self-importance, exhibited thinking patterns that were infected with components of power and control due to a poorly functioning ego. Keep in mind, I considered myself as superior to those around me, even in prison I refused to take a subordinate role and acted as if I were a guest in a high-class hotel. This meant while doing little to achieve anything of significance I still carried a tremendously inflated idea of myself. Actually, I believed I either was or would be the best at whatever I chose to involve myself in, thinking of myself as always right; I felt others had to change and see things my way. I thought adversities experienced by others should never happen to me. Ironically, it was my own pretentiousness, the misguided view of how the world should treat me, that caused a day full of put-downs.

GK During your life of criminality, given all you've described thus far, did you have awareness or concern about your profound insensitivity?

FJA Along with refusing to assume obligations and responsible initiatives, having failed to perform as society expected, I demanded every consideration for myself but seldom did a kind act or considered what others thought, felt, or expected. This self-centeredness also included having little regard for rules, laws, and social mores. As such, and because of the impossibility of simultaneously being responsible and involved in crime, many aspects of thoughtfulness remained beyond my realm of experience. For instance, I failed to understand how rules served to help society. Additionally, disregarding laws and people enabled me to preserve my self-image by closing my mind and then viewing others as being favorably disposed toward me—another manifestation of defective thinking. Then again, disregarding others also avoided my risk of being confronted with ideas opposing my own position. That is, I did not discuss topics but rather imposed my own view. As a result, I became deaf and blind to responsible opinions, my entire existence was patterned predominantly by self-delusion.

GK Do you recall any specific public display of this disregard and misperception?

FJA When traveling from Los Angeles to Oklahoma in 1984 I would enter convenience store parking lots at breakneck speed, under the guise of having been in an extreme rush. I then stormed into the store, hustling around to gather supplies, even when having to elbow past others or use menacing postures. My intent was to ward off criticism, and to deflect comments or conversation in conflict with my carefully contrived self-image. My rudeness resulted in everyone in the store desiring to get this madman out of there as quickly as possible (letting me move to the head of the line where the clerk proffered friendly comments). Of course, I misconstrued these actions as others having been favorably disposed toward me by thinking they saw what a rush I was in so let me go first. Then again, had I been subjected to an insult at the time I simply would've considered it "proof" of what an unfair world I was forced to endure.

GK Killing your thirsty ego and rebuilding a positive self-image must've been a real chore?

FJA Remember, I had always mistakenly believed the evil and injurious acts I committed were forgiven by what I viewed as my many good qualities. For instance, after having committed a string of burglaries—of enough harmful impact to have ended in television coverage (including some of the victims telling of the pain from their losses)—I felt compelled to minimize the damage I had inflicted. Thus, I recalled how on the night preceding these news reports I'd resisted temptation to steal my mother's car, then considered my having used the money I really wanted to use for drugs to repay a loan, and finally made an empty promise to myself to look for a job within the next few days…all misconstrued as righteous acts. Having reflected on these "good qualities" I was able to assuage any lingering guilt and continue on my merry way. So yes, it was a radical fight to slay ego and responsibly build a positive self-image, many of the correctives we've discussed thus far were pure torture to implement.

GK Given the admittedly warped nature of your thinking method, in what ways did you overcome the view of your criminal self as good?

FJA Absent from my convoluted logic was any acknowledgment to repay loans, seek employment, and not steal were everyday acts to the responsible person, these acts possessed no especial value. Consequently, by having erroneously elevated the ordinary to the extraordinary, while also having relegated my victims to the status of those who could easily afford to be ripped off (as fat cats who deserved it), I imposed a false sense of worth and ethics upon myself and my victims. This misappropriation of self-righteousness was a favorite tactic in my arsenal of self-delusion; writing about it now, years later, I can so clearly see just how ridiculous, desperate, and pathetic I was.

As is readily evident, these misguided views of good qualities were absolutely necessary in order for me to pardon past evils and to contemplate future crime. Thus, it was essential to strip away what I once viewed as my benevolent attributes in order to make crime impossible to sustain; my daily phenomenological reports uncovered innumerable attempts by myself to build up my professed positive traits and to minimize the devastation caused by my deviant thinking. By recognizing these endeavors as errors, I was slowly able to dismantle my view of self as a good (criminal) person.

Writing about it now, years later, I can so clearly see just how ridiculous, desperate, and pathetic I was.

GK And the next step?

FJA I contrasted my criminal acts and their effects with my few paltry good deeds and their lack of impact. One way in which I performed this task was by comprising a balance sheet of good and evil; in every instance, the scales were overwhelmingly evil and negative. To this I added daily moral inventories of my conscience, thusly forcing me to dwell on the harm I had caused and of how I had wasted my life.

GK In what other realms did your criminal thinking patterns create problems for yourself and others?

FJA Certainly with sexuality. There existed a great desire to prove myself sexually but fears of inadequacy persisted. Even when having performed proficiently I believed I was inadequate and would become angry if having suffered a put-down. I would often misconstrue intimacy as the onset of a long-term relationship and once the other person went on their way I'd erroneously believe it resulted from my sexual shortcomings and felt completely rejected.

GK Did this contribute to crimes you committed against children in California?

FJA The many fears of sexual deficiency did give rise to fantasies involving children, the reverie sexual attack on a child engendering total control over an inexperienced person. That is, because of doubting my sexual prowess the ideas involving sexual conduct with kids provided the sought-after total mastery and precluded any criticism. Also, the thought of winning a virgin existed as a victory in that it meant acquiring a pure person, achieving what no one else had, and included fantasies of sex with someone who had no one with whom to compare my performance.

GK So what consideration(s) went into thoughts of sex and/or sexual partners?

FJA There was an absence of any discrimination when considering sexual partners, it was almost as if sexual activity were a requirement; I preferred to pursue excitement in other ways, via different forms of conquest, yet felt obligated to appear interested in sexuality in order to preserve my persona as macho. As a result, sexual desires themselves were very shallow—with gratification resting mere in the thrill of banal fantasy or masturbation (i.e., without need for another person, and all the attendant potential for failure or inadequacy). Therefore, it was rare when what concerned a sexual partner would concern me.

GK So you found effective tools of manipulation and power at a young age, risky behavior for sure.

FJA The indiscriminate selection of sexual partners often led to homosexual encounters; however, these contacts were rarely for sexual purposes. For instance, as a teenager I became involved in homosexual acts either for monetary gain or the sense of control over generally much older partners who possessed positions of prominence in the community. These liaisons usually included being picked up while hitch-hiking in the Bel Air neighborhood, the ultra-rich section of Los Angeles, and allowing myself to be orally copulated or involved famous rock stars in hotel suites. So, the homosexual act was relatively insignificant and, since I wanted not to be considered homosexual, I justified these encounters by claiming the "passive/feminine" partner was "queer" but not myself, the "masculine" partner. In my more than sixty years I had only one girlfriend and, with the same person, enjoyed sexual intercourse with one female.

GK Were there other activities you used to pursue sexual satisfaction?

FJA I sought the semblance of gratification through perversities such as voyeurism and invading the privacy of others in my mid-teens when looking in windows, hoping to see women in various stages of undress and occasionally witnessing sexual activity. Obscene phone calls existed as another control operation; I'd randomly dial numbers until locating a voice I found desirable, to then pursue prescribed responses (this usually included fear and shock).

Most of the time I was so active in crime that sex became inconsequential. I'd conceal encounters of a homosexual nature and fantasies about children from my criminal cohorts, pursue the need for power and control mostly through criminal ventures, and then lie about all the sex I'd supposedly been getting with beautiful adult females, making up story after story.

GK Did having been the repeated victim of sexual assault play any role in your admittedly perverse sexuality when in California?

FJA Great insightful question. PTSD compelled sexual promiscuity and caused an adverse response to sexuality. The four assaults in a five-year span made the act of sex somewhat repulsive to me, even though subsequent to the initial age fourteen molestation I engaged in homosexual activity; PTSD is a complex disorder and, tragically, found me victimizing a seven-year-old boy when I was twenty-four…one of the most horrid acts possible and for which I have never forgiven myself.

GK Why do you think you became interested in sexual offenses when you knew of the pain it caused you?

FJA First, I had absolutely no idea of the inextricable connection betwixt my assault sexually and having molested a child, what is patently obvious now somehow had escaped detection then. Secondly, for me the interest resided in lashing out against society, rather than toward an innocent boy. Maybe a little like killing in a video game being unreal, I just failed to realize the thorough harm I'd inflicted.

GK Continuing with the sexual arena, can you define your general attitude in the 1970's – 1980's?

FJA I viewed sex as merely one more way to strive for power and derived little pleasure from the sex act itself, sexual release was not my goal—my aim resided in establishing myself in a dominant role. Furthermore, I did not seek companionship or friendship through sexual relationships but simply saw partners as a body rather than as a person and believed they belonged to me and possessed no rights of their own. The sexual patterns I engaged in resembled the patterns of other crimes; for instance, I acted boldly when committing a robbery and in my attempts to conquer a sexual partner.

GK How else did you use (abuse) sexual relationships?

Ten Myths About Sex Offenders

1. Sex offenders will always keep offending.
2. Treatment doesn't work.
3. Most sexual offenders are strangers
4. Banning known sex offenders from places where children congregate, protects our children.
5. Tougher laws are the only solution.
6. Lock 'em up, throw away the key.
7. Mandatory minimum sentences work.
8. Sex offender registries protect children.
9. Tracking devices on sexual offenders keep us safe.
10. The experts say strong, repressive measures are necessary to keep sex offenders from re-offending.

http://nationalrsol.org/resources/ten-myths-about-sex-offenders

FJA As mentioned, sexual pleasure and release did not constitute my main goal, nor did who or what my sexual partner was of importance. I generally accepted whatever was available. For example, while not homosexually oriented as a life preference, homosexual acts were common because I sought a quick thrill and desired any action. This was prevalent in prison, where access to females was virtually non-existent, but homosexual involvements were even more common with older men when I was a teenager because I was able to obtain a power surge from managing someone much older, the acts were profitable, and an opportunity for new experiences existed. I often hitched rides down Sunset Blvd., from where I lived in Brentwood to Hollywood, and most of the time rich older men picked me up. Or once in Hollywood I'd hang out near the ritzy Roosevelt Hotel until some "dirty old man" propositioned me. Whether in a car on Sunset Blvd. or in the Roosevelt I achieved a sense of control from having powerful men desiring to orally copulate me, especially since I put a wad of cash in my pocket every time.

GK In addition to these gay encounters, were there any other sexual behaviors in which you engaged?
FJA The short of the long is no, at least not in terms of actual contact. I did engage in fantasies about sex with inexperienced children who could not evaluate the adequacy of my sexual performance. For me, sex used to truly be just another exploitation operation and search for power.
GK Continuing amidst the sexual arena and your previously perverted thinking and action patterns, I'd like you to please elaborate on your new attitude and beliefs toward sex.
FJA To have merely established acceptable sexual outlets I would never have been able to refrain from or eliminate my criminal sexual patterns in thought and action. My carnal immorality existed only as part of my irresponsibility and I needed to address it within the context of other criminal thinking and behavior patterns; like deception, intimidation, exploitation, control, and injury to others. Absent having forcefully and irrevocably dealt with specific sexual factors I would have been unable to produce even a single change in my sexual patterns.

Interestingly, I experienced outrage over events having not gone my way and which were seemingly unrelated to sexual themes—for instance, my having been stuck in a traffic jam or being denied a job—this generally prompted ideation of control scenarios and could end in fantasies involving sexual domination. Thus, I now understand in far more comprehensible terms how having merely expended focus on abstention from inappropriate sexual thought and action would have left me ill-equipped and unable to deal with underling pressures. Only after having searched my daily phenomenological reports for occasions where I sexually fantasized about exerting power and control after having suffered some perceived affront did I achieve the all-important self-disgust. It was this advancement in my program for change that led to the implementation of new, healthy sexual patterns.
GK Do you have any idea why your sexuality became so firmly connected to thinking about crime?
FJA The fact that sexuality had always been an expression of my broad criminal patterns meant I had to repress discussion on erotic topics when having initially embarked on the change process. This was of paramount importance in developing the ability to shut the door on criminal patterns triggered by irresponsible sexual ideation. For example, I had to uncover contributing roles that power, control, ownership, and super-

optimism had played in my sexual fantasies to expose how conquest, not sexual intimacy, had nearly always been the goal. These insights subsequently resulted in my having assumed a perspective that included a near constant reflection of how I had spent a lifetime injuring both myself and others. Clearly, my review of past patterns was crucial in having developed full awareness of the widespread devastation my sexuality had inflicted; this eventually enabled a firewall for inappropriate sexual thought, talk, and behavior.

GK What other avenues of healing distortions of sexual thinking errors did you use?

FJA Additional correctives to combat misguided perspectives of sexuality included meticulously avoiding any situation in which my irresponsible pursuit of sexual ideation became likely. In furtherance of this I had to monitor what I read, watched on television, and how I interacted with others.

GK You know, for years I couldn't watch TV programs with children because I felt shameful and guilty about being a bad parent.

FJA I can understand that.

I also examined my daily journals closely to correct any attitudes suggesting focus on machismo or sexual conquest. I would then put myself in the position of others and consider the injuries I'd previously inflicted. While watching a somewhat sexually suggestive television show one evening (hence, temptation toward conquest and control) I began to be inordinately irritated by the incessant chatter of other prisoners. Soon thereafter thoughts of physical confrontation arose, but I was able to turn off the TV, drown out the noise by listening to music through headphones, and contemplate past harm I'd inflicted under similar circumstances.

I was able to more completely understand how having pursued a misguided sense of manhood had violated the rights of others.

GK And as you got more practice at identifying your errors?

FJA Eventually, as correctives began to be more immediately and consistently applied, I was able to more completely understand how having pursued a misguided sense of manhood had violated the rights of others. This resulted in no longer needing to defend my "manhood" as I realized both physical and verbal conflict were a badge of cowardice. The implementation of correctives also enabled me to base my sense of pride on the small achievements I had made; such as attendance at and completion of degree programs at Ohio and Cal. State universities, saving and budgeting money, not injuring others, and living responsibly. As criminal patterns were replaced with responsible initiatives I developed self-respect, something that cannot be taught but rather emerges as a consequence of change.

GK What about forgiveness, have you been able to accept forgiveness of self? I know that was a difficult one for me.

FJA No! Take three examples: had I not been trying to purchase marijuana in 1970 at age fourteen I would not have been picked up and molested; in 1980 I forced a young boy to engage in oral copulation; and the horrendous treatment of my blessed mom and dad all linger in consciousness; how can any of that be forgiven? I do possess hope because forgiveness, rather than a single moment in time action, functions as a process…I am on the path of forgiveness.

GK Considering the injury you committed against others, did you ever place yourself in their position?

FJA As a criminal, I tragically did not put myself in the position of others—had I been a responsible citizen confronted by the presence of such an unseemly character as myself, I also would've been anything but favorably disposed toward the vulgar deviant and would've done whatever necessary to have facilitated a quick exit.

GK How cognizant were you of psychological and/or physical injuries you imposed on others around you?

FJA In addition to the failure to have put myself in the position of others I also took an extremely narrow view of injury I had inflicted; a perspective generally limited to serious bodily injury, failing to consider emotional damage, fear, and inconvenience. While physical harm did comprise one aspect of the damage I inflicted I failed to consider the untold anguish I brought to so many people.

Take, as an example, while attending high school on Catalina Island I ended up in a fight with my best friend. After having struck him with a front kick, I then knocked him to the floor with a roundhouse kick. My friend suffered bruising on his jaw, a broken tooth, and a concussion. However, even more damaging was the emotional injury; this boy was never the same after enduring this vicious attack; his studies suffered, he never again really trusted anyone, a friendship had been destroyed, and within a month he left school. Sadly, at the time I was blind to all of this emotional injury.

GK Just wondering, as part of your healing process did you ever try to locate this person and apologize?

FJA This was on Catalina Island, so I had to await returning to the mainland to seek out this classmate (several teachers had answered some of my inquiries about his welfare). Once home I did gain contact information, however, attempts to speak and apologize to him met with firm resistance by his parents. I regret having never been able to apologize to him.

GK What other examples do you remember?

FJA More general examples of my failure to consider the injury I inflicted on others includes the harm to children at school as a consequence of my disruptive antics having interfered with their learning opportunities and the injuries imposed on neighbors from whom I stole. Not until I had been the victim of a burglary did I comprehend fully the sense of loss and personal invasion. Also, theft and vandalism to businesses resulted in widespread injury, such as having customers pay higher prices and even the closing of some stores. Of course, accompanying these financial injuries was the untold personal emotional damage these victims suffered.

GK You failed to realize any of the serious-non physical injuries?

FJA Despite devastating and enormous harm I'd inflicted on so many people I did not see myself as having caused widespread emotional harm. In fact, I actually regarded myself as the injured party because my objectives had been interfered with. Then, if confronted with the injury I'd inflicted, I blamed others or minimized the harm done; I believe all hardened criminals possess these outlooks.

GK When assuming responsible thought patterns, I'm wondering how contemplating the harm you inflicted on others played any role?

FJA Changes in my perception of personal and social responsibilities, from none to building responsible experiences, were invariably in constant altercation with my cognition process. I had to learn to take someone else's thinking into account, to become sensitive to and aware of their needs. This helped me to correct the absence of an accurate and cumulative knowledge of people, the inability to consider the thoughts of others. By learning to consider the thinking processes of others, I could then cease approaching people from the perspective of only what I wanted in every circumstance. Obviously, this was a significant and essential shift to foster my new perceptions of responsibility. The use of my phenomenological reports to illuminate the errors in my daily life provided innumerable opportunities to apply correctives, such as putting myself in the position of others, to learn to view and value people in a balanced way, and understand how responsible persons saw me. This consideration of others nurtured my comprehension that it was reasonable for them to have seen me as a criminal, and to have harbored a sense of fear and suspicion. One productive exercise for my onset of considering perspectives of people was to place myself in the role of crime victim to envision self-disgust toward criminal action; this quickly built responsible thinking.

GK Okay. But that seems to perceive others from an intellectual viewpoint, I was hoping to hear a little about physical and emotional injury you caused.

FJA As part of considering the tremendous injury my thinking and behavior inflicted, I had to realize there existed no such thing as a harmless crime. To succeed at change, I needed to consider every type of injury, tangible and intangible, as possible consequences of any crime. Hence, I came to experience how my family, victims and their families, the local community, and society in general were all victims.

This led to a realization of how I had victimized and harmed my own family. As a result, I was left with no choice other than to see myself as I was...

Initially, I considered both past and present patterns of thoughts and actions, but as change progressed I began to focus on only current thinking. It was essential to visualize and process all irresponsible ideas exposed by phenomenological reports as inflicting extensive emotional injury to others if or when implemented. My objective was to apply this perspective before violations occurred. Correctives such as this were most effective once I understood the full impact of a criminal act (including violations such as lying and its potential resultant injury).

GK You certainly undertook a broad view of injury, actually, the whole range. How else did you learn from the harms you committed?

FJA Another corrective considered how I would react if

someone close to me had been injured by a crime. This led to a realization of how I had victimized and harmed my own family. As a result, I was left with no choice other than to see myself as I was: a depraved and out of control criminal. I was then able to develop both self-loathing and remorse, which led to my implementation of further change and existed as yet another deterrent to inflicting injury.

As the process of change progressed I made reparations when possible. The supreme example lies in the continued making amends to my parents prior to their 2008 and 2010 deaths. I began regularly telephoning and writing them, inquiring into what I could do to help them. My absolute obedience to them truly demonstrated to my loving parents the profound changes I had made. A couple of weeks before my dad's passing he wrote a Mother's Day card to my mom saying "Litzel, this is truly a wonderful Mother's Day, our son has finally grown up." The reparations felt good and fueled further change.

As I ceaselessly applied correctives and deterred violation, consideration developed in advance of various consequences for criminal thinking; this meant my conscience became operative and I developed a genuine compassion for others.

Interviewer Note: We have thus far discussed in depth the traits Frank possessed as a criminal, and have also briefly touched upon the overwhelming adverse influence defective thought patterns held over him. The following conversation picks up on this by exposing how Frank (and every criminal) operated with a closed mind, it supplies in detail many of the thought processes he possessed as a criminal. These warped thinking patterns became deeply ingrained; they were employed automatically and inevitably resulted in significant disaster for both himself and those around him.

GK Would you agree that your closed mind would have continued to prevent you from healing and changing your ways until you were permanently incarcerated or dead (aside from your current predicament)?

FJA Yes, an open mind is fundamental to the change process and has three basic components: (1) disclosure, (2) receptivity, and (3) self-criticism. As for myself, I operated with a closed mind, which, in the context of communication, was akin to going for a physical examination but refusing to undress or give blood

A few words from George on Sexual Offender Recidivism Rates

Sexual Offender Recidivism Rates: 5% or 35%?
Studying these statistics has been the most tedious aspect of this project. Naturally, people project the percentages that favor their advocacy–I just wanted the real numbers: good luck!

Recidivism rates increase over time, any article not including the span of years is hiding something. Another critical consideration is what kind of sex crime, internet or violent rape?

The 15-year recidivism rate for incest offenders is 13 percent; 24 percent for rapists, and 35 percent for pedophiles of boy victims.

A meta-analysis of 95 studies involving a combined sample of 31,216 sex offenders over 5-6 years. The average recidivism rate for another sex crime was 13.7 %. https://www.smart.gov/SOMAPI/sec1/ch5_recidivism.html

The bigger question is, how many sex offenses did these sex offenders commit between release and arrest. It's estimated that only 36% of (age 12 and up) sex crimes are reported. And, many prosecutors' plea bargain sex offenses to non-sex offenses: good luck!

samples. As a result, rather than disclosure, receptivity, and self-criticism, I dealt with others through omission, assent, diversion, circumlocution, exaggeration, and distortion. And yes, it took coming to death row to shock my mind into receptivity, to become open to the change process.

GK Let's try to take these one at a time, and please begin with disclosure.

FJA For criminals, disclosure must be avoided at all costs, revealing my thinking would have placed me in jeopardy for past, current, and future crimes. Moreover, exposure of my thinking would have ruptured my inflated self-image. Others could not be allowed to critique my ideas or know my fears and vulnerabilities. I even went so far as to have intermittently contemplated suicide rather than risk full disclosure. For example, at age fifteen I was placed in a psychiatric hospital where I felt extremely vulnerable at such a young and immature stage in life. I did not want to disclose my thinking, which at that time mostly involved ways to convince the doctors "I was all better" and ideas on how to get stoned. However, without full disclosure I was at the mercy of my captors. This generated a profound fear of remaining in that nuthouse for a long time, and momentarily having seen no avenue to success led to the contemplation of suicide.

GK Oddly, I shared your non-disclosure values. My mother would drill into my brain "do not disclose family affairs to strangers." People who had known me for years will admit, "I knew George but I didn't really know him at all." Anyway, what about receptivity?

FJA I also had to avoid receptivity, something I accomplished by being a selective listener. I would listen only to what I deemed to be of importance to me and reject the rest. People were always telling me what to do in regard to responsible living—parents, teachers, bosses, etc. However, I certainly held no interest in living responsibly. I often sat in class and contemplated my next burglary or other felony while the teacher talked about matters in which I had no interest. Rarely would I pay attention to the lecture, my mind craved excitement. Of course, among my criminal cohorts' crime existed as the topic, and I suddenly listened attentively. Insofar as anyone who sought to guide me in a responsible direction was concerned, I seldom acknowledged their ideas had any merit. This made most attempts to influence me futile. My basic position was: "I've made up my mind, don't bother me with facts."

GK And the third factor, self-criticism?

FJA In addition to having avoided disclosure and receptivity, two of the components required for an open channel, I also angrily rejected censure directed toward myself. Self-criticism, the third constituent of an open mind, is absolutely essential to the process of change. While I readily criticized others, I rarely looked at my own performance to assess shortcomings and make improvements. Because of this arrogance and sense of uniqueness I would not adapt to the world and failed to fulfill obligations. In fact, I demanded others accommodate me, required others to cater to me and my desires. One time, after a series of especially dumb miscalculations, a criminal co-conspirator began offering me some suggestions. I took this as an unreasonable critique of my ability to plan criminal enterprises, so I "punished" the offending party by demanding he carry out endless demeaning tasks for the rest of the evening.

Disclosure, receptivity, and self-criticism, as processes that would destroy my fragile self-esteem, were out of the question.

GK How did you cultivate an antibody to your closed mind?

FJA As alluded to, the corrective resides in having to develop a wide-open mind/channel. That is, without total disclosure, receptivity to the viewpoints of others, and self-criticism I could not have engendered change. Moreover, openness was only able to be put into operation daily after the abdication of control had begun and this facilitated my learning about emotions.

GK You referenced again the open-mind ingredients. Let's review each; start with full disclosure from the perspective of corrective agent.

FJA In considering disclosure, I normally would reveal only material I perceived as beneficial to myself and concealed the rest. Consequently, as I began my program for change I initiated a rigorous routine of journaling (phenomenological reporting) so no aspect of thought or conduct would be withheld. Total disclosure existed as the most important and effective corrective for my previously closed way of functioning.

GK And the next component for wide-open channels, receptivity?

FJA I continually viewed myself as having known everything and I consistently rejected any view from others. As a result, it became extremely difficult to learn a way of thinking in which I subordinated my own misguided views and became open to the perspectives of others. Quite simply, change could not transpire until I opened myself to opinions from others regarding how I functioned.

GK What about self-criticism?

FJA In considering self-criticism, I had to abandon my victor/victim view and adopt an attitude enabling me to learn from every situation. It was important for me to stress I was fully accountable for whatever happened, because the assumption of full responsibility led to self-criticism, resulting in correction. It was this continuation of self-critical thinking, alertness to old patterns of thought/action, and the assumption of accountability that resulted in a responsible way of life.

GK I notice outside of working on this project you sometimes don't handle criticism well. Everyone is careful not to criticize you when joking around for fear you'll attack with verbal abuse—they walk on eggshells so to speak. So, you may think since others don't criticize you that you've mastered criticism. That's not the reality.

FJA Interesting. I do see myself as occasionally falling into a victor/victim role with inmates on death row. Having suffered for decades as a victim of verbal and physical abuse, one of my defense mechanisms centers on seeking to avoid attack by assuming a victor stance. Rather than to have not mastered criticism, I see the defense from fears of abuse severing the potential for enjoying beneficial input from prisoners. Even when well along in the change process, we must be ever vigilant to watch for and correct lapses! Thank you for your help with this.

GK No problem. Using one of the wide-open channel constituents, please give an example of developing the openness necessary for change.

FJA An example of closed vs. open channels of communication is how as an extreme criminal I would only disclose details of an event that tended to support my skewed perception. One day I cut someone off in traffic, cussed at them, made obscene gestures, and hurled threats. When recounting the event that evening to a fellow parolee, I contended it was the other driver who had functioned inappropriately as a way to justify my offensive actions as acceptable and even honorable. Of course, having discussed this occurrence with someone who was as misguided and mad at the world as myself guaranteed reinforcement of my thinking error patterns as a way of life.

In contrast to this was the difficult onset of full disclosure, as I embarked upon my process of change. For instance, rather than to have selected another criminal with whom to have discussed my experience I chose a responsible person to speak with, such as my wife, priest, or parents. The conversation then took on a completely different tenor as I openly shared each and every detail of the event, as an academic exercise, without any attempt to slant things one way or the other. This produced a straightforward recounting of facts to go over with my chosen responsible person; this enabled their pointing out where I had acted irresponsibly. It was this kind of practicing openness that both corrected erroneous thinking patterns and helped in my more accurately assessing daily phenomenological reports.

GK Tell me, how did you react to having been arrested?

FJA I would first protest about the injustice of being taken into custody; I harbored the misbelief that justice resided in not getting caught and injustice existed as interference with my plans. To me, from my entitled position, the inherent "injustice" was having been apprehended rather than slapped on the wrist and let go.

The harm my criminal acts inflicted were of no issue, no concern to me. One reason I came to believe in such distorted concepts sprang from the fact that getting caught for a crime was in stark contrast to my view of myself as a good person. Furthermore, I saw myself as helpful to society rather than as a criminal. Remember, I often engaged in acts of benevolence enroute to or after crimes. Consequently, I possessed no shame, there was no consideration or thought of the injury done, and little concern for my own family existed. Occasionally, I would ask myself: "How could I have gotten caught?" However, my "concern" merely considered why I'd been apprehended rather than why I had resorted to committing a criminal act. My main concern after arrest (while in county jail) was on getting out and being free. I sustained myself through expectation of release and the excitement resulting from scheming my liberation.

GK In what way did you seek release, what options were available to you?

FJA Upon capture I was initially sure family or friends would arrange for bail. Actually, I believed those close to me were obliged to bail me out and once freed I generally possessed little to no worry—there was a long time between release and trial. My mental state included the delusional thought pattern that my arrest never happened. In fact, even as I awaited release the prevailing theme was the "injustice" of getting caught, I simply believed I should not be accountable to anyone. I would then launch into a bevy of supposed excuses such as:

Everyone did it.
I was led into doing it.
I had associated with the wrong people.
I never had a chance in life.
I needed the money.

The list of excuses was endless and I was never at fault.

Not only did I consider getting arrested as a grave injustice to me, but upon being jailed believed there existed an immediate need to correct the unfairness of having been locked up.

GK I'm sure 98% of arrestees share your belief on this one.

FJA True! While I had broken the law, something that I felt was my right to have done, I now believed the law must be inviolate when I invoked it. In other words, I both broke and used the law to get what I desired and had an army of imagined and real tactics at my disposal. This tinkering with the system at every turn, and occasionally winning, existed for me as a series of triumphs. I insisted on my constitutional rights then enjoyed added satisfaction from having played games with the system. In my warped criminal mind, it was this gamesmanship, this making fool out of others, where so much excitement resided.

GK You've mentioned occasions when you maneuvered out of custody, but what of the times when you were convicted and sent to prison?

FJA Even if convicted, my games and manipulation of the system continued. I studied criminal procedure and law, was a very effective jailhouse lawyer since 1974, found legal loopholes (for myself and others), and then filed appeals. The successes on appeal provided an extreme thrill and sense of control.

> 35.8 percent of sexual assaults occur when the victim is between the ages of 12 and 17. 18 and above, 30 percent.
>
> https://www.nsopw.gov/en-US/Education/FactsStatistics

GK And once you began to serve your sentence?

FJA Some of the above transpired once in prison, but an example of my having abated and manipulated the impact of incarceration was my having viewed transfer from the juvenile justice system to adult prison as a promotion, a mental state through which I turned adversity into triumph. The more secure and more notorious the prison the bigger build-up I enjoyed. For example, having done several months in the hole at Soledad (an extremely violent prison in California) produced a great deal of status. I then acquired more "cred" from spending six more months in the Management Control Unit at Tracy (another "gladiator school" in California, also known as DVI). However, none of that compared to the thrill and sense of prestige and pride I experienced upon being moved to San Quentin, one of America's most infamous prisons. Now obvious, my confinement was simply viewed as an arena in which to continue my criminal lifestyle.

GK Prisoners who possessed the "happy to be in prison" attitude, like you did, displayed they are truly lost souls. They have no intention of changing who they are.

FJA Very accurate. For me, once released I only differed in how fast I returned to "action"—my determinant factor having been my overriding need for excitement and re-establishment of control. Thus, parole and probation were never deterring factors or concern; these simply existed as other obstacles to surmount. This meant eventually old patterns resurfaced, and confinement became a revolving door; the average time I spent free from incarceration was four to six months.

GK So you were in a serious downward spiral, headed for a life sentence eventually. I mean it's obvious you weren't getting any better at not getting caught. Right?

FJA Actually, being captured wasn't much in my stream of thought. And in regard to my view about absence of accountability, what I actually thought, both prior to and during the course of a criminal operation, would never correspond to the stories I fed authorities. I related self-serving stories, used various explanations for my own benefit, and responded in any way that would best serve my interest. I recall one night when I attempted to break into a place of business by entering through the roof. Just as I was about to climb through the skylight I heard a voice calling me, upon peering over the edge I discovered it was the police. I immediately began a song and dance about having messed around with a friend who tossed my wallet on the roof. Of course, once my "friend" got finished ratting on me, my story fell apart.

GK Once a citizen becomes a felon, as far as the cops on the crime scene are concerned, this criminal has not the presumption of innocence afforded to a non-felon under the same circumstances. Everything you say in response to their interrogation is considered a lie until they verify it as the truth.

FJA Amen. I would also attempt to learn as much as I could about my interrogators and examined them at least as closely as I was examined. I assessed the beliefs of my inquisitors, then employed one of two general methods of presentation: (1) playing the victim of forces outside of myself, or (2) being the victim of feelings and various aspects of my personality. Again, I told any story to reduce personal jeopardy. For instance, I had severe mental illnesses since at least age fourteen, however, to have revealed this would have constituted a severe put-down. Nevertheless, when held accountable for crime I readily suffered the indignation of revealing my mental illness in order to pursue freedom. Or, as another example, I perpetuated the myth of wanting to be caught even though I actually did everything within my power to assure the success of a criminal enterprise.

GK Besides having become a jailhouse lawyer, in what other ways did your same basic patterns continue in confinement?

FJA Once in prison I had to establish myself as a force to be respected and also endeavored to set up excitement via criminal talk and action. This often took the form of exaggerating the number of crimes I had committed, the proceeds amassed, and sexual conquests I'd supposedly enjoyed. I also became a source for drugs; what mattered to me was I was seen as a big shot.

GK Share some more of your survival attitudes while incarcerated.

FJA When pursuing excitement in prison I reacted with righteous indignation if interfered with. If faced with punishment I generally responded by having employed either "insight," as a way to mitigate penalties, or antagonism. I viewed discipline as an injustice, so if punished, even when deservedly so, I claimed I'd been mistreated.

I would do almost anything for a thrill in confinement, and if something went wrong I blamed and criticized others. For instance, I once planned an attack upon a guard but he quit prior to the mission having been completed. Consequently, I chastised several prisoners for the failure when it actually was my fault. Thus, my inflated image of self-precluded any possibility, in my mind, that I was to blame.

GK Prison is a great place for scum such as you were; crimes done in prison that'd you'd get 5 years for on the street got you 30 days in the hole or less. Plus, you receive all the accolades from fellow prisoners.

FJA Even in lockup I pursued criminal enterprises, I found it posed a better challenge due to the significant restrictions and snitches. There were several times when I ██████ and the thrill was extreme. Then, upon success, I was able to play drug kingpin. This all indicates how the common misperception of my having been taught crime while in prison was a fallacy; jail neither taught me crime or induced me into it. However, there were lessons on getting away with illegal actions more easily.

GK So, would it be safe to say imprisonment made little if any dent in your life as a criminal?

FJA There were times when I didn't engage in crimes while incarcerated. When confined and isolated from society I occasionally engendered new views, but these invariably turned out to be transient. Later on, in prison, or when released, crime was never foreclosed (even though it was frequently postponed temporarily). Prison by itself will never rehabilitate the mentally ill or hardened criminals.

GK So, what was life like between your episodes of crime?

FJA There were periods when I did not actively engage in criminal enterprises. However, during these momentary lapses I still possessed the thought patterns that existed when actively participating in crime. As such, I still treated both the world and others as my property; still motivated by control and excitement. Although I was temporarily not committing crimes for which I could be arrested, I was still an active criminal in my mental process. What these so-called non-criminal phases constituted was merely an omission of any overt offenses—crimes in the assault, sexual, and property categories—while still participating in parallel fields. For example, "criminal substitutes" and "periods of remission" were not phases in which I did not engage in crime but rather existed as alternatives to my overt criminal action.

GK Speak a little more about your criminal substitutes.

FJA For me, a criminal substitute was an action, or series of actions, in which power was sought for its own sake. Therefore, if not pushing for control through crime I found other ways to pursue power via criminal substitutes. Everywhere I went, even in confinement, I tired controlling things because achieving influence over others existed as a key to establishing self-aggrandizement.

GK So control was one substitute?

FJA Yes, one example of this was despite having been sent to prison for sexual assault on a minor I still manipulated situations in a way enabling me to assume a position of respect. This began by misinforming other prisoners about the circumstances of my crime, I'd pled guilty to kidnapping and told others this occurred during a robbery. Having thusly established an "honorable" commitment offense I then functioned as a gangster and instilled fear in most other prisoners, thereby having commanded a great deal of respect.

GK And your reward for gaining control was respect from fools?

FJA Yes, and at the same time power achieved legitimately provided no excitement. I could have used my knowledge, experience, and intelligence to work in the prison library, which would have provided a position of influence over other prisoners, but this type of control was worthless to me. I craved power through manipulative means to function as an alternative to crime and to produce the sought-after excitement.

GK Describe some additional forms of your substitutes.

FJA Criminal substitutes covered a wide range of activities; including driving at high speeds and in reckless manners, dominating conversations, an interest in enforcement (such as by inventing anti-theft devices), propulsion into the limelight, and helping others. For instance, I would assist others by being a reformer, advisor, and source of knowledge, not to be mistaken for an interest in social causes. Instead, I became involved with others because of the resultant excitement from having been in a position of dominance. That is, I rarely did anything favorable for others unless the result existed as a criminal substitute, and this reveals why I did something for others only for self-serving purposes. I didn't view helping others as a way of life.

To sum it up, criminal substitutes were merely momentary states, and I inevitably returned to old patterns of irresponsibility and arrestable behavior.

GK Where for you these criminal substitutes served as an alternative to criminal action (i.e., still enabling a pseudo-criminality), did there reside moments wherein even this ceased temporarily?

FJA The period of remission was a state in which I was less active in crime. Reasons for entering this condition often included a fear of getting caught or dreading a return to jail. However, while in a period of remission I still engaged in criminal ideation and irresponsible behavior.

GK Thus, some remnant of crime, in action and/or thought, loitered within. What else would urge this decreased yet still active state?

FJA I would also enter this temporary state of suspension when consumed with self-pity as a consequence of having become relatively unenthusiastic about life. Additional reasons for entering this phase were impairment by illness and injury or becoming occasionally burned out on crime. Yet despite all of these prevailing reasons this mental state never lasted long. Eventually I demanded greater excitement. Thus, when an opportunity for excitement arrived my sloth immediately vanished. I recall having had knee surgery while in prison and feeling very sorry for myself as I convalesced in the hospital ward. Of course, as soon as a pal of mine suggested raiding the medicine cabinet, I lost all sense of self-pity and enthusiastically went about constructing a plan.

GK Were there any advantages to states of remission?

FJA One must also consider how periods of remission enabled me to sponge off others and/or the government. This fit in with my criminal personality, because I preferred not to work and was able to get what I wanted on my terms without having to comply with society's demands. This parasitism was criminal excitement, since I was able to outwit the system.

GK Didn't you experience any crime free periods?

FJA In a state of momentary purification I wished to eradicate my past, to purify myself and become good. The object was to blot out my criminal history. This condition would occur both in and out of confinement and existed as a sincere state that could last for weeks. "Getting a conscience" played a strong role in my entering this state and reveals why momentary purification was characterized by an extreme sense of morality and perfectionism, a period wherein I'd try to avoid the slightest infraction.

GK Did any of these periods contain a religious theme?

FJA The initial expression of this temporary stage often involved a religious conversion, but not necessarily a Christian one. Before being released from prison in 1978 I played at being involved in several belief systems (such as tarot, astrology, yoga, and so on). Of course, this ended up as mere intellectual practice and knowledge; these teachings never penetrated my surface of consciousness or became a way of life for me. This shows that in my religious experiences criminal thought was still evident and I had not become a person of humility.

> The negative path of a violent mind is not to be understood by the peaceful mind.
>
> One guy here on the row wanted to be housed in Dog cluster (with his fellow gang members). Dog is where the real worst of the worst reside. The first chance he got he stabbed a 70-year-old man 40 or 50 times out at the basketball court. The old man lived, the guy was moved to Dog and the basketball court recreation was canceled for the rest of us.
>
> A normal human is no match for a true criminal.

GK What, if any, benefit did these exercises in intellectual fodder have for you?

FJA I would also latch onto teachings that were concrete and easy to implement, and would then try to convert others as a way of achieving influence and to build myself up. Thus, it became easy to mistake these episodes of self-centered momentary purification for true conversion or change. However, rather than adopt teachings as a fixture in my life, I usually promoted myself more than my religious message and ultimately violated my ideals and the principles I espoused. I would then inevitably return to old patterns and active crime.

GK As a component of PTSD there dwells the precinct of suicide, precisely how did this apply to you?

FJA While I experienced sporadic suicidal thinking, attention must be focused on whether I was genuinely contemplating suicide, or merely engaging in a phony gesture to recruit sympathy. Sometimes I superficially cut myself if I could be sure those in authority would be well aware of my action; the reason being, to assume control and elicit sympathy by altering my position from arrested criminal to disturbed child.

GK When the contemplation of suicide manifested, how did this unfold?

FJA I was not a happy person, possessed no peace of mind, and was chronically dissatisfied. For example, I always had to extricate myself from an unending series of problems and often became angry, both of which triggered a righteous indignation because my world was not catering to me. This meant having developed an anger that raged against society, because I was unhappy with what life had brought me. I always felt I was destined for number one, but this ideal now seemed forever out of reach. Consequently, suicide was perceived as a resolution for lacking self-esteem, and this "reasoning" occurred with the greatest frequency while imprisoned.

GK Was this emergence of suicidal ideation commonplace for you?

FJA Well, true suicidal thinking would have been a prolonged condition and, because of having to transcend fragmented states of mind, was a rarity for me. Additionally, I was deterred from committing suicide by a fear of death, as well as from having considered the devastation my parents would've experienced.

GK And yet you were unable to see the continued devastation by your parents from your years of craziness and crime?

FJA May God forgive me, no. This is perhaps the single greatest regret in my life, how I devastated my precious parents.

GK In what ways did you transcend limbo states?

FJA When having experienced remission, etc., these were soon followed by what I perceived as despondency. Moods such as this so-called depression could not be the topic of consideration, I had to instead focus on the thinking before and during these mind-sets.

When I reached a state of limbo during my change process, I

believed I was worthless and viewed my solution(s) as engaging in irresponsibility. By way of example: I experienced a despondent frame of mind one afternoon while in the prison recreation cages. Other inmates had been ridiculing me, and I began feeling worthless. The temptation to employ tactics to boost my status in the eyes of other prisoners, and to improve my morale (such as by yelling or even throwing rocks), was nearly overwhelming. However, once I ignored this mood and began to consider that the thinking had precipitated the situation, I was able to apply patience, the single most effective corrective in altering this thinking error, and thusly produced accountable judgment.

GK How else did you combat these states of limbo?

FJA Part of considering my thinking involved responsibly reading my results of past states of limbo. This included the realization of these moods having always resulted in crime, then remaining aware that my persistence in similar states of suspension would produce the same outcome. As I considered past results of limbo states, and future outcomes if maintained, I could then direct my thinking toward how responsible people had regarded me as I progressed in positive change. The realization of their having commended me in many ways for having endeavored to actually change acted as a strong bar against the view of myself as a transparent nothing and facilitated exits from the limbo state.

GK Being a transparent nothing- boy, that brings back memories of my limbo days. It's easy to feel terrible about oneself when you wake up on death row every day. Were other remedies applied?

FJA Yes, absolutely. Other correctives included having learned to treat fluctuating moods calmly and rationally, as well as having implemented the avoidance of sympathy elicitations, an occurrence having always inevitably led to a tendency to exploit situations. In a straightforward manner, I had to consider my choices: either enduring the suffering of change, returning to crime, or committing suicide. These choices, along with emphasizing misconceptions about myself and reevaluating the assets I'd previously underrated, effectively enabled my transcending of limbo states.

CHANGE YOUR THINKING – CHANGE YOUR LIFE

GK Insofar as deterrents, what, if anything, slowed your active involvement in criminal thought and action? Seems like you were a runaway train.

FJA Occasionally, during initial phases of a criminal enterprise, I experienced internal and/or external deterrents. Consequently, internal deterrents prevented some crimes by having existed as those components within my conscience that functioned like restraints. An example of this would be the time I planned to kill a drug dealer who had sold me a very impure quarter pound of cocaine. Somewhere in the depths of my conscience I understood that murder, due to its categorical finality, existed as something in which I must never participate. As a result, my plans to execute the drug dealer were immediately abandoned. On the other hand, external deterrents acted as sporadic bars to crime because they gave rise to a fear of apprehension. In other words, I may have suddenly felt an inexplicable foreboding just prior to the commission of a crime or determined a particular operation harbored an unacceptable possibility of arrest. In either case, deterrents would have caused me to pursue other plans. Of course, because of severe fragmentation neither internal nor external deterrents operated consistently.

GK Please detail the internal deterrent concept.

FJA I did have a conscience, but it was usually not functional. Even if it was operational, I was frequently able to overcome restraints within my conscience by putting emphasis on what I would not do. For instance, having stopped short of murder (supra)—rather than to consider all I had done. Additionally, I suppressed internal deterrents and maintained the image of myself as a good person through the use of sentimentality, religion, and acts of compassion. But there still remained times when conscience stood in the way of what I craved: excitement and power via crime. Of course, these momentary appearances of conscience (internal deterrents) never lasted and were almost always thwarted.

GK And external deterrents, detailed?

FJA With external deterrents, the basic question was not the propriety of any contemplated act but rather if I'd get caught. Other concerns included whether I would be injured, maimed, or even killed during the proposed enterprise. Also, if recently imprisoned, I may have initially been more cautious upon release, but only for a short period of time, if at all. As can be seen, none of these external deterrents focused upon any consideration other than my own well-being.

GK In other words, neither internal nor external deterrents stemmed the flow of criminality? At least not consistently?

FJA I should also point out, in regard to deterrents, despite how well my parents raised me I still began a life of crime at age fifteen. As my violations continued to increase in severity and frequency, previously existing deterrents were cut off. My main point of focus became fear of getting caught, rather than any sense of morality, and because I didn't believe I would be arrested, stiff sentences were not effective deterrents. Then again, even if jailed, there existed belief I would never be convicted, or even if convicted, I believed only an extremely light sentence would be imposed. As mentioned previously, personal experience bore this out. Moreover, often the increased possibility of apprehension merely led to more calculation and even provided a twofold personal triumph: having committed a crime while overcoming risky conditions. Circumventing alarms and motion sensors, watching for security, and so on, all served to enhance the theft experience. The afterglow of having pulled off a successful heist, while having braved such dangerous circumstances, lasted for days.

GK Please provide more specifics on the cutting off of deterrents.

FJA Additional methods I employed to overcome deterrents were erosion and cut off. Erosion was a mental process through which I slowly eliminated internal and/or external deterrents until the craving to commit crime overrode any deterrent. The result was my desire to engage in illegal behaviors won. For example, I initially felt that to steal drugs from my grandmother constituted an act too depraved to consider. Then, after several days of having thought about all the excellent dope she possessed, and the attendant fun it would provide, along with the belief she really didn't need all those drugs (some had been there for over twenty years), internal deterrents were eroded and consequently I yielded to desire.

GK Are you saying transcendence of deterrence was a process?

FJA As this example revealed, the gradual process of erosion would occur up to a point and then cut off would happen. Cut off allowed instant disposal of both internal and external deterrents, enabling me to commit my desired illegal action. Thus, severance, cut off of deterrents, occurred prior to engagement in criminal acts. Moreover, my severance of deterrents was not automatic, cut off existed as a process that was generally under my control and implemented by choice; unless PTSD intervened.

GK Then a process, which you identify as erosion, transpires and culminates in the death of deterrence, which you label as "cut off," correct? Please discuss "cut off."

> Corrections officials once thought they had time to prepare for this, but something unexpected happened. Federal data shows that prison inmates age more rapidly than people on the outside–because of the stress, poor diet and lack of medical care–so much so that their infirmities qualify them as "elderly" at the age of 50.
>
> Op-Ed excerpt New York Times 1-3-17

FJA In regard to cut off, it becomes important to distinguish it from both suppression and repression. Cut off, at least in one respect, acts to eradicate fear whereas suppression merely functions as the conscious decision to exclude specific ideas from present thinking, such as when exorcising thoughts of sexual crimes from one's mind. As for repression, this involves relegating memories of painful experiences to the unconscious mind, for instance, my banishing thoughts of having been sexually assaulted from consciousness. Also of importance must be how my search for triumphs and conquests cuts off deterrents, even those having resulted from prior experience, as well as how the act of cut off exists as its own triumph. That is, when shutting down deterrents, much of what was previously valued (e.g., physical safety, not getting caught) becomes eliminated, a significant step in the need to expel the internal deterrent of conscience and the external deterrent of fear, prior to implementing criminal schemes.

GK Well put. Now, once deterrence has been expunged, please identify the next link of criminal thought en route to a felonious act.

FJA Once deterrents had been cut off, and just prior to my execution of a crime, I generally experienced a state of nervousness and state of excitement. This can be compared to the state of arousal immediately preceding a big race, having a baby, or riding a roller coaster. Another common feature, as an immediate precursor to the actual commission of a crime, was the return of fear along with a decrease of my insuperable confidence. This renewed fear had to be forcefully dealt with through an exacting application of cut offs. For instance, one night I sat waiting for security guards to make their rounds so I could break into a stereo store. Fear arose so I brought to mind how many times I'd gotten away with far more dangerous crimes and thought about the enjoyment of my new stereo system. Cut off had been surgically applied, I was again ready for action, and super-optimism had returned. Of course, the emergence of fear itself had been exciting and doubled the challenge, which made my crime even more exciting and desirable.

GK You alluded to part of my next question, your thought process subsequent to a successful heist.

FJA After the commission of crimes I generally remained in the same geographical area, I regarded running as demeaning, and it diminished the thrill. In fact, remaining and traveling within the area where I'd just committed a crime added to the dimension of excitement. There was a time when I purchased wrecked VW vans and stole VW vans in good condition to then place the VIN (vehicle identification number) and license plates from the junked van on the stolen van. One day, while driving one such VW van just blocks from where I'd stolen it, I stopped for a red light and was confronted by a woman who insisted I had her van. The commotion attracted the attention of a cop, who ended up checking the VIN and plates but could do no more. As I drove away the woman stood there helplessly and watched her van disappear. Wow, sure reinforces how depraved I became.

GK Did any other thoughts appear with frequency post-crime?

FJA Another common occurrence after the commission of a crime would be re-experiencing my fear of apprehension. My fear would last from several minutes to several days, however, unless an immediate danger of capture existed, my fear engendered a tremendous sense of triumph from the successful completion of a crime.

GK Can you give me an example?

FJA After stealing quite a few [redacted] (censored due to ARS 13-4202-A), I remained in fear of arrest for several days, even though my likelihood of apprehension was pretty slim. But my fear soon turned to excitement, and I remained charged for nearly a week as a result of having ripped off the U.S. government for some dangerous drugs.

GK You just said the, rather than our, government. Was this personal detachment intentional and, if so, how do you now feel about the American Government and your position in society?

FJA Absolutely, the distance from American government was intentional. My previous intense dislike of government has significantly mellowed. However, tremendous distrust remains. Consider the political corruption in the USA now, 2016-17. On a personal level, my incarceration on death row for several decades, while innocent, resulted from and continues because the government fabricated evidence, acted wrongly and maliciously! In general terms, government constantly functions dishonestly, obtrusively, and with disdain toward its citizens. I do feel a connection to society; however, there remains the belief that some of society and all of government sees me still as an enemy of the State.

GK Anything else to add?

FJA Occasionally, post-crime activity included additional crimes; however, a far more common occurrence involved using the proceeds to play the big shot and enjoy a power thrust. These festivities usually included covering costs for alcohol and drugs, hiring limos, renting luxury hotel suites, and other extravagances. As I celebrated and played top dog, I generated additional excitement by bragging about my exploit to criminal cohorts. Of course, each time I related my tale more embellishment occurred; deterrence had vanished.

GK Please give a more complete explanation on restraint, or suppression, and change.

FJA Given restraint from criminal thinking and action was indispensable to the modification process. Focus had to fall upon the necessity of dismantling all underlying thought that functions as a precursor to crime—this being the cornerstone of my program for change.

GK Let's talk about your lessons and difficulties in learning restraint.

FJA The necessity to have cultivated and sustained restraint was vital, because my extreme concreteness caused transient deterrents to have been insufficiently adequate to produce lasting change.

Take, as an example, how fear functioned as the most useful external deterrent, but never by itself induced alteration of my thinking on a permanent basis. I could rarely begin to recall the times when I had aborted a criminal enterprise because of fear. The external deterrent of fear in no way negated the rampant, unceasing incipient thinking existing as the foundation of my criminal action. While deterrents were extremely useful, they were not a cure-all. More complete procedures of restraint required development, like the maturation of detailed reasoning as a method through which my criminal ideas were able to have eventually been preempted by responsibility. Only then were deterrents applied automatically, to serve as effective restraints leading me to the pursuit of an overall upright and moral view of normal life.

GK Experiencing the critical necessity of restraint, how did you cultivate this virtue?

FJA Restraint was developed as I extracted my mental content from daily phenomenological reports, learning my many criminal musings could never be taken lightly. The failure to immediately forestall my very first thought in a fantasy would have made the application of deterrence later far more difficult. To further these objectives, I found four basic steps worked best for me:

1. Aborting crises.
2. Disposing of and preempting persistent criminal thinking with a reasoning process.
3. Taking moral inventories when no criminal thoughts came to mind.
4. Automatic deterrence (a state wherein if an irresponsible thought arose I'd dismiss it without effort; e.g., "that pack of cigarettes looks alluring" being immediately rebutted by "tobacco is unhealthy," "those aren't mine," etc.).

I learned these processes in combination with correctives for my thinking errors, this being essential to my having been able to change.

GK I know you experienced many occasions when restraint was in dire need, how did you abort disaster?

FJA As I initially embarked on my process of change my thinking contained a constant stream of criminal ideas, a crisis situation persisted. Therefore, it was crucial for me to intensify cognizance on the perils of my criminal thought; realizing my first step was to regard my every thought as dangerous, without any requirement for an elaborate review of past experiences. This process is similar to touching a hot surface: trial by fire.

GK Please elaborate on this "every thought is dangerous" tactic.

FJA This strategy—being an initial deterrent focusing on the extant consequences of my thought or action in question (injury to others = trouble for myself)—linked my incipient criminal thinking with immediate punishment. However, while this tactic was effective early in my change program, it did not eliminate irresponsible thinking; overall, it was insufficient as a long-range tool. This initial bridle to violation fit my concreteness by having extended from precise thoughts that resulted in specific crimes to particular thinking error patterns. It was an extremely useful first strategy and stepping stone; serving as a temporary, vital and indispensable emergency measure to deal with crises.

GK What were some of your more advanced techniques to restrain rage?

FJA As mentioned, over time I had to progress beyond simpler deterrents (i.e., my fear of punishment), which required

> Serval months of insomnia are distressing enough, but when insomnia becomes chronic, lasting six months or longer, it can wreak serious physical, emotional and social havoc.
>
> In addition to excessive daytime sleepiness, which can be dangerous in and of itself, Dr. Avidan reports that chronic insomnia "may result in disturbed intellect, impaired cognition, confusion, psychomotor retardation, or increased risk for injury." Understandably, it is often accompanied by – depression either as a cause or result of persistent insomnia. Untreated insomnia also increases the risk of falls and fractures, a study of nursing home residents showed.
>
> Excerpt from an article by
> Jane E. Brody
> New York Times 1-17-17

imposing more effective restraint through the use of responsible adult reasoning. In furtherance of this I began to use methods of prevention requiring an application of reason in two stages:

1. Drawing on experience to establish and strengthen self-disgust.
2. Applying lessons of the past to the future.

My first stage involved a post-moral assessment after any violation(s) or series of criminal thoughts while the second stage required my using all I learned to engage in reasoning before the fact. This strategy was very effective in having illuminated my criminal thinking; as I increased sessions to twenty minutes or longer my productivity finally reached satisfactory levels.

GK Were there any further techniques?

FJA At this juncture I'd surpassed my rudimentary crisis intervention phase, and moved on to more formidable avenues of restraint, I was on the way to having altered my criminal personality. This means as I consistently and consciously applied the principles of this new stage of my change program I developed a more stable view of myself, one in which disgust with my past self was purposely pursued. This enabled self-repulsion to remain vivid and act as a responsible guide for future thinking and action; advances in my change through relabeling of self-occurred only once I ceased to review the details of my criminal performances and instead contemplated the physical and emotional harm I had inflicted on others (society, my family, and myself). This deterrent became totally effective when actual experience was applied to thoughts of the future—meaning preparation was a major area of focus when having studied daily phenomenological reports.

Having learned to effectively dispose of criminal thoughts by having installed restraint, either during or just prior to a crisis or violation, indicated I finally reached a point in my program for change in which a reasoning process had provided me the ability to exercise earlier awareness, to employ cognizance prior to situations having arisen. Nevertheless, the danger still existed, I could find memories of past exploits exciting and return to criminal thought patterns. This necessitated my use of preemptive deterrents that considered my future probabilities even before criminal thinking occurred. By becoming aware of what was likely to unfold I placed myself in a position from which I was able to have attacked incipient deviant and irresponsible ideation.

Applying a defensive posture of preemptive and anticipatory restraint I also had to proactively redirect thinking. Once criminal thinking had been deterred something had to replace it; there could be no vacuum of thought. Initially my redirection of attention was contrived, I had to temporarily choose what to contemplate, however, focus eventually turned automatically to responsible pursuits (like Greek Orthodox Christian theology) and preemption enabled the simultaneous and habitual redirection of perception.

GK How often did you do a moral inventory to track your progress?

FJA I adopted the use of moral inventories, or examinations of conscience, several times a day to start; my daily phenomenological report existed as the vehicle through which I was able to conduct a detailed moral analysis of self. For instance, say I had experienced a negative interaction with an officer regarding policy, I would've soon thereafter written a factual account of the event documenting exactly what occurred; I also recorded all of my attendant thoughts and feelings. This journaling enabled me to conduct a moral inventory by reviewing what I said, did, thought, and felt for any sign of incipient criminality (e.g., was I merely seeking to assume control or trying to courteously resolve a legitimate complaint?).

GK Did this remain a mainstay in your change program, were other strategies implemented?

FJA Once I was somewhat advanced in my change program I developed the ability to implement this deterrent as an exercise in its own right by engaging in an examination of conscience whenever needed. This may have involved evaluating thoughts, words, and deeds as they occurred—such as in the above example, conducting an inventory while having interacted with prison personnel, rather than having waited; journaling it existed as part of a self-assessment during events.

Then again, I experienced occasions of a sense of futility as I took a moral inventory. The correctives for this required I direct all guilt and shame about my past, and my sense of having been generally overwhelmed, toward constructive options. Because of the wearisome nature of repeated moral inventories, once I advanced in my change program I spent less attention reflecting on past crimes and instead applied focus on imagining I was the victim of some of my past crimes. This eased the fatigue factor while having enabled me to maintain self-disgust.

GK What do you mean by "imagining I was the victim of some of my past crimes?"

FJA As I became well advanced in change I was able to accept the previously deviant features of my moral inventories as terribly regrettable facts of my life. I was able to come to terms with having been a criminal and having inflicted such extensive injury, emphasis shifted from having dwelt on the past to planning what had to be done to ensure present and future responsible functioning. However, the practice of taking stock of myself could never cease.

GK Does this infer total success in your change or must you still, even now, practice restraints?

FJA Eventually I began to function like non-criminals, only occasional irresponsible ideas had to be deterred. However, even when well advanced in change I still had intermittent criminal thoughts—which I'd once savored, elaborated on, and translated into action—entering and leaving consciousness without deliberate deterrents. For instance, suppose a wayward criminal notion, like the temptation to scheme my way around some prison rule had manifested, rather than willfully acknowledge my idea as irresponsible (to then consider possible hindrances and purposefully apply these impediments to violation), I developed the ability to perform these components of restraint habitually and without having to think about them. I eventually reached a stage wherein preventive measures did not require effort or conscious implementation but rather could be applied automatically. Of course, while the inception of automatic restraint demonstrates I had built a foundation of responsibility, it remains critical that I never become complacent. For instance, genuine indebtedness had to evolve into an ingrained and habitual pattern so it could be a natural part of my responsible living. To overcome deficiencies in the financial arena I had to initiate fact-finding (incoming funds, bills, other expenses, savings) and then transcend my demand for a guarantee of effort resulting in success. I had to acquire knowledge of there being no assurance (in this realm as well as in life) and needed to realize sustained initiatives were required in order to become a responsible adult, thus, the applied corrective was an attitude of humble doing.

Furthermore, to facilitate implementation of responsible initiatives I also had to overcome the fear of making a fool of myself. I had chosen to shun the responsible world and had few experiences and interests in common with dependable people. My phenomenological reports had to focus on all of the thinking and acting patterns limiting my trustworthy interaction so I could then learn by practice. That is, knowledge about trustworthy living and the process of change could not occur by osmosis, it had to be diligently pursued and experienced.

GK In regard to healing and changing, what was the trigger, the flip of the switch moment, that you looked in the mirror and said: "Frank Atwood...?" WTH?

What was the trigger, the flip the switch moment that you looked in the mirror and said: Frank Atwood? WTH?

FJA After years of study and introspection I learned each thought pattern existed as part of the totality of all thought forms or, put another way, each thought structure was interrelated with other ideation compositions. These thinking forms operated everywhere and were not merely restricted to crime; as a result, all of my thinking had to be brought out so it could be corrected, then, by identifying my criminal thought patterns these could be opposed and subsequently destroyed. The manner in which I exposed all of my thinking was through phenomenological reporting, a method that involved writing down my streams of thought on a daily basis.

GK You mean the key resides in changing all negative patterns of thought?

FJA Yes. The need to uncover and alter all thinking existed as one reason why behavior modification programs (such as drug rehab centers) constituted such an insufficient arena for change and was why at least one avenue for transformation had to include learning a new set of thinking processes. Only new thought patterns were able to correct my former thinking errors and enabled me to sustain a sense of self-disgust, an idea of just how rotten I had become. Moreover, having altered my thought process enabled fear, shame, and regret to function as cornerstones of responsible living and sustained change.

GK Why is it so difficult to rehabilitate hardened criminals? Provide a personal example, if you would please.

FJA While possible for a criminal to change into a responsible person, much of what has been applied to non-criminals (in terms of treatment methods) were not applicable to myself. Routine procedures for responsible people accomplished little because I was very different from law abiding patients in conventional therapeutic settings. For example, techniques for exploring "Early Life" proved to be insufficient to produce change in myself. I recall having been caught engaging in sexual activity at Atascadero

State Hospital, I participated in group therapy sessions to discuss how sexual repression in childhood had led to a distorted perception of sexuality as a means by which to excuse my in-custody sexual conduct. This "insight" enabled the criminal in me to escape punishment and even resulted in having been praised for having "benefitted" from treatment. This demonstrates how having taught me (the criminal) insight provided only more material for excusing and justifying misbehavior.

GK Does this infer you experienced little to no benefit from established therapy programs?

FJA The *Miller and Kenney Study* (1966) concluded that no one ever demonstrated success in treating delinquency by psychiatric techniques. This means that, at best, mental health care professionals experience very little success in treating criminal behavior, and explains why psychiatric hospitals were relatively unable to alter my criminality. In fact, psychoanalytic approaches only helped me to develop into a more sophisticated criminal and sociological programs were powerless to change my way of life or to impact my desires. Actually, I merely exploited these approaches for my own gain.

GK Well, then the obvious question becomes just how did you change?

FJA To produce responsible behavior I had to be equipped with an entirely new set of thought processes. This was because I operated from a base that was completely separate from responsibility, my mental consistency was very different from that of the non-criminal; I had become a different breed of person. To have described me from the viewpoint of a responsible person would have constituted imposing a frame of reference that would not have fit my reality so could only have produced an inaccurate portrait and failure in therapy. Keep in mind my personality as a criminal was comprised of extremely concrete thinking, apparent contradiction in thought and action, persistent fearfulness, the inclination to view myself as worthless, and having seen myself as either a victim or a victor. Additionally, I also believed I was a good person (not a lawbreaker or inflictor of harm) and considered myself as totally unique, which enhanced my sense of superiority. As an extreme criminal, all of these characteristics were very pronounced in myself.

GK What were your initial steps in the change process?

FJA In order to initiate change I had to become completely fed up with my criminal characteristics, then embarking on a conversion to an entirely new lifestyle had to occur; one including the total destruction of my criminal personality. That was in incredibly daunting task! I simply found the expectations of the responsible world to be meaningless and had consistently rejected my duty as a member of society. Then once I really decided to change I still viewed responsibility as nirvana, as a problemless existence—only after having become a responsible person could I comprehend responsibility as a way of life involving continual problems. In other words, change had to involve being taught what the responsible world consisted of. I had to learn to accept this new world as I found it and make the best of it...and stop demanding a different kind of world. Also, it was essential for me to learn within the context of real life situations, not merely intellectually or in theoretical terms. This proved to be extremely difficult given my inherently oppressive conditions on death row, of life in a supermax prison. [See Control Unit Prison Article In Back]. However, as I began to cease insisting upon what my idea of fairness involved and simply accepted the circumstances imposed upon me a responsible perspective developed.

GK Quite frankly, this seems like a monumental task, the alteration of your own process of thinking.

FJA I now see with greater clarity that changing my thought process was far more important than trying to reduce my number of violations; absent altering my thought process the reduction of violation would always have been short-lived at best. Again, the *Miller and Kenney Study*, regarding the futility of only treating symptomatic behavior, demonstrates why responsibility and change must occur in both behavior and mental alignment. For me this meant initially I had to confront myself with what I had become and then had to change my context while persistently struggling toward engendering trust, effort, interdependence, responsible initiatives, and time perspectives. I also needed to learn how to consider injury to others and use responsible decision making which, when consistently implemented, opposed and eventually replaced my old criminal thought patterns. Crimelessness without mental change existed as an impossible objective and any change would never have been sustained or completed.

GK In other words, inherent in any change program must be the thinking of not merely yourself but interaction with others?

FJA Let's consider an example of how the alteration of my thinking process impacted me. To begin with, the way in which I contemplated interaction with others took on completely different patterns. For instance, rather than construct relations intended to enable my taking advantage of and using others I began considering the feelings and wishes of people. One way in which this became especially pronounced was in my interactions with prison guards as I moved from perceiving them as contemptuous enemies toward acknowledging them as fellow human beings with hopes, dreams, and needs. My shift in perspective initiated a whole new way of being as I exited a world of perpetual combat with those I encountered daily and embarked upon a path of thoughtfulness and harmony.

GK How can your degree of change, or need for continued effort, be determined?

FJA There exists no foolproof system to evaluate my extent of change and my process of modification can never be considered as having been completed. However, some indications of progress include:

A. Less complaining.
B. Less posturing as victim/victor.
C. Disassociation from criminals.
D. An attitude that includes seeking help.
E. Increased self-criticism.
F. Elimination of violation.

What Parents Should Know

Not all sexually abused children exhibit symptoms–some estimate that up to 40% of sexually abused children are Asymptomatic.

Also, sexually abused males tend to not report being victimized, which may affect statistics. Males tend to feel societal pressure to be proud of early sexual activity.

American Psychological Association. http://www.apa.org/pi/families/resources/child-sexual-abuse.aspx

GK What I perceive as one roadblock to change pertains to prison life being filled with criminals retelling their exploits. Can you speak to this?

FJA The thinking process had to become my primary focus. This meant all consideration of behavior or crime which resulted from negative thought patterns I had possessed needed to become residual. To have listened to prisoners boasting of crime, or to have recalled past conquests, would have merely induced excitement; thusly stimulating additional criminal thinking. For example, in the months after my arrival on death row I was an avid fan of police and crime programs, like "Cops," even though this generated severe criticism from other criminals—watching police action on television existed as an unpopular pastime here. Only years later did I realize the ardent desire to view those shows arose from a desperate need to engage in voyeuristic and pseudo-criminality. That is, having been locked away from direct participation in criminal enterprises I sought to vicariously engage in crime by catching the action on television.

Furthermore, if having allowed myself to recall past crimes I would have only considered those that were relatively harmless. In other words, I would only have focused on the tip of the iceberg of violation, a blunder that would have enabled the perpetuation of a one-time favorite fallacy: I was a good person.

GK How did choosing to turn away from criminality in thought impact your view of self?

FJA I was extremely reluctant to destroy my criminal mind-set and way of living, after all, it was what had justified the despicable deeds I had routinely engaged in and to have adopted a responsible viewpoint would have exposed me as a worthless nothing. Treatment and change were the last choices I wanted to consider.

GK So what most everyone takes for granted you had to learn for yourself (being ill-equipped for "normal" functioning)?

FJA Concepts such as tax withholdings, budgeting, income, insurance, rent, and so on were completely foreign to me...by choice! I recall a time when my parents, in an attempt to assist me in achieving responsibility, co-signed a car purchase I made. The idea was for me to look for and maintain a job, to learn how to fulfill obligations (in this case, monthly car payments), and to take on the responsibility of ownership (e.g., arranging for car insurance and maintenance). Of course, I treated this like everything else, as a criminal enterprise; predictably, I defaulted on car and insurance payments, ignored necessary repairs, never looked-for work, and turned this intended lesson in responsible living into both a disaster and a free ride at the expense of my parents. Any attempt to have changed without the necessary thought process became one more unmitigated disaster.

GK Despite embarrassment, you had to choose to adopt

different thought patterns, correct?

FJA I opted to take new thinking patterns as a habitual part of my daily life and this process enabled me to adopt a change from lifelong thinking errors. In other words, only then could I learn correctives and utilize a wide-open channel of communication; the implementation of full disclosure, listening with an open mind, and self-criticism. Consequently, change involved choosing to do what was responsible, whether or not I was interested, liked it, or obtained a guarantee of success.

I should also mention, when learning a new thought process, I repeatedly refocused on my ultimate choices, such as what kind of life I wanted or whether I even wanted to live. Also, when I resisted responsible decisions, I had to consistently recall my three options: crime, suicide, or change. Keep in mind my choice to learn new ideation constructs constituted merely my initial step in change, this choice only became effective upon implementation, meaning the putting in place new patterns of thinking existed as my most difficult decision.

GK Is this a matter of choice, or, simply will power?

FJA Will power, when directed toward a responsible directive, this was totally foreign to me. I had repeatedly scorned responsible people and objectives throughout my entire life. Will power involves endurance and cannot be taught by someone else, it must be personally experienced from within as a new pattern of thinking. For me, will power and endurance had to include giving up the role of playing the big shot; of seeing myself as the unique number one and believing I could be an overnight success. It also meant abdicating my delusion of power and control, then living as an ordinary person. Finally, my will power needed to endure, to involve doing what was required to achieve responsible objectives, whether I felt like it or not. Obviously, my developing perseverance required tremendous self-discipline and, in the change process, played a dominant role in early and middle changes.

GK You previously referenced phenomenological reporting, a concept with which I am unfamiliar. Please explain this.

FJA While studying human consciousness and pursuing methods of change, I encountered a process known as phenomenological reporting. Phenomenology is the description and/or or classification of observable facts and events that are subject to change; this relates to (i) epoch, the indication of a new time or event onset that is marked by a specific period of time, (ii) transcendental conditions of human experience as determined by the mind, and (iii) reductionism, reduction to simplest forms. This approach, phenomenology, considers how one's mind progresses through variant stages; this looks at the fixed point from where a new process of unfoldment begins and distinctive development ensues. When applied to experiences in life, phenomenology enables that which is registered in consciousness to be reported. In other words, phenomenological reporting encompasses a procedure wherein raw data of thinking can be recorded.

GK And how did you implement and utilize the process of phenomenological reporting?

FJA As I engaged in my change process I implemented three forms of phenomenological reporting, or three ways of recording thinking and events: (1) in a chronological, continuous manner, (2) in thematic fashion, and (3) as they occurred. These daily accounts of what I experienced, when made as soon after thinking and events as possible enabled the exposure of thinking errors. Of particular interest was my incipient thinking, even if temporarily eliminated by erosion and cut off, I could now clearly see how it recurred and found expression later in criminal acts.

Let's consider an example: I may have suffered a put-down, perhaps a potential employer expressed concern over my prison history or a store clerk hesitated to assist me because of my rudeness. Events like these would prompt thinking errors like "everyone is against me and will never give me a chance." I'd then begin to contemplate ways I could retaliate against society, a process involving criminal thinking (planning a criminal act as payment for having been "wronged"). Finally, even if my plan to commit a crime was not immediately carried out, there still remained the perceived mistreatment by society and concomitant thinking, both of which would persist until criminal ideas were eventually put into action. My thought of one moment often became the irresponsible criminal action of a subsequent instant.

GK Did it also interfere with the thinking you just explained?

FJA Had I neglected to record initial events and ensuing thinking in my daily phenomenological reports, it would have remained impossible to have exposed my unreasonable suspicions of societal abuse, and ridiculous justifications for criminal behavior would have remained covered. This shows it was crucial for me to comprehend my experiences by using the raw data of phenomenological reports, rather than self-serving interpretation. I had to train myself to record my thinking so contents in my mind became available, a process involving eliciting details of my thinking to learn an elaborate set of deterrents. This then led to an elimination of my criminal thought patterns. In other words, I had to write down (capture) every thought that passed through my mind; the data could never be limited, and the focus had to remain in the present.

GK Please explain a little further this discipline of documenting thousands of thoughts.

FJA Training myself to conscientiously supply the raw data of my thinking and action can be visualized as having created a printout of my ideas, a printout enabling me to see my cut off of fear, my scheming, my lack of endurance, and my failure to plan for the future. Additionally, the mere process of authoring phenomenological reports throughout each and every day developed self-monitoring, self-discipline, and self-criticism, assets which assisted me in remaining alert for criminal thought patterns as I focused on the intent, purpose, and objective of my thinking.

The daily recording of thought and action also let me expose thought patterns that needed to be altered, by enabling me to select a single error, and to then perceive it as one manifestation in a broad pattern in my life of constant occurrence in my thinking and action. This once again demonstrates that the outcome or consequences of my behavior could never be the initial consideration. That is, I could not attempt to explain effects by attributing causes after the fact. To have considered results and imputed causation simply would have retarded the change process. The far more effective method for perpetuating modification was to probe the ongoing thinking that had been recorded in daily phenomenological reports to expose intent, purpose, and objective. Only then could I introduce corrective concepts and apply them to comparable thinking and action patterns, as well as throughout all aspect of my new life.

GK In the reprogramming of thought and conduct what did you perceive as the overarching concern and/or need?

FJA Part of my program for change involved the pursuit of responsibility by conscientiously forcing new thinking patterns, so I could begin to become an effective and constructive person of integrity. Given that responsibility had to go beyond crimelessness, it was necessary to fully engage in the daily phenomenological reporting of thinking patterns and to then implement the correctives. This meant uncovering thinking errors, removing them, then replacing the resultant void with responsibility.

GK Insofar as correctives, were these generalities or specifically formatted?

FJA The correctives for thinking patterns I employed had three basic functions: (1) serving as deterrents to crime, (2) preventing irresponsibility, and (3) replacing old thought patterns to provide a foundation for new processes. Thus, my new thought patterns, developed through extreme determination, became the basis for my new way of life.

GK Did your correctives function on just an intellectual level or was emotion included?

FJA Good question, the pursuit of eliminating criminal characteristics could not focus on feelings, I had to concentrate on thinking. If attention fell on sensation, feelings, and emotions, I would have resorted to these when held accountable in order to excuse my actions. Moreover, feelings are intangible and cannot be phenomenologically reported with consistency, could not have served as the basis for change.

GK Please explain more about the difficulties of changing each and every aspect of yourself.

FJA Interest in total change had to be self-nurtured and this emerged by experience, from knowledge arising from experience. This indicates I had to develop an interest in responsible living by substituting correctives for criminal thought processes. Thus, to initiate responsible thinking a start had to be made, a venture I embarked upon by choosing acceptable leisure activities. Once initiative had been exercised, and something had been given a fair trial, I found my interest persisted.

GK I find the modification process so encouraging, please share more of what you experienced during your program for change.

FJA I encountered a variety of experiences throughout my process of modification. It would be impossible to relate all of them, or even a majority of them. However, I hope we will discuss elements of what my program for change involved, and I intend to provide a list of characteristics within myself in order to evidence change is possible, even for hardened criminals, and to chronicle some of my modifications I've been able to make over the years.

GK What was your greatest barrier to change?

FJA The greatest obstacle to change I experienced was my firmly entrenched opposition to change itself. One common manifestation of this involved having repeatedly expressed desire to begin therapy or enter a rehabilitation center merely as a way to avoid confinement; no intent to have genuinely participated accommodated these seemingly honorable assertions. Moreover, if having been confined I frequently made duplicitous declarations about wanting to engage in some form of positive programming as a way to facilitate my release or to be housed in a more desirable location.

GK I imagine this cycle of resistance continued until landing on death row?

FJA Yes. Prior to contemplating a program for modification (this was in California, in the 1970's) I'd spent four years locked up when a new law allowed authorities to petition a court annually to continually extend my maximum sentence. I convinced a judge to release me to a substance abuse center, yet even though my failure to follow through would mean a return to custody I left the program earlier-in opposition to treatment and change.

GK When you first began your change program, you were so lost, more so than me. It must have been a huge challenge to hang onto any thread of reality?

FJA When I was initially motivated to change myself in the 1990's, there existed significant obstacles as a consequence of underlying self-manipulative schemes having infected my perceptions about my improvement of thinking and behavior patterns. Consider how I had viewed ultimate personal change as a state of crimelessness rather than as assumption of responsibility, or my misbelief that I could have achieved required objectives through my own meager means. Furthermore, initial motivation was tainted by my having gone along with the program (assent) merely as a way to have avoided antagonizing authority figures (parole officers, prison counselors, courts, etc.). I generally provided only what I believed was required and did nothing more. This underscores the importance of my needing to continually evaluate whether I was being truthful at any given time, and recognizing how all my thinking errors constituted imposing obstacles to change.

Even after I'd begun to adhere consistently to my program for change, I repeatedly wondered why I had to endure what I perceived to be an inordinately prolonged, rigorous, and extremely dull process. During these early stages of change, I persisted in daily failures to realize the problem was the whole person, not just a particular criminal pattern. I still possessed no experience in functioning responsibly; I had to learn about accountability in much the same manner as a child; a slow and arduous process I had to pursue diligently, despite my inclinations to resist or rush change.

GK Did you experience any "honeymoon" syndrome?

FJA Once I embarked on a sincere attempt to change I became diligent, enthusiastic, interested in learning and made a genuine effort. One reason for this was because I saw self-improvement as easy to accomplish and was certain I would perform magnificently; besides, the program was something new and initially provided excitement. This constituted what was my honeymoon phase during which super-optimism existed as a predominant feature. While in this brief stage I experienced a temporary absence of violation and reduction in criminal thinking.

GK What year did you begin your change program, and how long did it take to complete it?

FJA I've not kept my notes, but I believe the onset was around 1993 and I still actively participate in it, the program will never be complete, nor will it end.

Thinking back, I recall how eventually the excitement wore off and the change process became grueling and tedious—the honeymoon ended. Soon thereafter I grew disenchanted, began to function with a closed mind, and was less perseverant in making and reviewing phenomenological reports. This led to again becoming immersed in complaining about situations and criticizing others. Rather than being self-critical, prior thinking errors reemerged, and I believed liberties could be taken with the program. Because I had temporarily been free of violation, I grew overly optimistic about the degree of change having occurred, and decided I could skip a report or commit one small lie. All of this demonstrates how I had been misled by the harmony of the honeymoon; reentry into a life of crime was not far off at this point.

GK This sounds like a critical juncture in your process, how did you proceed?

FJA One way in which I was able to abandon the letdown of the honeymoon having ended was by remembering my program for change was a lifeline; it existed as the sole method by which I could ever pursue a life of responsibility. In having established my program for change as a lifeline, I adopted two keys: (1) intensifying and sustaining self-disgust, and (2) developing self-denial.

GK Having experienced my own soul searching and

reprogramming of self, I can see where someone in your own position would need to cautiously dip your toe into these pools of self-disgust or risk drowning in sadness and depression. How did you manage to stay afloat?

FJA As I sank further into my change program, my lifeline (the process itself) functioned as a life preserver. The key was to focus on the program, to trust it, as the means by which to avoid drowning in waves of sorrow. For example, as I conjured up vivid pictures of my sordid past, rather than to solely dwell on these, I was subsequently able to generate a fear of what I might do to myself and others at the present time or in the future. I began to realize no amount of good deeds could ever cancel out even one criminal exploit, and no matter how many positive traits I possessed, they were all totally eclipsed by my rampant criminality. As can be seen, only as I gained more responsible experiences could I develop the capacity to have contrasted my current and past life without being overwhelmed by sorrow, a method by which I caused self-disgust to intensify, as I used self-loathing to prompt additional responsible experience, along with implementation of the change process.

GK And how about the necessity of self-denial?

FJA Self-denial was critical. Throughout the process of change, I had to refrain from doing many things I wanted, and I needed to also contemporaneously engage in practices I detested. This was an excruciatingly agonizing procedure. By far the greatest single act of self-denial was the elimination of criminal excitement. In fact, as I restrained myself from this excitement I actually experienced psychosomatic symptoms—dizziness, headaches, stomach distress, and sweats, similar to an exorcism! Nevertheless, I could offer myself absolutely no sympathy; it was far better for me to have suffered these maladies than to have engaged in violation. Furthermore, I had to fastidiously avoid seeking any medication in an attempt to have assuaged these disorders. Pharmaceutical intervention would have only attacked the external manifestation, rather than the underlying basis. The corrective for having abated my severity and intensity of psychosomatic reactions resided in the reduction of my expectations and pretension.

There were times when I faltered under the restraints of self-denial, as well as the austerity of pursuing responsibility. This required having to repeatedly invoke my long-range perspective to stay focused. To learn the importance of maintaining a protracted outlook was essential; I required a far-reaching view to remain focused on basic issues as I avoided diversions from any momentary rigors of self-denial.

GK Having spoken rather extensively about the tools essential to change, just how did you translate these necessities into practice?

FJA In order to more systematically, and thoroughly effect change, three types of implementations were required:

The first was reporting. That is, total disclosure, receptivity, and self-criticism.

Stranger Danger?

Only 25 percent of female victims of rape/sexual assault were victimized by strangers and 12 percent involved a weapon.

http://bjs.ojp.usdoj.gov/content/pub/pdf/cv10.pdf

The second involved an alteration in thinking, especially in regard to deterrence and moral inventories.

Finally, the third required full activation of all correctives. This could be seen through the changes in my thought patterns and by ensuing responsible conduct.

In addition to having applied these three correctives, I also needed to learn that when modifying thought and behavior, all decisions had to be based on my new logical induction. I had to develop the ability to process ideas rationally, needed to begin exercising sound judgment. Along with having invoked reason, I also meticulously avoided justification, to ceaselessly ensure feelings/emotions never dominated my judgment. I was then, as a result of doing, able to authentically learn about both myself and the outside world. Endeavors must rely upon the insight I had developed as a consequence of practicing responsibility.

Finally, the implementation of change, the restraint of criminal thought and action, could not have occurred without having continually applied my four basic deterrents: aborting a crisis, disposing of /preempting criminal ideation via reasoning, moral inventory, and automatic deterrence. The application of these deterrents exists even today as an active process. Their full implementation provided me with the capacity to overcome adversity, a cornerstone of any successful and permanent positive change.

GK It seems to have required tremendous discipline to have maintained strict adherence to all deterrents you discussed so far.

Any advice?

FJA Both effort and endurance were absolutely necessary throughout the modification process, and had to be continuously stressed, so I could learn and eventually implement what had previously been a foreign type of thinking. What this entailed was going beyond the mere intellectualization of these requirements by having incorporated them as habitual aspects of daily life. As long as they remained only theoretical precepts (not put into use) they compelled little or no result. This demonstrates why methodical responsible thinking and controlled action were mandatory elements in my program for change. In other words, the requisite discipline had to be cultivated by emphasizing life's smallest details over and over again, to put into practice what had heretofore been merely conceptual. Thus, it was my consistent examination of minute details of what appeared to be trivial issues, that demanded and taught me self-control. This meant even valid attempts to have departed from my newly established regimen had to be closely scrutinized, regardless of the degree of change attained thus far.

As previous patterns of irresponsibility continued to be amended, I then had to establish intermediate targets (or sub goals) along the way. The purpose of sub goals was to enable these baby steps to make will power a functional asset, by establishing something concrete through which I could then judge accomplishment. However, such achievements in themselves did not constitute change. There still existed my potential to hijack these deeds into something where my overriding objective was to simply look good. Instead, my emphasis had to firmly reside on the process of attainment rather than on the accomplishment itself. As such, my program for change required a steady, plodding elimination of criminal thinking and action patterns. In this way, from early on in the adjustment process, I could begin to understand that a responsible life involved assuming one burden or task after another. Only in this manner was I able to actualize the business of altering multiple errors at the same time, and for an extended period.

GK How did you maintain enthusiasm while voiding self-contentment?

FJA Once I had deterred overt violation, and learned to enjoy a few positive modifications, I began to view myself as a totally changed person. This marked the onset of complacency and precluded generating new initiatives or vigorously attacking daily problems. As a result, my mind began to slowly close, the ensuing egotistic overconfidence was not obvious to me. It was noticed only once a significant erosion of responsibility and several prison disciplinary infractions had occurred. This all too frequent trend toward complacency made it imperative for me to realize my having changed one pattern was only an initial step. The entire spectrum of thinking and behavior had to be altered while hubristic precepts had to be preempted.

GK Can you give a specific example of complacency and your triumph over it?

FJA One effective method I found for abrogating complacency was to consider potentially adverse situations. For example, the contemplation of results flowing from the briefest cessation of daily phenomenological reports—like my immediate influx of incipient criminal thinking, clinging to desire for excitement, pursuit of criminal enterprises, devastating aftereffects, etc.—functioned to promptly restore diligence. In this thought zone, I was able to focus on hardship rather than smugness. I could avoid disaster by ensuring possible negligence would not become a reality. This I accomplished by employing daily phenomenological reports as a means for self-criticism, for the preparation of eventual tribulation, and to determine what still required change. Despite these tools with which to combat lethargic tendencies, I still suffered occasional consequences of complacency. However, these experiences then enabled me to more fully realize I did not have it made and that my continued perseverance was essential.

GK Are you speaking here of incipient thinking's dangers?

FJA My having argued over my thinking not serving as an arrestable offense completely failed to recognize how my thoughts precipitated my actions, were integral sequences to any flow of events. Therefore, my having neglected to deter incipient capricious criminal ideation resulted in rampant irresponsible behavior and violation. That is not to say illicit action was inevitable. My aggressive implementation of my program for change, and tireless attack of each embryonic irresponsible inclination, deterred infraction and facilitated change. This demonstrates how the long and arduous struggle toward responsibility was ameliorated, once I eliminated incipient criminal thinking.

For me, my criminal thoughts were as criminal as the act itself. I found that a successful corrective for defeating this precursor of evil machinations involved repeated focus on my phenomenological reports to explore the results and impact of incipient irresponsibility. This tactic acted as a learning tool and retarded inherent unaccountability from developing into something more serious. In addition to this, I also abstained from using alcohol and drugs, because of their tendency to mitigate restraints and to function as facilitators to violation.

GK Wait! They have alcohol on death row?

FJA For those willing to risk detection and poisoning, yes--alcohol can be brewed in a death row cell.

GK You mentioned temptations to halt your program for change, due to misbelieving full rehabilitation had transpired or some other falsehood. How did you battle this provocation demon toward disaster?

FJA My ongoing desire to stop my program for change was expressed in different ways, the most frequent being a declaration I was ready to stand on my own two feet. Actually, this pronouncement had to be construed as an expression of boredom, disenchantment, and a belief that the implementation required was more than I felt to have been necessary. I was really displaying a reluctance to surrender fully to the modification process.

This refusal to have fully immersed myself in the business at hand forced me to make a critical choice: whether to resign from my program permanently, temporarily, or not at all. Of course, I was then able to consider how even the slightest deviation from altering my thought and action patterns would be disastrous. I could then immediately return to full implementation of the required elements for complete change.

GK How about the need for steadfastness? I think you've spoken about having to apply rigid dedication, but would you please address this a bit further?

FJA It was absolutely necessary. My program for change required a definitive understanding of my having no option other than to continue. I had to comprehend that any slacking off or drug use would mean immediate failure—a lax attitude would have irreparably weakened effectiveness. This meant I had to be uncompromising in requiring myself to meet all of my program's standards. The burden to function responsibly had to be repeatedly placed on my shoulders, regardless of how I believed I'd been wronged and despite whatever objectionable obstacles existed.

Firmness and steadfastness had to be established

straightaway, a requirement I accomplished by having immediately refused to accept excuses for my irresponsibility. Instead, I assumed an unapologetic and moralistic posture. I was then able to perceive firmness as demanding an unyielding insistence that my change required full implementation and my utter priority and commitment.

GK You briefly alluded to interaction with other prisoners. I'm wondering about this at various stages throughout your change process, both from your perspective of change and attitudes toward other inmates.

FJA Okay. Let's look at the attitude harbored by hardcore criminals toward me, once I began my program for change, the attitude possessed by myself toward unchanged career felons as I continued to undergo modification, and the attitude of non-criminals toward myself as I proceeded with the change process.

GK Cool. So, begin with unchanged criminal toward yourself?

FJA In my experience, generally most criminals who were not engaged in altering themselves—those who choose to remain unchanged and heavily involved in criminal thinking and action—reacted with great skepticism toward me once I embarked upon my process of change. There were some unchanged criminals who viewed me as sincere, however, they all doubted my implementation of required elements and that my desire would endure. As for the vast majority of unchanged criminals, their overriding opinion involved the belief I was not sincere and only intended to score points by conning authorities. This often gave rise to suspicion and a lack of trust, they became concerned with whether I would disclose information about past, ongoing, or future crimes; be it my own criminal action or theirs. Thus, most unchanged criminals made sure their conversations about illegal actions and the actual commission of violations were kept from me. In fact, occasionally I was even considered to have been an informant (a rat) by some dedicated criminals.

Once those who continued to ceaselessly think about and engage in crime began to observe change in myself many of them viewed me as having been brainwashed, others attempted to entice me back into a life of crime, and some saw me as becoming weak (they questioned my manhood). A few even attempted to attack me physically. On one occasion, a self-professed gangster offered $1200 in drugs and cash if I would draw blood on a stool pigeon I lived near. When I repeatedly rebuffed his proposition, he tried to slice me with a razor blade,

threw rocks at me, and had others spit on me.
GK Wow. Okay, and as for yourself toward unchanged prisoners?
FJA I initially continued some association with unchanged criminals, even after having instituted ingredients for change. However, as thinking and action patterns were actually modified, I began to refrain from engaging in conversations involving violation. The reason for this was twofold: (1) I needed to remain as far away as possible from any and all criminal involvement, in order to preclude temptation, and (2) I simply no longer had anything in common with unchanged criminals. If encouraged to engage in criminal talk, I usually espoused an anticrime position, and occasionally even went overboard by having assumed the role of reformer (a criminal substitute).
GK I can't imagine that went over well.
FJA As my modification progressed I was able to continue minimizing personal involvement with unchanged prisoners. Nothing remained to sustain previous common interactions. Eventually I began to share the same attitude toward unchanged criminals as most responsible people held, and wanted no contact at all. I became direct and outspoken to make this clear to those who continued any involvement with criminal or even immoral pursuits.
GK Finally, the attitude of non-criminals toward yourself?
FJA Generally, I found responsible people possess one of two drastically different attitudes toward changing criminals. Some are highly skeptical, often to the point of cynicism, and unwilling to offer any help, while others go overboard to provide aid—though in many cases these well-meaning folks are exploited and may turn skeptical. My experience has been that responsible people maintain their suspicions of me, even to the extent of refusing to believe I could or did change; I've had to accept this attitude. My focus has always had to remain on the fact that the smallest departure from total responsibility would lead to disastrous effects for myself. Consequently, I've had to remain prepared to be blamed erroneously for things simply because of my past; unjust suspicions and accusations are now foreseen and expected.

Another prominent and appreciated experience from responsible people consisted of perplexity and astonishment. Upon having openly revealed my past and then sharing my ongoing efforts to continue with the change process, I have often been regarded with respect for both my candor and effort.

GK Of course we're conducting this interview from death row. I'd still be interested in more comments about personal arenas for change. Do they transcend prison walls?
FJA Yes, here's an interesting point: when reviewing daily phenomenological reports, to deter ongoing criminal ideation, I also consider my role with others along with focus on patterns of thought. (i.e., immoral tendencies, etc., are investigated.) Whether contemplating interaction with prison staff, performance at the university or other involvements, the concerns and correctives were equally applicable and essential--change is a total package. Included must be change in patterns involving work, finances, female interactions, and friendships, so my process can be implemented anywhere.
GK Hmm, how about considering these arenas one at a time? So, work?
FJA I had to construe work (as a university student and an author) as a realm for implementing what had been learned daily in my program for change. This included the development of work and study skills (such as the ability to study and work without supervision), discovering how to work and cooperate with others, recognizing and accepting my limitations, and coping with a variety of knuckleheads, pressures, demands, and obstacles.

The discipline required in both university and work was demanding, as I learned to handle criticism, rely on my self-control, relate to hardcore murderers, and handle bias. Success was dependent upon having derived a positive impact from my work, and as a result of finally finding something gratifying in the process itself.
GK Let's now look at monetary fields.
FJA I had to learn to value and manage money, something that could not be taught, but rather had to be developed by implementing correctives for thinking errors. For example, the desire to play big shot by distributing every last penny I possessed had to be deterred. This required bringing to mind budgetary concerns: I had to purchase textbooks for classes and help my wife with bills. I simply had obligations. Consequently, there existed a need to experience financial responsibility. One corrective I implemented was having to account for all of my money, both income and expenditures, an endeavor which initially required seeking out assistance from my wife and parents to draw up and strictly adhere to a budget. As I gained experience in this monthly process, I developed an appreciation of and ability for

handling money.

GK Having referenced difficulties in relations behind bars as a changing criminal, how did social relationships serve as a setting for change?

FJA Once I'd severed ties to the criminal world (i.e., my old acquaintances) a deep sense of loneliness materialized. A partial remedy for this included taking the initiative to meet new people, but for me this constituted more challenges. For the first time in my life I had to build responsible relationships, meaning I needed to base interactions on common interests, trust, and concern for others. However, my prior life as a criminal provided little in common with responsible people and subjected me to a great deal of wariness by them. I had to consistently apply correctives for thinking errors; learn to fit my responses to a specific situation, and simply let both change in myself and trust from others develop. This was a slow but extremely rewarding experience.

GK Relations with women?

FJA Having previously perceived women as sex objects posed quite an obstacle. I had to start from scratch to locate and relate to mature women as friends rather than as potential sex partners. However, once I found levelheaded and moral women to interact with, they became additional vehicles for change. I was able to abdicate control, function interdependently, fulfill obligations, and implement other correctives that were essential to a responsible adult relationship. My entire approach changed as my thinking patterns were altered, and this positively impacted other aspects of my life.

GK What about relations and change outside of prison?

FJA I'm sorry, I've no personal experience; however, I believe the same rigorous program for change would apply.

GK How would you define the progress you've made? What virtue is prominent as a result?

FJA As a result of persistence, initiative, and endurance having been continually applied as I progressed on my program for change, I was slowly able to build a new life. Finally, a sense of self-respect began to emerge that was based on an authentic acquisition of a moral character, something which had not come easy and was highly valued.

My new life and honestly earned self-respect, along with a developing sense of inner cleanliness, eventually led to genuine liberation, to an interior freedom resulting from no longer having to endlessly deter criminal ideas. Then I became afraid of losing all

I'd attained. I no longer sabotaged evolving relationships with my family or other people. Fear became functional as a guide to responsible living. Undoubtedly, my emerging self-respect indicated a major success in the process of change; for me it was truly the onset of a productive and satisfying existence.

GK Let's conclude with discourse on major indicators of change.

FJA As can be seen from self-respect having been a significant development in the reconstruction process, change encompassed far more than merely crimelessness and participation in work, education, and religious programs. What the amendment of my entire way of existence demanded, and the key indicator of alteration having occurred, was the emergence of new thought patterns resulting in modified behavior. In other words, the extent of my participation in the change process, and the attitude I fostered, were accurate indicators of my degree of change. As I began to make headway, my mind remained wide open. I developed a self-critical attitude, and functioned with clarity rather than with vagueness. Along with this, as an early sign of change, there was the disappearance of tactics I once used to block effective transactions with responsible people.

Dream patterns also revealed the extent of my progress. There were three overlapping phases: first, I continued to experience comprehensive criminal dreams in which violation remained exciting; second, while criminal content remained, there was the actual use of deterrence within the dream—at this stage the dream visually became a nightmare in which I was either arrested or became the victim of an offense; third, dreams involving violation began to diminish and were replaced with those containing elements of daily concerns about family, work projects, and interactions with others.

GK That's fascinating. I too experienced re-programming on dream levels. You're in the middle of a robbery while dreaming, and must grab yourself and say "Stop! Put that cash back and apologize to those people."

Anyway, what areas of your change are you now able to derive satisfaction from?

FJA I'd say financial prudence, living a predominantly austere life, limiting romantic relations to one person, and still regarding myself as requiring continuation of my change program. Along with these conventional modifications I also experienced a sense of accomplishment from the decrease of angry reactions, abdication of control, and cessation of power thrusts. At this point in the change process I still apply my four basic deterrents as needed. However, the first two (aborting a crisis and preempting/disposing of criminal thinking via reasoning) are not needed as often, while the last two (moral inventories and automatic deterrence) have remained mainstays in my life.

GK Perhaps, in conclusion, you could restate the changes you've made and that we've covered.

FJA As a way to review the several dozen conversions I've worked on, yes, let's enumerate these. However, please keep in mind this list is in no way exhaustive, and is merely provided in order to aid the reader in determining how to gauge alterations in thinking patterns and resultant behavioral modifications:

1. An open mind.
2. Elimination of the victim stance.
3. Expulsion of the "I can't" attitude.
4. Achievement of a time perspective.
5. Putting forth consistent effort.
6. Placing myself in the position of others.
7. Cessation of injuring others.
8. Fulfilling obligations.
9. Eradication of the ownership attitude.
10. Generating responsibility on my own.
11. Enabling fear to guide action.
12. Basing interests on personal, responsible experiences.
13. Gaining interdependence.
14. Achieving trust (being trustworthy and trusting others).
15. Replacing pretensions with reasonable expectations.
16. Utilizing sound decision making.
17. Redistribution of energy.
18. Elimination of anger.
19. Replacing criminal pride with self-respect.
20. Discarding state-of-limbo thinking.
21. Removing the unique number one attitude.
22. Disposal of criminal power and control.
23. Acquiring excellence (not perfectionism).
24. Sustaining and expressing sentimentality responsibly.
25. Excluding inappropriate sexual ideation/fantasies.
26. Employing conceptual thinking.
27. Ceasing fragmentation.
28. Eliminating suggestibility (cutting criminal ties).

29. Changing sexual patterns.
30. Rooting out complacency.
31. Avoiding super-optimism.
32. Annihilating criminal tactics.
33. Implementing deterrents (especially moral inventories).
34. Cultivating responsible relationships.
35. Maintaining responsible money management.
36. Developing effective educational/work performance.
37. Refusing to defer ethical obligations and required initiatives.
38. Displacing criminal thinking and action.
39. Enduring adversity.
40. Accepting responsibility.

GK Frank, as a fellow death row inmate, I fully understand the recriminations your candor throughout this interview will create and commend your desire to help others.
FJA Thank you George, for both your compliment and the opportunity to mutually embark upon efforts to assist people. I pray God blesses our humble endeavor.
The End.

AFTERWORD

This comes to you at the very last minute possible. The book is at prepress and the publisher tells me mail it out today or it won't make it in the book.

Frank's health continues to deteriorate. Eighty percent of death row's population moved to another location. We're able to move around semi-freely, no cuffs or leg iorns and there are contact visits–the upgrades end there as explained below in a press release titled: Write Your Congressman–For Toilet Paper.

It's been three weeks since Frank and me parted ways and it's not like him not to write. I've sent two letters/e-mails to his wife and heard only that Frank's not doing well.

If you'd like to follow the progress visit VictimlyInsane.com and look for press releases and articles. Thank you for your interest.

Write Your Congressman–For Toilet Paper
FLORENCE, ARIZONA, UNITED STATES, August 16, 2017 /EINPresswire.com/ -- Lt. Anderson (a prison guard) tells famous author, George Kayer and other inmates on Death Row, "If you don't like the rules here, write your Congressman."

Tensions are rising and sphincters are tightening among Arizona's death row population who were recently moved (July 19th) from supermax facility at Browning unit to Central unit, another maximum custody facility.

"If you don't like the rules here, write your Congressman', said Lt. Anderson to a group of Death Row inmates seeking toilet paper."
— Lt. Anderson, Central Unit

The problems stem from the Arizona Department of Corrections (ADC) failing to honor the conditions promised to Inmates when the ADC lost yet another lawsuit by an inmate.

George Kayer, America's most published prisoner was refused a roll of toilet paper along with other inmates. Lt. Anderson (a prison guard at Arizona's Death Row) said: "If you don't like the rules here, write your congressman."

The ADC was supposed to transfer it's death row population to a lower custody, level four yard with more privileges. Instead, the ADC tricked the inmates, sending them to another max custody unit with less, not more privileges.

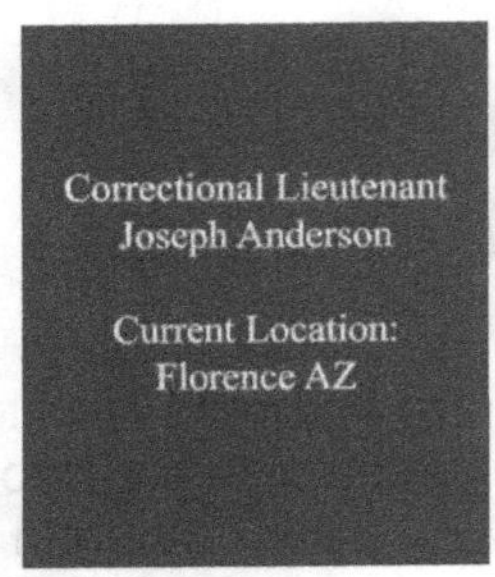

Correctional Lieutenant
Joseph Anderson
Current Location:
Florence AZ

"If you don't like the rules here, write your congressman" said Lt. Anderson to a group of Death Row inmates seeking toilet paper. One of those prisoners is America's most published prisoners- oops.

Placing some context to Lt. Anderson's quote: "Write your Congressman", Mr. Kayer, Roger Murry, (the author of Life on Death Row) and a few other Inmates were attempting to ask Lt. Anderson serious questions on August 10th 2017.

"Anderson being in a position of authority we hoped he'd have some much needed answers to our squalid living conditions," said Kayer.

The cause for much of the unrest is that the prison store at Central unit, unlike Browning unit, refuses to sell Death Row prisoners toilet paper among numerous other items promised in the lawsuit. And, Central unit passes out one ply toilet paper only once every ten days– period.

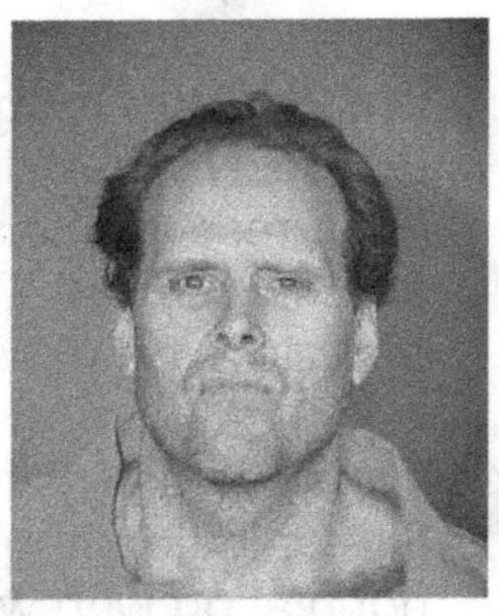

Scott Nordstrom is the man who moved Death Row. On July 19 the AZ DOC moved Death Row when Nordstrom won the conditions of confinement lawsuit March 3, 2017. See Nordstrom v. Ryan 2:15-CV-02176-DGC-J2B (10.29.15) and Id.

"I feel like we've all been tricked, including the judge. Guys here are killing six to eight large cockroaches in their cells everyday! My cell rarely gets below 88-90 degrees and cells here are 6x10: dog kennels are larger.

Look, employee attitudes flow from the top down. All these problems can be solved with one signature and 30 minutes on a computer."

APPENDIX

GLOSSARY

- A -

Admin.: Prison Administration, at the local level: a Warden, Deputy Warden, or Associate Deputy Warden. At the prison's headquarters (Central Office in Phoenix) the Admin. involves the prison Director's level.
ADW: Associate Deputy Warden, serves directly under a Deputy Warden.
Analytic Persuasion: A method of reasoning relying on analysis to reach or bolster strongly held opinions.
Antecedent: That which precedes an occurrence or cause.
Antisocial Personality Disorder: In general, a mental illness wherein sufferers exhibit, among other things, pervasive abuses of others' rights. In Frank Atwood's specific case, the prerequisite of having been diagnosed with conduct disorder by age fifteen was not met; consequently, experts for Frank testified he did not have this disorder.

- B -

Belly Chains: A chain around an inmate's waist (secured by a padlock) and having handcuffs attached on either side. These serve to restrain prisoners whose medical condition precludes the use of handcuffs behind the back.
Brentwood: Where Frank was raised in Los Angeles; this locale is next to ultra-rich Bel Air and Beverly Hills.
Browning Unit: Prisons in Arizona are arranged in Complexes (several Units comprise a Complex), and Browning is one of the Units in Eyman Complex.

- C -

Cellblock Six: A Unit in Florence Complex (a few miles from Eyman Complex); locale of death row from 1986 to 1997.
Closed Custody: Inmate housing level with limited movement and work opportunities; created to minimize public risk of harm to - and by - inmates; death row has been reduced from maximum to closed custody.
Chow Hall: A centralized area, separate from housing buildings, where prisoners go for meals.

Complex: A standalone cluster of several Units constitutes a Complex, (e.g., Eyman Complex includes five Units).
Concrete Thinking: The perception of people, institutions, and events as separate, isolated entities, (e.g., school as a discrete location sans conceptualization of preparation for life).
Condemned Row: Also, death row, where inmates sentenced to death reside. Used as an adjective to identify someone sentenced to be executed.
Conduct Disorder: A mental illness defined by a continued pattern of action that violates the rights of individuals and society.
Confirmation: The Episcopal Church confirms adherents at about age twelve via a ceremony to indicate faithfulness to and knowledge of its tenets.
Con of Assent: (Con as in confidence "con artist") Providing apparent agreement, when inwardly opposing views are held; a means of deceiving someone (especially authority figures).
Contagion Theory: In general terms, peer pressure; being influenced by external forces.
Cortical Immaturity: An organic brain disease affecting a person's behavior.
Criminal Causation: Reasons for crime; organic, sociologic, and so on.
Criminal Substitutes: Action(s) other than overt crime to satisfy the craving for control and excitement; usually involves something enabling dominance.
Cut Off: A process of consciously extinguishing deterrents prior to committing a criminal act.

- D -

Deterrents: Obstructive factors to crime on external and internal levels: (1) internal deterrence functions as a restraint to crime based on conscience; (2) external deterrence generally involves fear of being caught.
DW: Deputy Warden, the chief Unit Administrator who works under a Complex Warden, or Unit Warden in the same cases.

- E -

Equivocation: Defined by ambiguity, so as to communicate in vague, noncommittal terms or manner.
Erosion: The process of eradicating internal/external deterrents; occurs between deterrence and cut off.

Evaluating Interrogators: Examining an inquisitor during interrogation, looking for characteristics that would help a suspect manipulate the interviewer so as to avoid revelation of information.
Exactitude: Being exact, perfectionistic in action. Meticulous precision.
Eyman Complex: One of a dozen or so Complexes in the Arizona Department of Corrections' prison system, each with several units.

- F -

Fedex: A prisoner whose job is pod porter or porter. Their delivery of items from cell to cell gave rise to the moniker based on the iconic Fed Ex®. The practice violates prison rules, but porters nevertheless risk accepting pay or gratuities from inmates to supplement their 10 cents per hour income.
Flagitious: Shamefully wicked or particularly heinous.
Fragmentation: Rapid changes in thinking, frequently resulting in starting but never completing activities. It can impact a person's opinions of objects, situations or other people (e.g., one instant someone is a friend, the next moment a foe). The key is "rapidly changing."
Frontal Lobe Dysfunctions: An organic brain disease characterized by alteration in aggression or other functioning.
Front Cuffing: The use of standard handcuffs to restrain an inmate while his hands are in front of him. The default restraint method is handcuffing behind the back.
Fishing: The use of a line to pass items between cells in lockdown units.

- G -

Genetic Causation: A form of criminality based on inherent, genetic factors.
George/Henry Clusters: In Browning Unit, there are twelve Clusters (A-L), each Cluster holds six pods, and each pod houses ten prisoners. George and Henry are where condemned row inmates were housed after moving to Browning Unit in 1997.
Greek Orthodox Christianity: The original Christianity established by the Son of God in the first century and spread by Apostle Paul, et al, c. 50-54 in Asia Minor (now Turkey) and Greece. It is Greek, or Eastern, Christianity, as distinguished from Western (Roman, Latin) Catholicism and Protestantism. First century Christians all knew the Faith as an interior purification/illumination via God's grace, whereas the West

deviated from this Truth to undertake an intellectual pursuit (i.e., "knowing" God through one's fallen human mind).

- H -

Hereditary Causation: Crime due to inherited factors.

- I -

I Can't: A stance actually meaning I won't (I don't want to), used to escape distasteful thought or action.
Ideation: To ideate, to form an idea.
Inimical: Something harmful, or hostile.
Insuperable Confidence: Also called super-optimism; a criminal's state of extreme confidence, giving rise to the belief that they will not be caught for the crime they are about to commit.

- J -

Juvenile Facility: Commonly known as Juvenile Hall, "Juvie", where inmates under the age of eighteen are held.

- K -

Kite: A form known as an Inmate Letter; used to communicate in writing with prison staff, or a note informally sent to someone else (usually to another prisoner).

- L -

Levels: A ranking of degree of security in prisons. An inmate sentenced to death will be classified as Level 5 maximum custody or Level 4 closed custody.

- M -

Maximum Custody: Inmates posing the highest public and/or institutional risk are assigned to a Level 5 maximum custody building where they average over 23 hours a day locked in a cell.
M'Naghten Rule: The insanity defense basis stipulating that one cannot be held criminally responsible if unable to understand his/her actions or to know an act is wrong.
Momentary Purification: A temporary state during which a lapse in the commission of overt crimes occurs.

- N -

No Internet Access: Prisoners on death row in Arizona have virtually no access; no MP3, iPhone, email, texts, or Google. Communication is by visitation, mail, and phone, while research is via books, magazines or news programs.

- O -

Obfuscation of Communications: Tactics employed to interject confusion in communication for the purpose of withholding sensitive, secret data, often relating to culpability.
Oedipal Guilt: In general terms, guilt from sexual desire.
Open Yard: A prison environment in which Level 3 or lower (medium or minimum custody) prisoners are housed, and where movement to recreation, work, etc. is virtually free-flowing.
Organic Causation: Crime stemming from biological conditions, such as brain damage.

- P -

Parasitism: The habit of constantly taking advantage of others.
Patterns of Confinement: Methods and strategies of a particular inmate defining how he/she functions in prison.
Phenomenological Reporting: Applied herein to the daily journaling of thoughts, feelings, actions. A basis for exposing and studying behavioral or thinking errors so that correctives can be applied.
Pod: The ten-man living area for inmates in Browning; each Cluster contains six pods; included in each is a 22' x11' exercise pen with 20' high solid concrete walls and a mesh ceiling.
Positivist Movement: A c. 19th century science studying the cause of criminality, be it biologic, sociologic, genetic, etc.
Post-Traumatic Stress Disorder: (PTSD), a major mental illness impacting daily functioning. Onset transpires from experiencing trauma (war, sexual assault, emotional or physical abuse, etc.), and sets of intrusion symptoms ensue (anxiety, rage, avoidance, et al.) that severely disrupt functioning. Frank Atwood developed PTSD from four sexual assaults as a teen.
Psychoanalysis: A school of psychology studying how childhood experience impacts thinking patterns in later life. A method of studying the mind and treating mental and emotional disorders based on revealing and investigating the role of the unconscious mind.
Psychosomatic: Physical ailments generated by emotional or mental causes.
Put-Downs: Perceived insults stimulated by situations in which loss of control transpired.

- R -

Rear Cuffing: Handcuffs applied while a prisoner's hands are behind his/her back; the method of restraint in maximum custody, unless medical conditions dictate otherwise.
Responsibility: The aim for criminals; a state of dependability and accountability emerging as the process of change unfolds.

- S -

Skoufo: A Greek Orthodox head covering symbolizing God's protection and encouraging humility by its wearer.
Sociologic Causation: Understanding crime as instigated from external sources; societal conditions, environmental factors (e.g., poverty), familial and other relations, etc.
Store: Inmate Commissary; available items are significantly limited for all maximum custody prisoners. Merchandise can be purchased weekly and limits range from $60-$100, depending on privilege level.

- T -

Thematic: Often, but not necessarily, restricted to communication where a set motif for topics dominates.
The Row: A euphemism for death/condemned row.
Time Perspective: In the current work, this refers to awareness of the amount of time spent on a specific task.

- U -

Unchanged Felon: A criminal who maintains his negative path and criminal thought patterns.
Unit: A building within a Complex; for instance. Browning, a max custody Unit holding 800-900 inmates.

- V -

Vainglory: Excessive pride, often displayed in a grandiose manner. Used herein to indicate the attitude of perceiving oneself as a unique number one.
Victim Stance: The attitude of a criminal who concocts specious reasons to excuse unlawful acts, blames others for his transgressions, or attempts avoiding accountability in other ways.
Victimly Insane: A term covering the various mental disorders associated with having been a victim of crime.

- W -

Warden: The top official of a Complex, supervises the chief Unit leader (Deputy Warden).

PERSONAL COMMENTS ABOUT SEXUAL ASSAULT RESEARCH; SPECIFICALLY, IN WHAT CIRCUMSTANCES ARE QUESTIONS ASKED.

As a 20+ year resident of Death Row and having been arrested a few times, I've had plenty of experiences answering a questionnaire on a clipboard. When a criminal of average intellect is being processed into county jail or prison and staring at a questionnaire; the last thing a criminal will do is check off a box that would possibly trigger a red flag, thus creating more problems or charges and potentially delaying one's release.

How arrestee's answer specific questions about their sexual abuse as a child will vary considerably due to their circumstances:

1. What drug they're high on.
2. Level of intoxication.
3. How well they understand their Miranda Rights.
4. The number of hours or days after arrest.
5. What crimes they're currently being charged with.
6. Who asks the questions, the police officer or the defendant's attorney.

The importance of who asks the question may be evidenced in comparing two similar studies/questions, one by the Bureau of Justice Statistics (BJS) in April of 1999. View at:
https://www.bjs.gov/content/pub/pdf/parip.pdf

In the chart labeled, prior abuse of correctional populations, by sex, it reads 16.1 percent of males in state prisons had been abused.

*Answers provided by Inmates and Probationers.

In a more recent North Carolina study by Baumgartner and Neil (2017), reviewing 1435 capital trials (mitigation evidence?) 77.9 percent of defendants provided evidence of at least one (abuse) adverse childhood experience (ACE).

"According to our research, Death Row Inmates were far more likely to have suffered the more traumatic ACE's such as sexual abuse."

The North Carolina Study moves us closer to more accurate numbers but their case studies were from 1999 to 2016. My theory is older criminals like myself still believe in privacy and many of the questions asked are nobodies damn business. Today's generation posts their whole life on social media and have little to zero understanding of my concept of privacy.

As this new generation of people–criminals cycle through the jails, courts and prisons, our statisticians are receiving more accurate (truthful) data to questions of abuse.

From my experience, I knew the best source of data to my questions was Mitigation Specialist. These folks spend more time with capital case defendants than anyone else, and it's their job to identify abuse in their client's backgrounds.

APPENDIX 1

POST-TRAUMATIC STRESS DISORDER AND MENTAL ILLNESS

Post-Traumatic Stress Disorder (PTSD)

PTSD is a major mental illness that can cause impaired functioning (p. 19 at li. 4-5).

Expert testimony in October of 2013 served as the culmination of evaluations of Frank Jarvis Atwood (FJA), along with reports and depositions. Of special import must be the qualifications of each expert.

FJA's legal team retained Dr. Donna Schwartz-Watts (changed post-remarriage to Schwartz-Maddox). This eminently qualified, nationally renowned psychiatrist brought the following superlative qualifications:

- Possesses expertise, specializes in sexual disorders (p. 8 at li. 9-15).[7]
- Studied sexual disorders under a top expert (p. 8 at li. 15-18).
- Was granted a Rappeport Fellow Scholarship. Only four promising forensic psychiatry residents in the U.S. received this honor that year, (p. 9 at 6-7, 9-11, 14-15).
- As a Rappeport Fellow Dr. Schwartz-Maddox was mentored by the same paraphilia (sexual disorder) expert cited above (p. 9 at li. 20-21).
- From the onset of South Carolina's Sexual Violent Predator (SVP) statute in 1999 Dr. Schwartz-Maddox conducted all evaluations for 6-7 years (p. 9 at li. 24-25; p. 10 at li. 1-4).
- Treated SVP's for South Carolina's Department of Mental Health (p. 10 at li. 5-7).

[7] Page and line cites reference the 07 October 2013 hearing transcript; United States District Court (District of Arizona), Case No. C-98-00116-TUC-JCC.

- Presently performs SVP pre-release evaluations for the Department of Mental Health (p. 10 at li. 11-15).
- Worked at the Department of Juvenile Justice, the Department of Corrections, and the SVP unit (p. 12 at li. 10-12).
- Currently treats patients with PTSD and treats victims of childhood sexual trauma (p. 12 at li. 21-25).
- South Carolina's National Advocacy Center trains all U.S. Attorneys. Dr. Schwartz-Maddox writes reports for their training and serves as a mock defense expert (p. 13 at li. 18-21, 25; p. 14 at li. 2-4).
- Dr. Schwartz-Maddox trains lawyers at the South Carolina Attorney General's Office on Internet sexual crimes (p. 14 at li. 4-6).

The government called psychologist Dr. Erin Nelson, whose credentials merely included:

- A psychology doctorate degree from Argosy University, lowly ranked at 209 out of 217 programs by the Social Psychology Network (p. 4 at li. 13-15; p. 83 at li. 4-5, 7-8).[8]
- Currently treating one PTSD patient (p. 176 at li. 18-22, hearing transcript).
- Currently treating one sexual abuse patient, the same PTSD patient (p. 176 at li. 23-25; p. 177 at li. 1-2).
- Has not published anything on PTSD, sexual trauma, effects (p. 214 at li. 13-18).
- In 2013 was treating only two patients (p. 214 at li. 3-5).

The distinction between preeminent expert and unqualified government servant could not be more obvious and unequivocal.

Both Dr. Schwartz-Maddox and Dr. Nelson testified at the fall of

[8] This fact has been extracted from Dr. Nelson's August of 2013 deposition.

2013 hearing about PTSD generalities. Here's a summary:

The highest causes of PTSD are war and sexual trauma (p. 65 at li. 20-24; p. 216 at li. 14-16).

Up to 80% of PTSD sufferers have a co-morbid condition (p. 66 at li. 2-4).

PTSD involves pre-trauma risk factors, the trauma, and post-trauma risk factors (p. 79 at li. 3-5, 7-10).

Pre-trauma risk factors include childhood emotional and mental health problems (p. 79 at li. 11-18; p. 217 at li. 8-10).

FJA's mother endured a miscarriage and FJA at age 8 developed emotional and mental troubles (p. 80 at li. 18, 21-25) [pre-trauma risk factor].

FJA's sexual assault at age 14 [1970] satisfies, on its own, PTSD gatekeeper criterion (p. 20 at li. 9-10; p. 218 at li. 14-19) [the trauma].

Law enforcement personnel forced FJA to testify against his attacker in 1970 (p. 25 at li. 18-20; p. 158 at li. 13-17).

He suffered three additional assaults at ages 16 and 19 (1972 and 1975) (p. 162 at li. 10-11)[9]; underwent continued pressure for sex in-custody as a teen (p. 162 at li. 12-19) [post-trauma risk factors].

The pre/post-trauma risk factors FJA experienced increased the likelihood of PTSD (p. 217 at li. 25; p. 218 at li. 1-3; p. 222 at li. 1-4).

Within a year of FJA's initial age 14 rape he was being treated by a psychologist for PTSD and had been hospitalized in two

[9] This cite, and the ensuant one (re sexual pressure), are from Dr. Nelson's June of 2013 evaluation.

psychiatric institutions (p. 97 at li. 18-21, 24-25).

Post-Traumatic Stress Disorder, in addition to pre/post-trauma risk factors, possesses a set of eight criteria (A-H). Much hearing testimony centered on these factors and how FJA met each of them. It is precisely here that we learn of the mental illness he suffered and continually strives to overcome. Consequently, as the means by which to rip the façade off FJA, to clearly observe the depth of his disorder, the remainder of this section will focus on FJA fitting all PTSD criteria.

1. Criterion A

This item requires exposure to sexual violence (p. 20 at li. 3-5).

FJA was kidnapped and molested by force in 1970, at age 14; the perpetrator was convicted (p. 20 at li. 9-10; p. 23 at li. 16-18; 22-25; p. 24 at li. 1-2, 14-17).

Three additional assaults were experienced by FJA, two at age 16 and the other at age 19 (p. 118 at li. 1-6, 10, 15-20; p. 33 at li. 7-10, 12-15; p. 33 at li. 16-23).

2. Criterion B

Here dwell "intrusion symptoms." FJA has two (p. 40 at li. 21-23; p. 41 at li. 4).

When reminded of his sexual assaults, he experiences intense and prolonged distress in the form of anxiety, a psychological manifestation (p. 41 at li. 5-11, 13).

FJA suffers physiologic distress by fearing attack, so exits his cell less often (p. 41 at li. 19-21; p. 42 at li. 6-7; 19-20).

These reactive (to cues of sexual trauma) manifestations of fear and anxiety are observable and were evidenced by the Minnesota Multi-Phasic Personality Inventory Two test (MMPI-2)—anxiety as demonstrating PTSD (p. 94 at li. 4-11, 22-23; p. 95 at li. 1-2, 4-5).

3. Criterion C

This pertains to avoiding stimuli associated with the sexual trauma (p. 43 at li. 21-23).

The first of two avoidance features for FJA is not dealing with distressing memories and thoughts; the other involves avoidance of interaction with inmates (p. 43 at li. 23-25; p. 44 at li. 3, 5-9).

4. Criterion D

Here reside negative alterations in cognition, how one thinks (or the mood experienced), and FJA suffers several (p. 44 at li. 10-13, 15).

- He blames himself for his sexual assaults (p. 44 at li. 20-21; p. 111 at li. 3-6, 10-12).
- Endures a persistent, exaggerated negative belief of himself and the world (p. 44 at li. 16-17).
- The inability to trust authority after the rape. (p. 44 at li. 18-20).
- Rebelliousness and anger; demonstrated by explosive outbursts with little or no provocation; demanding body language; presentation of hostility (p. 44 at li. 2-25; p. 45 at li. 3-6; p. 58 at li. 13-14; p. 215 at li. 22-25; p. 216 at li. 1, 4-5).

5. Criterion E

This is a marked alteration in arousal and reactivity; that is, an alteration linked to the sexual trauma that demonstrates visible physiologic manifestation (p. 56 at li. 9-10, 16-19).

FJA displays:

i. Irritable behavior (p. 56 at li. 20).

ii. Angry outbursts with little or no provocation (p. 56 at li. 20-21).

iii. Verbal or physical aggression toward people or objects

(p. 56 at li. 21-22).

iv. Inability to regulate emotions (p. 222 at li. 10-13).

v. Hypervigilance, scanning of environment for danger (p. 57 at li. 7-9; p. 222 at li. 1-19).

vi. Sleep disturbance (p. 58 at li. 1-2).

vii. Reckless, self-destructive behavior:

viii. Extreme substance abuse (p. 90 at li. 9-11, 18-20).

ix Prostitution (p. 27 at li. 16-18, 23-24; p. 28 at li. 16, 22-24; p. 59 at li. 13, 15-16; p. 60 at li. 2-3).

x Dangerous driving (p. 216 at li. 6-9, 12-13).

xi Self-harm (p. 223 at li. 23-25).

6. Criterion F

Symptoms must persist for over one month (p. 63 at li. 10-11, 15) [age 14 sexual trauma to 2013 MMPI-2 test obviously transcends one month].

7. Criterion G

PTSD impact impairs functioning (p. 63 at li. 10-11, 22-23).

FJA's daily life has been disrupted by PTSD in three ways:

a) Occupational: FJA possesses virtually no employment history (p. 64 at li. 8-13).

b) Societal: FJA endures social impairment and was treated while in Atascadero State Hospital

(p. 64 at li. 20-23; p. 65 at li. 1-2, 8-9). Additionally:

- A 1973 psych report identified FJA as providing inadequate, ineffective social responses, is PTSD numbing (p. 46 at li. 6-8, 15-17, 23-25; p.47 at li. 1-3).

- A 1979 psych report found FJA harbored great anxiety, evidencing social inadequacy and an absence of social skills (p. 48 at li. 13-17, 19-20; p. 49 at li. 1-2).
- Atascadero records document a lack of social skills (p. 58 at li. 7, 14-15).
- The MMPI-2 test points to FJA's introversion, shyness, difficulty in meeting others, and uneasiness in social situations (p. 96 at li. 2-8).

c) Educational: FJA suffered significant impairment in this realm, was even said to have required professional help in 1973 (p. 89 at li. 4-8, 15-16, 21-22); moreover, subsequent to sexual trauma FJA attended six private schools (p. 88 at li. 21-22).

8. Criterion H

PTSD did not occur due to substance abuse or a medical condition (p. 65 at li. 10-12) [neither expert asserted drugs or medical as a source of FJA's PTSD].

Mental Illness

Noteworthy must be the categorical falsity of government's attempt to misdiagnose FJA with antisocial personality disorder and pedophilia.

Antisocial Personality Disorder: The fact of FJA not having been diagnosed with conduct disorder prior to age 15 precludes FJA having the antisocial diagnosis (p. 91 at li. 13-14, 23-25; p. 92 at li. 1-4, 7).

Consideration of an antisocial diagnosis for FJA needs to

account for the substance abuse and avoidant personality disorder co-morbidity negating an antisocial personality disorder (p. 92 at li. 9-11, 14-17).

Avoidance is inconsistent with antisocial. Those with antisocial personality disorder are extroverted and enjoy more relationships than does FJA (p. 96 at li. 13-16).

Both FJA's post-sexual trauma interpersonal difficulties and failure of the MMPI-2 test to cite antisocial personality disorder negates diagnosing FJA with this mental illness (p. 94 at li. 12-13; p. 219 at li. 5-10).

Pedophilia: Reasons to not diagnose FJA in this way included:

a) His prior convictions being old with few details, so questions remain (p. 68 at li. 12-16).

b) Atascadero identifying FJA's sex offending as a consequence of teen rebellion and extensive substance abuse (p. 69 at li. 3-4, 8-11, 17-19, 22-25; p. 70 at li. 1-2); treatment involved much therapy on FJA's relations with his parents to reduce rebellion potential (p. 70 at li. 13-15, 17-18).

Other Mental Illness: FJA records demonstrate rampant mental health debilities:

- 1974 pre-sentence report notes the ordering of a full-scale psychiatric study and indicates the obvious need for treatment.
- 1979 parole report spoke of FJA's psych treatment requirement.
- 1979 parole recommendation on FJA's need for psych treatment and meds.
- 1981 probation report documenting at age 16 FJA required psychotherapy, for bizarre behavior displays, and a court ordered psych evaluation.

- June 1984 parole notice of conditions showing a history of psych problems necessitating outpatient care requirements.
- May 1987 pre-sentence report validated FJA's history of significant mental problems since his early teen years.

Interestingly, the MMPI-2 test evidenced elevated anxiety levels for FJA, which are not inconsistent with PTSD; yet the test did not support an antisocial personality disorder diagnosis (p. 27 at li. 23, 25; p. 28 at li. 1-2, 4-6, 15-18; p. 29 at li. 3-5, 10, 17-19).[10]

During Dr. Nelson's June of 2013 evaluation of FJA, discourse transpired regarding his drastic changes having spewed from the initial sexual trauma at age 14 ½ and concomitant PTSD: Prior to having been kidnapped and raped, FJA attended one elementary school for grades 1-6 and was congratulated for high grades along with outstanding conduct, which included participation, as a most valuable player, in Pop Warner football, Little League baseball, and ice hockey. Yet, after having been traumatized, he attended six schools over a three-year period, his model behavior turned into counterculture attacks on governmental installations and extreme substance abuse; his musical talent (FJA played trumpet, cello, and piano) became involvement in the decadent rock music scene; attendance at St. Albans Episcopal Church morphed into practice in occult movements; family activities were traded for crime. The day to night drastic, sudden change due to PTSD is clearly evident.

A final point must be made: FJA was found, by government's expert and the MMPI-2 test, to be totally candid and honest (p. 188 at li. 3-4, 11, 16-20; see end of Introduction).

[10] These cites are from Dr. Nelson's deposition, August of 2013.

CONTROL UNIT PRISONS

BY FRANK JARVIS ATWOOD

In the 1840's, Charles Dickens toured the Eastern State Penitentiary (an isolation prison) and remarked: "I hold this slow and daily tampering with the mysteries of the brain to be immeasurably worse than any physical torture of the body."

Control units are supermax prisons designed to control the thinking of prisoners through carefully contrived sensory deprivation tactics and focusing of the prisoners' attention on immediate concerns. It is precisely these strategies that disable prisoners via a psychological, physical, and spiritual breakdown as the means by which to compel mindless compliance. These exercises in demoralization expose prison officials as master manipulators of inmates' lives; with this control over housing assignments, medical care, food, property, mail, recreation, and other conditions, each prisoner is relegated to government imposed inferiority in order for authority's goal to be met: the crushing of the human spirit and hope.

The concept of employing isolation and sensory deprivation as methods to control prisoners originated in the 1820's with the Eastern State Penitentiary, in Philadelphia, with the construction of the "Pennsylvania Model" prison (the prevailing belief centered on solitary confinement inducing remorse and rehabilitation). However, it soon became evident, use of these conditions compelled mental collapse and insanity. The 1830's found Charles Darwin visiting an isolation unit, observations prompted him to explain: "the prisoners seemed dead to everything but the torturing anxiety and horrible despair." Upon the heels of these devastating portraits of solitary confinement flowed literature in Germany, between 1854-1909, which concluded that isolation resulted in hallucinations (visual, auditory, tactile, and olfactory), disassociation, hysteria, agitation, motor excitement, aimless violence, persecutory delusions, self-harm, and psychosis (J. Ganser, *Arch Psychiatr Nervenkr 1898*). These condemnations culminated in an 1890 U.S. Supreme Court decision; sensory deprivation and solitary confinement caused violent insanity, the Court denounced the practice and in 1913 confinement in isolation was officially abolished.

Tragically, in 1962, a professor of psychology at the Massachusetts Institute of Technology, Edgar Schein, suggested physical, psychological, and chemical techniques could be utilized against prisoners to alter behavior and attitude. Schein was an internationally known expert on psychological coercion, having conducted extensive studies on the torture and brainwashing techniques used on American prisoners during the Korean War. Schein proposed the isolation and sensory deprivation of prisoners to destroy socialization and to sever links with the outside world – because humans validate their existence and personality through contact with others the imposition of solitary confinement visits detrimental impact upon the human psyche. Schein's unconscionable form of psychological disorientation was called the "Muttnik Principle" by psychologist Nathaniel Braden, it also came to be known as the "Psychology of Invisibility" (the purposeful removal of others to curb self-validation).

Others built on Schein's atrocities by suggesting the use of powerful psychotropic medications to mentally isolate and physically control prisoners. University of Michigan psychologist James V. McConnell followed up on this suggestion with an article entitled *Criminals can be Brainwashed (Psychology Today*, April 1970), which was followed by Harvard psychologist B.F. Skinner's 1971 book, *Beyond Freedom and Dignity*, in which he discussed manipulating the mind like clay.

These ungodly developments soon received support from former U.S. Bureau of Prisons Director Bennett's determination that the prison system served as an ideal locale for human experimentation on brainwashing. Consequently, federal prison psychologist Martin Groder transferred prisoners to solitary confinement; if compliance ensued then privileges were granted, otherwise, the psychological torture continued. Prison authorities aimed at sensory feedback reduction to create predictable cracks in prisoner's mental defense mechanisms, fissures they filled with government propaganda. Jessica Mitford, in *The Torture Cure: In Some American Prisons it is already 1984* (Harper's, August 1973), detailed results of a laboratory experiment designed to test the effects of sensory deprivation on the mind:

> Sensory deprivation, as a behavior modifier, was the subject of an experiment in which students were paid twenty dollars to live in tiny solitary cubicles with nothing to do. The experiment was to last at least six weeks, but none of the students could last for more than a few days. Many experienced vivid

> hallucinations . . . [and] the students were fed propaganda messages. No matter how poorly the messages were presented, or how illogical the messages sounded, the propaganda had a marked effect on the attitudes of all students – an effect that lasted for at least one year after they came out of the experiment.

The initial federal lockdown unit was Marion, Ill., an experimental project for developing programs to mentally break prisoners; by 1983 prisoners averaged 22 ½ hrs. daily in their cells. The early 1980's also witnessed various states erecting control units; by 1996 there existed more than forty control units housing some 15,000 prisoners, an abomination into which the feds rejoined when opening Administrative Maximum in Florence, Colorado, in 1994 (prisoners received three hours of recreation three times a week).

Biderman's Chart on Penal Coercion (reprinted in 1983 by *Amnesty International's Report on Torture*) divided the systematic torture tactics into eight sections (each section possessing two subsections, one labelled "Purpose" and the other identifying "Variants"). The remainder of this article will concentrate on Biderman's blueprint.

1. Isolation
   Purpose: Deprivation of support from other prisoners and the outside world to both obstruct the ability to resist and compel absolute dependence on captors.
   Variants: Use of solitary confinement through isolation, partial isolation, or group isolation.
2. Monopolization of Perception
   Purpose: Fixation of attention on immediate predicaments and the elimination of stimuli competing with captor propaganda.
   Variants: Isolation, lights on in cells 24 hrs. a day, restricted movement, bland food in limited amounts, and furtherance of sensory deprivation via windowless cells.
3. Induced Exhaustion & Debility
   Purpose: Weakening the physical and mental ability to resist.
   Variants: Reduced caloric intake, exploitation of pre-

existing injuries, sleep deprivation, exposure to climate extremes (e.g., no coat, gloves, or head cover in freezing conditions), and intentionally inadequate health care.

4. Threats
   Purpose: Cultivating anxiety and despair.
   Variants: Verbal threats, occasional physical assault by guards, rewards for compliance, disclosure of confidential information to trigger abusive attacks by other inmates, use of random searches, and urine analysis testing.
5. Occasional Indulgence
   Purpose: Motivation of compliance, deterring adjustment to set conditions.
   Variants: Doing favors, constant fluctuation of attitudes (e.g., cessation of cell searches, making small talk, extra recreation) to make knowing what to expect impossible.
6. Demonstration of Omnipotence
   Purpose: To evidence the futility of resistance.
   Variants: Officer confrontations toward inmates, failure to follow written policies, trumped up disciplinary charges, and indefinite assignment to supermax (the snitch, parole, or die, one's sole opportunity for control unit departure).
7. Degradation
   Purpose: Guards showing prisoners the cost of resistance is far more damaging than capitulation to one's self-esteem, reduction of inmates to animal level concerns.
   Variants: Impositions on personal hygiene, a filthy environment, demeaning punishments, lack of privacy (even when using toilet), and taken out-of-cell only when restrained and under guard escort.
8. Enforcement of Trivial Demands
   Purpose: Development of compliance habits.
   Variants: Strict adherence to petty rules, seizure of authorized property, destruction of items during searches, and fabricated disciplinary reports.

Today's foremost expert on the results of solitary confinement, Harvard Medical School faculty member Dr. Stuart Grassian, authored an article in 1983, *Psychopathological Effects of Solitary Confinement*, wherein he described barbarous consequences from prison sensory deprivation conditions. In general, Dr. Grassian pointed to restlessness, banging on walls and yelling (as seen with caged animals), incoherent states of confusion, assaultiveness, hallucinations, disassociation, and withdrawn hypnoid states. Some data resulted from his study of prisoners in a control unit for an average of only two months; imagine 10, 20, 30 years – it's happening! Dr. Grassian observed cutting, other methods of self-mutilation, hypersensitivity to external stimuli (lights causing discomfort, noise inflicting irritation), perceptual distortions, derealization, partial amnesia, degradation of memory and concentration, paranoia, and fantasies of aggressive revenge (torture/mutilation of guards) – Dr. Grassian found that 80% of prisoners in solitary confinement suffered massive increases in pre-existing mental illnesses and developed symptoms associated with reduced environmental stimuli, a psychiatric condition characterized by above cited symptoms.

The *American Journal of Psychiatry* confirmed Dr. Grassian's conclusions and the current article's author (having been in supermax for over thirty years) experiences, in addition to the pathologies supra, headaches, poor impulse control, depression, anti-social attitudes, and personality changes. Undoubtedly, control unit prisons cause severe mental breakdown, and do so with the full knowledge of government; rather than corrective action, government enacted the Prison Litigation Reform Act to specifically exclude lawsuits by prisoners for mental damage absent physical injury. Our government, your congressman, has consciously sanctioned both psychological torture and its resulting devastation on our sons, daughters, and neighbors in control unit prisons.

Mr. Atwood is a victim of child rape, was arrested in 1984, ended up on death row, and since then has resided in supermax prisons. He earned a three-year theology degree from an Orthodox Christian seminary, a bachelor (as a pre-law English major), and a master in literature. Frank has also written several books on Eastern Christian theology. Please visit www.churchfathertheology.com. Two books are due out in 2017 about Mr. Atwood's life: Freebird Publishers and Macheras monastery (in Cyprus) publisher.

FJA Mental Illness

Sex Offenses
1976 Atascadero State Hospital (ASH) record related these to rebellion/hostility by FJA toward his parents.
1977 ASH record noted teen rebellion and drugs, advising therapy on family relations.

Mental Problems
June 1973 - school report: FJA needs professional help.
February 1975 – Atascadero State Hospital report on FJA at Resthaven psychiatric hospital at age 15 in 1971.
1974 – pre-sentence report on full-scale psychiatric study ordered and FJA in obvious need of treatment.
May 1979 – parole report: FJA required to undergo psychiatric treatment, plus medication.
1981 – probation report: FJA at 16 demonstrated bizarre behavior: court-ordered psychiatric evaluation.
July 1982 – California prison report on FJA in-custody treatment.
June 1984 – parole condition notice on history of mental problems: requires outpatient care.
May 1987 – pre-sentence report: FJA history of significant mental illness since early teens.
January 2013 – Dr. Schwartz-Maddox report on FJA's PTSD diagnosis.

Psychiatric Medication

1975 Stelazine	2012 Buspar (still on it)
1999 Amitriptyline	2014 Nortriptyline
2008 Desipramine	2014 Tegretol
2011 Zoloft	2016 Paxil

Dr. Erin Nelson CV Review**

Doctorate from Argosy, an institution ranked extremely low (209 out of 217) by Social Psychology Network
Currently treating one patient with PTSD; same one has sexual trauma history.
Never published on PTSD, sexual trauma, and their effects.

** State's expert at 2013 hearing.

Dr. Nelson 6/26/13 FJA Evaluation

FJA saw Dr. Brandt at age 14 in 1970 (after rape) for sexual trauma and drug use.
Brandt recommended Melrose School (for emotionally disturbed kids), FJA attended from ages 14 ½ -15 ½.
Several months pre-1970 assault FJA tried barbiturates a few times and marijuana once.
The early 1970 initial drug use was pot once and downers less than a handful of times.
FJA was sexually assaulted 4 times and suffered continued sexual pressure.
FJA drastic changes from 1970 rape.

Dr. Nelson 8/15/13 Deposition

MMPI-2 test: Does not support antisocial personality disorder; elevated FJA anxiety levels consistent w/ PTSD.
Dr. Nelson knew of antisocial prerequisite. FJA not diagnosed with conduct disorder.

FJA truthfulness: MMPI-2 test, called by Dr. Nelson (who administered it) "the gold-standard personality test," which established FJA as truthful. Dr. Nelson also verified FJA was forthcoming and truthful.

Dr. Donna Schwartz-Watts CV[11] (9 pages) not included.

Overview of Dr. Schwartz-Maddox's Qualifications
Expert specializing in sexual disorders.
Studied sexual paraphilia (disorders); mentored by prominent expert.
Rappeport Fellow, an award given to promising forensic (i.e., how psychiatry and law intermingle) psychiatric students; only 4 in USA that year.
From onset of South Carolina sexual violent predator (SVP) law did all S. Carolina evaluations for 6-7 years.
Treated SVP's at South Carolina Department of Mental Health.

---

[11] Changed name to Schwartz-Maddox (remarried), is expert called by FJA at 2013 mental health mitigation hearing.

Currently does Department of Mental Health SVP evaluations.
At present working at South Carolina Department of Corrections SVP unit.
Now treats both patients with PTSD and sexual trauma histories.
The South Carolina National Advocacy Center trains all US attorneys; Dr. Schwartz-Maddox writes training reports and serves as mock defense expert.
Trains South Carolina Attorney General's Office staff on sexual predator internet crimes.

Dr. Schwartz-Maddox 9/19/13 Deposition

FJA self-mutilated c. 1972-75.
Personally, observed FJA hypervigilance. PTSD Records

Testimony re PTSD by Dr. Donna Schwartz-Maddox and Dr. Erin Nelson[12]

Highest causes of PTSD are sexual trauma and war.
Up to 80% of PTSD sufferers have an accompanying mental illness condition.
Risk factors for PTSD include pre-trauma, during trauma, and post-trauma experiences.
All three risk factors experienced by FJA increased likelihood of PTSD.
Pre-trauma involved emotional/mental problems developed at age 8 when mother miscarried.
Initial PTSD trauma when assaulted in 1970 at age 14.
FJA post-trauma: Forced to confront rapist in court at age 14.
3 more assaults (ages 16-19, 1972-75).
In-custody sex pressure as a teen.
FJA treated post-rape by Dr. Brandt for several years.
FJA two psychiatric hospital stays in 1971 (age 15).

1st PTSD Criterion (A)

Exposure to sexual violence is gatekeeper for PTSD.
At age 14 FJA molested by force, perpetrator convicted, satisfying gatekeeper criterion.
FJA testifying against rapist increased trauma.
Additional rapes increased PTSD probability.
FJA suffered steady in-custody sex pressure in teen years.

---

[12] Pp. 8-158 by Dr. Schwartz-Maddox and pp. 176-230 Dr. Nelson; noted on FJA edition.

Second sexual assault at age 16 in juvenile facility, 1972.
Third attack in 1972 while 16-year-old FJA was on vacation with parents in Aspen.
Fourth rape in 1975 at age 19 in Atascadero State Hospital (ASH).

2nd PTSD Criterion (B)

Intrusion Symptoms: FJA has two.
First: psychological distress from trauma reminder cues contributed to FJA suffering from anxiety.
Second: physiologic (physical) distress from trauma cues.
FJA fears attack and schedules his activities with that in mind.
Obvious are FJA's anxiety and his reactivity to cues.
Minnesota Multiphasic Personality Inventory-Two (MMPI-2) tests shows anxiety and PTSD.

3rd PTSD Criterion (C)

Avoidance of stimuli associated with the sexual trauma.
First: FJA avoids distressing memories and thoughts.
Second: Avoids physical effort, shuns interaction with other inmates.

4th PTSD Criterion (D)

Negative alterations in cognition- how thinking or mood is experienced.
FJA possesses several of these:

Blamed self for sexual assaults.

Endures persistent, exaggerated, negative belief in himself and the world.

FJA is rebellious, unable to trust authority.

5th Criterion (E)

Marked alteration in arousal and activity, tied to sexual trauma with visible physiologic manifestation.
For FJA:

Irritable behavior.
Angry outbursts.
Verbal/physical aggression toward people and objects.
Inability to properly regulate emotions.

Also, FJA is hypervigilant, scans his environment for danger.
Records are replete with sleep disturbance evidence.
Finally, reckless/self-destructive behavior:

Extreme substance abuse.

Prostitution.
Dangerous driving.
Self-harm.

6th Criterion (F)

Symptoms must persist for over a month. With FJA, persistence from age 14 to 61 certainly qualifies!

7th Criterion (G)

Must have impaired functioning.
FJA suffered impaired occupational functioning, resulting in virtually no employment history.
FJA also endures impaired social functioning:
1973 psychiatric report: FJA provides inadequate/ineffective emotional and social responses; Dr. Schwartz-Maddox identifies this as numbing from his PTSD.
1979 psychiatric report: FJA has many worries; Dr. Schwartz-Maddox expressed the significance as evidence of social inadequacy; tension headaches from stress contribute to his lack of social skills.
Atascadero State Hospital records document lack of social skills, poor self-image, trust issues.
MMPI-2 results point to FJA's introversion, difficulty meeting others, shy and emotionally distant, uneasy and rigid in social situations.

Finally, FJA experienced impaired educational functioning.
School records show six post-initial sexual trauma schools.
FJA's cognitive deficit [from PTSD] and anxiety caused concentration difficulty.
1973 school report stated the consensus is FJA needs professional help.

8th Criterion (H)

PTSD not due to substance abuse or a medical condition. FJA no history of applied drugs or medical treatment

Other Expert Testimony
RE: Antisocial personality disorder: Dr. Schwartz-Maddox would not accept this for FJA, mainly because FJA did not have the required conduct disorder diagnosis by age 15.

Neither a pattern of conduct disorder, nor any legal trouble prior to initial sexual trauma.

Antisocial also contraindicated by his co-morbid substance abuse.

FJA diagnosed with co/avoidance personality disorder, so antisocial inappropriate.

If antisocial, FJA would appear extroverted (not with avoidance) and having many more relationships.

FJA's interpersonal difficulties from PTSD negate antisocial diagnosis.

FJA did not register significantly on antisocial scale on MMPI-2.

Pedophilia diagnosis: Dr. Donna Schwartz-Maddox did not diagnose FJA with this.

Atascadero State Hospital records put FJA sex offenses in context of teen rebellion, extensive drug abuse.

FJA treatment team (physician and a psychologist) set sex offense trigger as teen unruliness.

Atascadero State Hospital treatment included therapy for FJA and parents to diminish rebellion.

ARIZONA CAPITAL REPRESENTATION PROJECT
101 East Pennington Street, Suite 201
Tucson, Arizona 85701
Telephone: (520) 229-8550
SAMUEL KOOISTRA *(Arizona license pending)*
SAM@AZCAPITALPROJECT.ORG

JACKSON & ODEN, P.C.
3573 East Sunrise Drive, Suite 125
Tucson, Arizona 85718
Telephone: (520) 884-0024
Fax: (520) 884-0025
TODD JACKSON ASB NO. 012202
TJACKSON@JACKSONODENLAW.COM

Attorneys for Plaintiff

UNITED STATES DISTRICT COURT

FOR THE DISTRICT OF ARIZONA

SCOTT DOUGLAS NORDSTROM, Plaintiff, vs. CHARLES RYAN, DIRECTOR, ARIZONA DEPARTMENT OF CORRECTION; JAMES O'NEIL, WARDEN, ASPC EYMAN; STACI FAY, DEPUTY WARDEN, BROWNING UNIT, Defendants.	No. ____________ **COMPLAINT**

The plaintiff, Scott Douglas Nordstrom, moves the Court for entry of judgment in his favor against Charles Ryan, James O'Neil, and Staci Fay and in support of such Complaint avers as follows:

NATURE OF THE ACTION

1. This is a civil action under 42 U.S.C. §1983 seeking declaratory and injunctive relief against Charles Ryan, James O'Neil, and Staci Fay (collectively, "Defendants") in their official

capacities for acts and omission, under color of law, which deprived and continue to deprive Plaintiff of rights secured under the Constitution and laws of the United States.

2. Plaintiff is a state prisoner in the custody of the Arizona Department of Corrections ("ADC"). Plaintiff is sentenced to death, and like all other condemned male prisoners he is automatically and non-discretionarily housed at Arizona State Prison Complex ("ASPC"), Eyman, Browning Unit under unique conditions imposed exclusively on prisoners sentenced to death ("death row"). Conditions on death row are marked by hardship that is significant and atypical when compared to conditions in the general prison population and conditions on other maximum custody units. Atypical and significant hardships experienced by prisoners housed on death row include highly restrictive living conditions in small cells that are constantly illuminated; reduced access to food and property available through the prison commissary; reduced visitation opportunities, including a total bar on contact visits—legal and non-legal; significantly restricted opportunities for recreation and exercise; fewer and lower paying work opportunities within the prison; no opportunity to participate in communal meals or group religious services; and other deprivations and adverse conditions. Plaintiff and condemned inmates like him are subjected to these conditions indefinitely, in Plaintiff's case for a period of almost two decades.

3. Under ADC policy, placement on death row is mandatory for prisoners, including Plaintiff, who are under a sentence of death, and ADC considers no factors other than that sentence when determining where to house such prisoners. The non-discretionary nature of this placement means Plaintiff is given no meaningful opportunity to challenge his housing assignment, nor does ADC conduct any meaningful review of his placement *sua sponte*. Because Plaintiff has a liberty interest in avoiding the atypical and significantly harsh conditions

of death row, Defendants' failure to provide a meaningful review and opportunity to challenge his placement there harms Plaintiff and violates his right to Due Process under the Fourteenth Amendment. *Sandin v. Conner*, 515 U.S. 472 (1995).

4. The grave conditions on death row have caused Plaintiff serious physical and psychological injury. Defendants are aware of the nature of death row conditions and the likelihood of injury, but through their deliberate indifference have failed to rectify them. This constitutes a violation of Plaintiff's right to be free from cruel and unusual punishment under the Eighth Amendment.

5. Plaintiff seeks declaratory and injunctive relief to compel Defendants to immediately end their mandatory placement of Plaintiff on death row and instead provide Plaintiff a meaningful individualized assessment and opportunity for rebuttal and, if appropriate, to alter Plaintiff's housing assignment to conform to the results of the individualized assessment. Plaintiff further seeks declaratory and injunctive relief to compel Defendants to rectify the unconstitutionally cruel and unusual conditions on death row which violate Plaintiff's Eighth Amendment rights.

JURISDICTION AND VENUE

6. This Court has jurisdiction pursuant to 28 U.S.C. §§1331 and 1343. This civil action seeks declaratory and injunctive relief under 28 U.S.C. §§1343, 2201, and 2202; and 42 U.S.C. §1983. Plaintiff has exhausted all administrative remedies as required by 42 U.S.C. §1997e(a).

7. Venue is proper under 28 U.S.C. §1391(b), because the Defendants reside in the District of Arizona and because a substantial part or all of the events or omissions giving rise to Plaintiff's claims occurred in the District of Arizona.

PARTIES

8. Plaintiff, Scott Douglas Nordstrom, is a death-sentenced prisoner in ADC custody currently residing on death row at ASPC Eyman, Browning Unit.

9. Defendant Charles Ryan is the Director of ADC, and he is sued herein in his official capacity. As the Director, Mr. Ryan is responsible for establishing, monitoring, and enforcing overall operations, policies, and practices of the Arizona state prison system, which includes the adoption of rules governing the classification and housing placements of inmates. A.R.S. §§31-201, 41-1604.

10. Defendant James O'Neil is Warden of ASPC Eyman, and he is sued herein in his official capacity. As Warden and pursuant to ADC regulations, Mr. O'Neil exercises direct and supervisory powers over the custody classification of prisoners housed at ASPC Eyman, including prisoners on death row. ADC Order 801.

11. Defendant Staci Fay is a Deputy Warden, and she is sued herein in her official capacity. Ms. Fay oversees the Browning Unit, which houses, among others, condemned male prisoners, including Plaintiff. As Deputy Warden and pursuant to ADC regulations, Ms. Fay exercises direct and supervisory powers over the custody classification of inmates at the Browning Unit. ADC Order 801.

EXHAUSTION

12. Mr. Nordstrom has exhausted such administrative remedies as were available to him.

FACTUAL ALLEGATIONS

13. Plaintiff is a state prisoner in the custody of ADC.

14. In 1998, Plaintiff was sentenced to death.

15. Since being sentenced to death, Plaintiff has remained primarily in the custody of ADC.

16. Since entering ADC custody, Plaintiff has been housed exclusively on death row at the Browning Unit, with the exception of brief periods during which he was temporarily housed in Pima County jail for the pendency of court proceedings.

17. Because he is under a sentence of death, according to ADC regulations Plaintiff may not be housed anywhere other than on death row.

ADC Inmate Classification

18. ADC classifies inmates according to a multi-tier "custody level" based upon the inmate's risk of escape or committing violence.

19. These custody level classifications range from minimum custody (least risk) to maximum custody (most risk).

20. In general, higher custody levels impose more restrictions and greater hardships on inmates than lower custody levels.

21. Conditions in the Browning Unit, which houses death row, are the most restrictive of any ADC maximum custody facility.

22. On information and belief, in most cases ADC uses pre-established risk assessment criteria for determining what level of custody is appropriate for a given inmate, based upon the risk posed by the inmate.

23. According to ADC regulations, all prisoners sentenced to death are automatically and irrevocably placed into maximum custody, regardless of where they would otherwise be classified under the prisoner risk assessment criteria.

24. Death row is a unique subset of maximum custody subject to rules and regulations distinct from and stricter than those imposed on other maximum custody populations.

25. There is no legitimate penological justification for the mandatory placement of Plaintiff on death row.

Conditions on Death Row

26. Because he is housed on death row, Plaintiff is subjected to harsh conditions that are atypical and significant in comparison to conditions in the general ADC prison population as well as conditions experienced by prisoners in other ADC maximum custody populations. For example:

27. Confinement: Prisoners on death row are kept in solitary confinement. They are confined to cells measuring 11' 7" by 7' 9". The front wall of the cell is made of perforated steel. The floor, ceiling, and remaining walls are concrete. The only fixtures in the cell are a hard sleeping platform, a combination sink/toilet, a desk, stool, and nothing else. All fixtures are made out of steel and are welded or bolted to the floor or wall of the cell. Cells are clustered together into "pods." Each pod consists of two rows of five cells, one on top of the other, with a common floor space outside the cells patrolled by guards.

28. Death row cells are constantly, brightly illuminated throughout the day, even during nighttime sleeping hours. Cells are illuminated by three forty watt bulbs and one seven watt bulb during the day. The seven watt bulb remains on during sleeping hours, ensuring that cells remain constantly illuminated with no periods of darkness. Inmates have no ability to dim or otherwise control the brightness of the lights in their cells. If they attempt to artificially dim the lights by, for example, hanging a towel in front of the light source, they are subject to discipline.

29. The brighter, forty watt lights are kept on at least sixteen hours a day, from roughly 6:00 a.m. until roughly 10:00 p.m. In practice, the period of brightest illumination is longer, with lights remaining on until the completion of 10:00 p.m. count, usually around 10:45 p.m. or later, while lights are typically first turned on well before 6:00 a.m. On Fridays and Saturdays, lights are left on an additional two hours, staying on until at least midnight.

30. Cells have poor airflow, leading to a foul and stagnant smell. During humid weather, the air in cells can become muggy enough to cause cardboard boxes to crumble and envelopes to seal. Cells are not air conditioned, but are instead cooled using evaporative cooling, also known as a swamp cooler. The swamp cooler is ineffective at controlling extreme summer temperatures and often contributes to the humidity problem. Because of the inadequate climate control, death row can become extremely hot during the summer months. These extreme heat conditions create a grave and unnecessary risk of adverse health consequences for the inmates subjected to them.

31. Death row inmates are infrequently provided the necessary supplies to clean their cells, allowing dirt and filth to accumulate.

32. There are no shower or other bathing facilities inside cells on death row. Prisoners on death row are permitted to use shower located outside their cells no more than four times per week.

33. Prisoners regularly remain in these cells up to twenty-four hours per day.

34. Inmates on death row are subjected to a strip search every time they leave their cell, be it for a legal visit, recreation period, shower, or any other purpose. During strip searches, inmates are required to remove all clothing, which is inspected by guards. Guards also inspect anything the inmate brings with them from their cell, such as a folder containing legal papers

for a visit with the inmate's attorney. During the strip search, the mouth, hair, ears, armpits, and genitals of the inmate are inspected. The inmate is required to bend forward and spread his buttocks, and guards will inspect the inmate's rectum for contraband.

35. Recreation: Out-of-cell recreation is permitted no more than four times per week.

36. Recreation sessions consist of 2.5 hours spent in an outdoor cage approximately the same size as the prisoner's cell. The cage is made of a heavy metallic mesh and is furnished with nothing but a water jug.

37. Recreation cages are not cleaned of debris, dirt, or standing water prior to use. Their concrete foundation allows water to collect and become stagnant with algae and mold. The standing water is a breeding ground for mosquitos, but Defendants do not provide insect repellant to Plaintiff or make it available for purchase.

38. Prisoners housed on death row are not permitted to use the recreation yard or other recreation facilities and are not permitted any kind of social recreation with other inmates.

39. Personal Property and Commissary: There are greater restrictions on the type and quantity of personal property a prisoner on death row may possess compared to other inmates. For example, a death row prisoner may own cassettes but not CDs, and he is permitted to possess fewer cassettes at one time than non-death row inmates. Death row prisoners cannot purchase a CD player.

40. Prisoners housed on death row are also more restricted than other inmates as to the type and quantity of food they may purchase from the prison commissary.

41. Prisoners on death row cannot purchase hats, sunglasses, winter jackets, or thermal clothing for use during outdoor recreation, nor will they be issued such clothing by ADC. Death row prisoners are also not issued and are not permitted to purchase insect repellant despite the

presence of significant numbers of mosquitos and other biting insects during outdoor recreation and inside the facility.

42. Despite policies to the contrary, inmates housed on death row are issued clothing, bed sheets and towels infrequently and in limited quantity.

43. The cells which house condemned prisoners do not include any shelving or storage space. Commissary and hygiene items, clothing, legal materials, and other personal property must be stored in cardboard bankers' boxes. Inmates may have no more than four such boxes in their cell at a time.

44. Visitation: Prisoners on death row are not permitted to have any physical contact with their visitors. All visitation with condemned inmates, including legal and family visits, are conducted in separate rooms divided by a glass partition.

45. Visits to prisoners housed on death row may last no longer than two hours, whereas visits to other inmates may last up to four hours.

46. Religious Services: Prisoners housed on death row may not participate in group religious activities, including group religious services. Individual cell front visits from approved religious volunteers are also not allowed.

47. Education: Other than special education classes, prisoners housed on death row may not participate in any educational programs provided by ADC, including GED or functional literacy classes.

48. By statute, ADC may not spend monies designated for prisoner education services on programs dedicated to servicing inmates housed on death row. A.R.S. §31-240(B).

49. Meals: Prisoners housed on death row eat all meals alone in their cell. They are not permitted to dine alongside other inmates, as in the prison mess hall. They are served reduced portion meals.

50. Prisoners on death row are prohibited from having any fresh or canned fruit as part of their diet. Death row prisoners are provided a drink powder containing no actual fruit as a fruit substitute.

51. Death row inmates are fed two meals a day. Schedules for the preparation and distribution of meals on death row are designed to accommodate institutional convenience rather than the needs of inmates. As a result, food is often prepared hours before it is served and is not kept warm in the interim, making lukewarm or cold meals the norm for death row inmates. Breakfast is served in the early morning hours, usually around 4:30 a.m. Dinner is typically served around 4:30 p.m.

52. Prisoners housed on death row are not permitted to have "food visits" where a visitor brings the prisoner outside food to be eaten during the visitation.

53. Employment: Work opportunities for prisoners on death row are severely limited. Inmates on death row are only permitted custodial employment as porters cleaning their own pods. They are not permitted to work as clerks, tutors, aides, drivers, or in any other positions available to other inmates. Because porter is an unskilled position and unskilled labor is compensated at a lower hourly rate, this restriction also limits death row prisoner's ability to earn income. Porter work is restricted to a two hour shift, five times a week. Porter assignments themselves are rare: because death row porters clean only the pod they are housed on, and because of the small number of pods themselves, even eligible death row prisoners may not be able to work as a porter.

54. Per ADC policy, all inmates performing work are paid at ten cents an hour until they complete a functional literacy course. Because condemned inmates are not permitted to take this course, there is no way for them to earn above this minimum wage.

55. Duration: Incarceration on death row is mandatory and indefinite. All other inmates housed under conditions similar to those on death row are there for punitive or security reasons, and over time they may be able to reclassify to a less restrictive form of custody. By contrast, prisoners under a sentence of death, who are housed in these conditions solely because of their sentence, will never be reclassified.

56. The conditions described above are the least restrictive conditions available for inmates on death row. Depending on their placement within an incentive program, many condemned inmates are subject to even harsher, more restrictive conditions. Notably, even inmates that have completed this incentive program and are eligible for the least restrictive death row conditions have no prospect of ever being reclassified to less restrictive housing.

57. On information and belief, the death row conditions described above, in part or in whole, create hardships that are atypical and significant in comparison with conditions in ADC's general population or with other maximum custody units operated by ADC. This atypical and significant hardship manifests through both the extreme conditions themselves and the extended duration of their imposition.

58. The death row conditions described above cause serious physical and psychological harm to inmates, including Plaintiff, who are subjected to them over an extended period of time. This harm includes, but is not limited to, adverse physical and mental health consequences stemming from the constant illumination, poor diet, and social isolation to which death row inmates are subjected.

59. Defendants are aware of the nature of conditions on death row and their effect on condemned inmates but have failed to take meaningful remedial action.

60. There is no legitimate penological justification for the severity of these conditions.

Review of Death Row Placement

61. Under ADC regulations, prisoners housed in maximum custody, including prisoners on death row, have their maximum custody status reviewed every six months.

62. Under ADC regulations, it is mandatory that prisoners sentenced to death be housed on death row.

63. Because his placement there is mandatory, review of Plaintiff's placement on death row does not offer a meaningful opportunity for him to challenge this assignment.

64. A hearing to review Plaintiff's maximum custody placement was held on July 9, 2014.

65. The result of this hearing was a recommendation that Plaintiff remain in maximum custody.

66. The hearing officers found no conduct on Plaintiff's part falling into behavior categories that would support placement into maximum custody.

67. On information and belief, the only rationale given for Plaintiff's continued placement in maximum custody was his death sentence.

68. Since being placed on death row, a period spanning more than seventeen years, Plaintiff has only been disciplined once, fifteen years ago, for failing to wear his prison jumpsuit after he sent both his issued jumpsuits to the laundry at the same time. Other than this single infraction, Plaintiff has a perfect disciplinary record.

69. On September 4, 2014, Plaintiff appealed his placement in maximum custody.

70. On October 10, 2014, Plaintiff's appeal was denied and maximum custody placement upheld.

71. Plaintiff's death sentence was again the sole rationale provided for his placement in maximum custody.

72. There is no legitimate penological justification for Plaintiff's continued placement in maximum custody.

COUNT ONE
Violation of Fourteenth Amendment Due Process Rights

73. The foregoing allegations are incorporated as if re-alleged herein.

74. The harshness of conditions on death row is atypical and significant in comparison with both conditions in ADC general population and conditions on other maximum custody units.

75. Under the Fourteenth Amendment, Plaintiff has a protected liberty interest in avoiding conditions such as the ones found on death row.

76. Because Plaintiff has a protected liberty interest, the Fourteenth Amendment of the United States Constitution requires that he be provided due process before this interest can be denied by state officials.

77. Current procedures for reviewing the appropriateness of placement under death row conditions do not provide meaningful review and are insufficient under the Fourteenth Amendment.

78. Defendants have violated and continue to violate Plaintiff's Fourteenth Amendment right to Due Process by failing to provide adequate process by which Plaintiff could meaningfully challenge his placement on death row.

79. Defendants' actions have caused and will continue to cause irreparable harm to Plaintiff and others similarly situated, for which they lack adequate remedies at law.

COUNT TWO

Violation of Eighth Amendment Right to Freedom from Cruel and Unusual Punishment

80. The foregoing allegations are incorporated as if re-alleged herein.

81. Conditions on death row collectively have caused and continue to cause serious physical and psychological injury to Plaintiff.

82. Defendants are aware of the nature of these conditions and their effect but have failed to remedy the conditions or their effect.

83. This failure manifests deliberate indifference on the part of Defendants.

84. This deliberate indifference to serious conditions that harmed and continue to harm Plaintiff constitute an ongoing violation of his right to be free from cruel and unusual punishment under the Eighth Amendment of the United States Constitution.

85. The harm these conditions have imposed on Plaintiff is so grave as to violate contemporary standards of decency.

PRAYER FOR RELIEF

WHEREFORE, Plaintiff, Scott Douglas Nordstrom, requests judgment against Defendants as follows:

A. For appropriate declaratory relief regarding the unlawful and unconstitutional acts, omissions, and practices of Defendants;

B. For appropriate equitable relief against all Defendants as allowed by the Civil Rights Act of 1871, 42 U.S.C. §1983, including the enjoining and permanent restraining of these violations, and direction to the Defendants to take such affirmative action as is necessary to ensure that the effects of the unconstitutional and unlawful practices and omissions are eliminated and do not continue to affect Plaintiff's or others' rights to liberty, due process of law, and freedom from cruel and unusual punishment under the Fourteenth and Eighth Amendments;

C. For an award of reasonable attorneys' fees and his costs on his behalf expended as to such Defendants pursuant to the Civil Rights Act of 1871, 42 U.S.C. §1988; and

D. For such other and further relief to which Plaintiff may show himself justly entitled.

DATED: October 28, 2015.

ARIZONA CAPITAL REPRESENTATION PROJECT
Samuel Kooistra*
(Arizona license pending)
**Arkansas Bar No. 2012272*

JACKSON & ODEN, P.C.

By: */s/ Todd Jackson*
Todd Jackson
Attorneys for Plaintiff

ADDITIONAL TITLES BY FRANK ATWOOD

2017 *And the Two Shall Become One*
Autobiography about Frank and Rachel Atwood. Being released in English and Greek late 2017.

2015 *Noetic Jerusalem*
Uses Church Father writings to teach about demonic attacks. On Amazon.

2012 *Gates of Hades Prevaileth Not*
On Amazon

2010 *Spiritual Alchemy*
On Amazon

2006 *West of Jesus*
Regina Orthodox Press, (out of print) 2nd edition Xlibris 2012.

Visit Frank's Website for a complete list of articles and books at ChurchFatherTheology.com

ADDITIONAL PUBLICATIONS BY GEORGE KAYER

According to Goodreads.com, Mr. Kayer has written 15 books. Since Nancy Mairs persuaded George to start writing again he has dedicated his life to creating desperately needed content previously unavailable in print for prisoners and their familes

A few publishing Highlights:

2009, George founded Inmate Shopper, the #1 prisoner resource the past five years. (since 2012)

2011, George created the first The Best 500 Orgs for Prisoners and Their Families.

2015, 500 Free Magazines. Written to help prisoners stretch the 20 cents per hour many prisons pay.

Mr. Kayer welcomes your comments at:
gkayer@freebirdpublishers.com
Victimly_Insane@yahoo.com
Text: 704-406-8682

FREEBIRD PUBLISHERS

SPECIALIZING IN PRISONER PUBLICATIONS

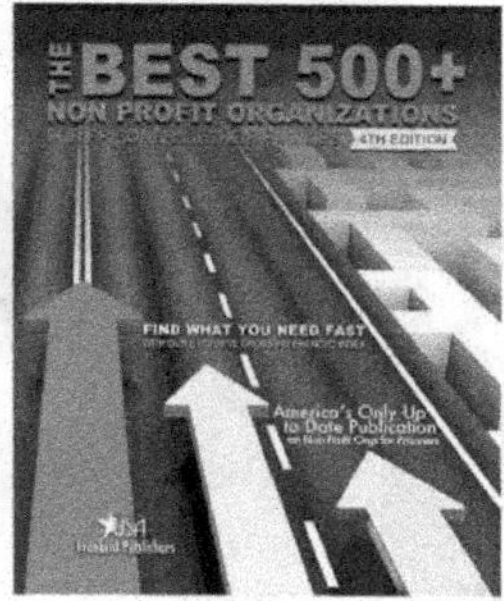

FOR MORE INFORMATION ON ALL WE OFFER
SEND 2 STAMPS TO: FREEBIRD PUBLISHERS
BOX 541, NORTH DIGHTON, MA 02764
TOLL FREE: 888-712-1987 TEXT/PHONE: 774-406-8682
WWW.FREEBIRDPUBLISHERS.COM
DIANE@FREEBIRDPUBLISHERS.COM

www.ingramcontent.com/pod-product-compliance
Lightning Source LLC
Chambersburg PA
CBHW072125270326
41931CB00010B/1670

* 9 7 8 0 9 9 1 3 5 9 1 8 9 *